Research Educa

370.78

before

4

0750704640

For Mum and Dad

Researching Drama and Arts Education:
Paradigms and Possibilities

Edited by Philip Taylor
With a Foreword by Maxine Greene

 The Falmer Press

(A member of the Taylor & Francis Group)
London • Washington, D.C.

UK   Falmer Press, 1 Gunpowder Square, London, EC4A 3DE
USA   Falmer Press, Taylor & Francis Inc., 1900 Frost Road, Suite 101,
        Bristol, PA 19007

First published in 1996

**A catalogue record for this book is available from the British
Library**

**Library of Congress Cataloging-in-Publication Data are
available on request**

ISBN 0 7507 0463 2 cased
ISBN 0 7507 0464 0 paper

Jacket design by Caroline Archer

Typeset in 10/12pt Garamond by
Graphicraft Typesetters Ltd., Hong Kong

*Printed in Great Britain by Biddles Ltd., Guildford and King's
Lynn on paper which has a specified pH value on final paper
manufacture of not less than 7.5 and is therefore 'acid free'.*

Contents

Contents

Acknowledgments

I rarely cook in, preferring the ambience of a restaurant, a good bottle of wine, a great discussion with a few friends. There have been many restaurants, bottles of wine, discussions and friends that have provided the backdrop for this book, too many to list here.

However, I would like to acknowledge Margot Ely, Cecily O'Neill, Donald Schön, and Nancy Swortzell who responded to selected drafts of this text and provided helpful advice on its content and structure. The friendships I've developed over the years have crystallized the ideas captured here, I especially note Ros Arnold, Jonothan Neelands, Gavin Bolton, John O'Toole, John Hughes, Alistair Martin-Smith, Wayne Fairhead, David Booth and Lowell Swortzell whose support always encourages me to go further. The colleagues and graduate students I have worked with have made me think more critically about research design, in particular I thank Kate Donelan, Judith McLean, John Deverall, Joanne O'Mara, Tracey Lee, and Christine Hoepper. The institute program which provided the genesis for this book was strengthened by the Second World Congress in Drama/Theatre and Education in Brisbane, July 1995, a landmark event which brought together over 1300 delegates from fifty-five countries. I am grateful to its convenors for their cooperation and input. I also acknowledge the generous assistance of the Fulbright Commission who contributed to the success of the institute.

My recent friendship with Maxine Greene, in my view one of arts education's most innovative and influential thinkers, has given me great personal and professional satisfaction; as have my conversations with David Hornbook at the Holborn Centre in London, who, although we rarely agree, manages to press my mettle in unique ways.

Of all these folks and institutions, though, I want to acknowledge Falmer Press and Malcolm Clarkson whose texts on qualitative research design and teacher research gave me such strength during the long, lonely hours while writing my dissertation in educational theatre at New York University, 1988–1991. What an honour to be now included in that Falmer library.

Preface

In July 1995, leaders and workers in drama and arts education from over ten countries gathered at Griffith University for a special event. Members from the American Alliance for Theatre and Education (USA), National Association for Drama in Education (Australia), National Drama (England) and the Arts Education Council of Ontario (Canada) were just a few who joined a diverse group of teachers, artists, policy-makers and graduate students from such diverse places as Scandinavia, Taiwan, South Africa, Spain, and Korea. In total, sixty-one delegates sharing a commitment to the ongoing and sustained inquiry into drama and arts education assembled in Brisbane, Australia, to canvass, debate and challenge the character of research activity.

The Institute of Drama Education Research, as the program came to be called, was convened because of the heightened focus that research was assuming on the educative agenda in the arts. Whereas in the past, drama educators prided themselves on their practice, on their ability to structure, direct and reflect upon improvised and performed drama, a growing feeling that practical work was now becoming redundant — especially in a political climate which emphasizes goals and outcomes — was resulting in strong dividing lines emerging. There were dangerous signs on the horizon that the future leaders in drama might never have led a classroom session with children, or, if they had worked in a school before, they were of a mind that such sessions did not constitute a valuable platform on which research could be launched.

In an academic world where the refereed article is championed, where the scholar is promoted often on the quantity of publications, no matter how beneficial these might be to the field, and where service and teaching are seen in conflict with research and advancement, is there a healthy future for drama and arts education? How could it be that the field could fall into the domain of the theoretician whose understandings are generated outside of a school context? What, if anything, could be done to rectify this trend? These were the important questions which gave rise to the Institute of Drama Education Research.

Drama educators have not positioned themselves naturally within the conventional boundaries of the research club. It may come as no surprise that many of the major writers in arts education, for instance, do not have a specialization in drama. Eminent thinkers like Maxine Greene, Elliot Eisner, David Best, Howard Gardner, John Dewey and Suzanne Langer, to name a few, were not trained as drama educators. As drama exists through a transitory and ephemeral medium, as it works through time, space and action, it is unsurprising that the configuration of the work demands an active and physical encounter. This demand may be one reason why the drama educator has been reluctant to write, and may account for the dearth of drama practitioners who are acknowledged leaders in arts education.

Drama educators may have unwittingly contributed to a distrust of research given their own value-laden prejudices about what researchers do and the meaningful application of research in practice. The following statement by one of the field's distinguished proponents, Gavin Bolton, in the 'Preface' to his book, *New Perspectives on Classroom Drama* (London, Simon and Schuster, 1992), echoes many of the concerns that practitioners experience when they encounter the word, research:

> Classroom-based writing is soon going to become something of a rarity. Too many key appointments in teacher education institutions are being filled by people who have little real classroom experience, yet they are the ones who have time and, indeed, are required by the position to write. In some universities . . . the myth that evidence of doctoral research has greater validity than evidence of sound practice is being perpetuated, so that instead of a Ph.D. being a proper culmination of years of teaching experience, it is not surprisingly seen by ambitious young people as the necessary starting point of their career.

While Bolton's attack on his juniors may seem a little severe, given that they are usually responding to the system that their elders have created, it does confirm a tension that has developed in the field.

So, the institute provided a forum through which the interaction between research, practice and artistry could be investigated. If research is on the public agenda, with tenure, job security and advancement dependent upon it, then we need to understand how to manage this interaction. As one delegate at the institute was to say to me, she had been suspicious of research for many years and was reluctant to see how it related to her work. Ironically, this same person was committed to ethnographic accounts of educational events and how such descriptions could yield valuable insights into teaching and learning, yet she failed to construe this interest as a scholarly one.

Unlike conventional conferences on research design, numbers at the Griffith University Institute were limited to provide the maximum opportunity for all delegates to investigate the major emphases and developments in research. Interestingly, this constraint caused some consternation, particularly among those used to presenting papers at large conferences. The institute was not a paper-presenting affair but a position interrogation. The aim was to critique different modalities of research design, to draw connections between them, and to probe how knowledge can be advanced by their application. The term *institute* was chosen specifically to describe this interaction. An institute connotes a body which produces and promotes educational advancement, a place where ideas can be investigated and new visions proposed. An institute can become a beacon through which emerging understandings happen, where stereotypical notions can be challenged, where new beginnings occur.

There have been many formative institute events which were designed to investigate the nature of knowledge within given disciplines or fields of understanding. The movement we know as critical theory, for instance, is said to have had its genesis within the Institute of Social Research in 1920s Frankfurt. There, under the leadership of Max Horkheimer, a group of leading thinkers examined the fabric of historical power structures and how the individual accommodated, transformed and manipulated these structures. This institute became a centre for applied research, where the like-minded could assemble to probe the construct of knowledge and the extent to which individuals could shape and control their destiny.

The 1966 Dartmouth Seminar in Hanover, New Hampshire, had a similar intent, although its focus was more on language learning education, and the extent to which contemporary notions of an English curriculum were fulfilling the needs of teachers and their students. In Dartmouth, fifty individuals, mostly from England and the US, challenged the traditional assumptions upon which current practice was based and explored how more dynamic learning encounters could be provided. The seminar was a milestone in language education and became a marker for widespread changes in English education. There have been many other landmark events in a variety of disciplines which have arrested the interest of the educational community for their innovative models, their future proposals, and the support systems they provided.

While it might seem bold to compare the Queensland Institute to those in Frankfurt and New Hampshire, they each shared a similar character. In each case, a small group of interested individuals willingly decided that it was time to investigate an aspect pertinent in their respective fields. Where professional lives are now ruled by huge conferences and conventions, institutes are dedicated to the intimate questioning of focused issues. Institutes by nature hold the field up for appraisal and can thoroughly critique the character of its work. In Brisbane, those whose careers had grown through their commitment to educational practices came together for the first time to examine in small numbers how their fieldwork — whether that field be the classroom, the theatre, or some other educational setting — interacts with formal and systematic inquiry.

Although opportunities had been provided elsewhere for drama and arts educators to share their research projects and papers, it was an unusual event for the formative *practitioners* in drama education to interrogate the purposes of research activity, and to understand how that activity linked to their commitment to practice. Furthermore, the institute responded to a growing international concern that drama and arts educators are expected to pursue a conventional model of research design which draws on standard notions of empiricism. These notions conform to a stereotypical paradigm which emphasizes linearity, control, measurement, and non-ambiguity. Although it is the case that such paradigms are promoted within the academy as familiar and acceptable, there is a danger that drama and arts educators may irrevocably misrepresent their work if they mindlessly adopt them.

The institute was convened, then, to assess what are the decisive features of research design. How do drama education researchers design their studies? Which research methods are appropriate for specific investigative questions? What are the major needs of drama education research for the twenty-first century? What is the nexus between research, artistry and practice? The program was structured on the principle that within educational contexts it is the young who should be the beneficiaries of our investigations. With this principle in mind, the institute included children's and teachers' work which raised numerous questions about design, especially in relation to data collection, analysis and reporting, as well as research ethics and presentation. Position papers were sent to delegates in advance so that a level of informed debate would characterize the program.

At the forefront of the discussions was the belief that drama education research operates within an artistic medium. The institute could not separate drama as pedagogy from drama as art. As the institute delegates conversed with one another about research paradigms and their possibilities, as they engaged with teachers working with children, as they participated in role-plays, and were audience to a solo performance from a local Brisbane actor, the constant thread of artistry powering the drama process was weaved. Maxine Greene has reminded us that research into the arts must release all those involved in the inquiry into fulfilling adventures and experiences, paying heed to notions of ambiguity, contradiction and struggle. And while these notions generated some strong reactions from the participants, especially when outcomes weren't clear or processes defined, there was a sense that our journey in Brisbane was a profound one, with many participants launched into a variety of investigative endeavours.

But, as Elliot Eisner (1985, p. 141) reminds us, knowing the outcome of the game tells us little about how the game is played, and one outcome of the institute was the recognition that the field requires more illustrations of how the game of drama and arts education research is to be or can be negotiated. If the game of drama education is now about survival of a research kind, how can that game be played in a way that furthers our practice, that relates to our artistic work, and thereby honours the life experiences of the children we teach?

This book provides a picture of that game but importantly it shares the views of experienced practitioners and how they construe their work as research. The contributors, mostly participants in the institute, have presented their own reworked musings around research design, they share their own evolving understandings of what research is and how it interacts with their practice. While they suggest possible paths that others might follow they do so knowing that the transient, yet crystallized, nature of the dramatic artform requires a reaching beyond the stereotype of conventional research, and the active pursuit of a paradigm that can release all those engaged in the research journey into a powerful investigative experience.

Researching Drama and Arts Education: Paradigms and Possibilities will provide important insights into how the research game might be negotiated, how we can design our studies, and, what support systems need to be established to enable us to document our work in an honest manner. It challenges many of the myths of research endeavour, especially in the arts, and it will constitute, I hope, an invaluable reference for those beginning and continuing their investigative work. For those fortunate to have been in Brisbane in July 1995, we were reminded of the commitment and dedication of the many teachers, artists, students and children who daily enter classrooms and construct drama experiences. This book celebrates their achievement but importantly provides a supportive lens through which we can understand and develop those experiences more fully.

Philip Taylor
Kangaroo Point, Queensland

Reference

EISNER, E. (1985) *The Art of Educational Evaluation*, London, Falmer Press.

Foreword

In the midst of a preoccupation with the measurable, with benchmarks and outcomes, new voices are becoming audible in the world of education. They are voices responsive to talk of the 'reflective practitioner', to novel modes of participant observation in actual classrooms, to the judgments of practitioners asked to think about their own thinking. This book marks an entry of drama education into what is emerging as a community of renewal and reconstruction in the western world. What with the pressures of institutions and grass-roots demands for quantifiable achievement, there is something remarkable about the articulation of what might be called 'progressive' or even emancipatory values in and around existing schools.

Perhaps for the first time, the world of the practitioner is being made audible and visible, as collaboration increases between universities and public schools. Teacher research is being encouraged; many teachers are going 'on line' to share narratives of teaching and learning. The very notion of story-telling as a mode of knowing is beginning to shake the foundations of traditional empiricism and objectivism. The focus is no longer on the object (the so called 'art work', the 'text') but on the transaction between the living human being and what is to be grasped, what is to be learned.

This book marks a watershed where drama education is concerned, since it represents an affirmation of the role to be played by drama educators in the emergent community. The very subtitle, 'Paradigms and Possibilities', indicates the fruitful dialectic in which Philip Taylor and his colleagues are engaged. The writers here are all well versed in the standards and demands of what is known as academic research. The Institute of Drama Education Research, which gave rise to this ground-breaking volume, engaged in the kind of interrogation and critique of existing research paradigms that indicated informed acquaintance with a whole range of modalities. The writers here are clearly not outsiders crying in the wilderness; they are among the more experienced and informed people in their field.

Philip Taylor sets the standard, and it is a high one. The chapters that follow are not only well and carefully honed; they are various and revelatory; some of them verge on the artistic. One of the crucial strengths, in fact, of this collection is its relevance for thinking about the arts in education, including but not limited to drama. There is all the difference in the world between writing *about* a performance of Tony Kushner's *Angels in America*, say, or Wendy Wasserstein's *The Heidi Chronicles*, or Hendrik Ibsen's *Ghosts*, and experiencing it as perceiver or as participant. Some of us have only just begun to recognize the freezing consequences of formalism or the enclosing of dramatic works in gilt cages of aestheticism. Some of us have only just begun to see the connections between the expanding dialogues about art 'as engagement', about 'reader response', and about what can happen in drama classrooms.

What follows is, must be, the kind of recognition that grants real significance to reports on, or descriptions of, or stories about, the lived situations in classrooms where drama is being explored or where particular works are being ushered into life. The chapters here are true to what the artistic-aesthetic asks of all of us: a willingness to be present as situated beings to created worlds. They are as-if worlds, illusioned worlds, with the potentiality of revealing unexpected dimensions of the lives we live together and apart. If they are to be opened, if they are to become accessible, those who come to them must be enabled to attend, to notice what there is to be noticed. They must be freed for live imaginative encounters with what is taking place around them or before them, freed as embodied beings, as thoughtful and wondering beings, as beings caught up in process, in the pursuit of possibility.

An enticing aspect of this book is its opening to the winds of possibility. In chapter after chapter, new windows seem to open as the ethnographic mode of inquiry is probed, or narrative, or the aesthetic, as new connections are forged between power and knowledge. This is in no sense a debunking book: the uses of academic research, even of quantitative research, are acknowledged. But the terrible falsifications and distortions of what might be called 'neo-positivism' are recognized as well. The dreary attempts at neutrality, the claims of being value-free, the intoxication with the measurable: all these are challenged, exposed, resisted. And that is the excitement of this book. The reader is summoned to open her/his own shutter, to envisage the heretofore unseen.

For the sake of the wide-awakeness of our students, for the sake of the mysteries and wonders of our art form, these chapters deserve attention and concern. If they work, they may arouse their readers to take on new responsibilities, to join the emerging community, to begin to transform.

Maxine Greene
Teachers College
Columbia University

Introduction: Rebellion, Reflective Turning and Arts Education Research

Philip Taylor

We are living in a desperate time in arts education. Across the globe, programs are being savagely cut, teachers' work is being undermined, curricula outcome targets and directives, rather than their processes, are forever in sight. National priorities invade local school communities, short-term contracts control teachers' professional lives, an eager band of obsequious officers evangelize uniform attainment. A new conforming scientism begins to breed a purblind complacency in arts education. Those who fought for and achieved their economic security show little interest in others who struggle to maintain a bare livelihood. Teachers are still the recipients of programmed curricula, students are still the recipients of the teacher's. Power games continue to be fought, intellectual insecurities still motivate, the arts are tentatively poised.

So what, you may ask, has changed in the last fifty years? Little, it seems, except a dangerous training climate where the great liberal and democratic thinkers of our times are being superseded by a disarmingly charming set of academics, bureaucrats, politicians and officials who point to the dark forces undermining our schools, our homes and our lives. These dark forces, they argue, can be corrected if a new general curriculum language is learnt with shared attainment levels, predetermined outcomes and common exemplars. The politics of fear begin to control the human educational destiny. Teachers and the children they teach are uncertain of their future and tenuously believe or are led to believe that if they place hope in the mandated or recommended curriculum, if they learn the new language, if they only did what they were told, their future will be assured. As the arts struggle to remain on the curriculum, as they continue to be relegated to the marginalized periphery, their leaders seek salvage in the politics of fear, they retreat to the new language, and promote a common global view of what the arts are and should be. Arts education learns to play the game of scientism.

In her formative essay 'The artistic-aesthetic and curriculum', written some years back, Maxine Greene (1978) alerted educators to the political forces which would eventually shape school curriculum in the arts. We now see these forces in action. They are demonstrated through the governmental arts agency which adopts a sanitized rhetoric, as well as the arts curriculum which embraces a political rather than an educative agenda. Arts educators are dangerously poised,

Greene warned us, when they seek salvage in a scientific rather than an artistic-aesthetic curriculum, and when they believe that discrete cognitive outcomes, and the separation of brain spheres, are more palatable to those encharged with directing educational policy. While Greene appealed for educators to construct learning experiences where students can struggle with the contradictions of life and tolerate the ambiguities of living, arts officers promote national curriculum statements and enthusiastically seek governmental funds which will implement them. Even the rapid advances in technology, such as the Internet and CD-ROM, become valuable to the extent that they can implement external attainment targets often set by business, government and industry.

In this climate, the implications for humanist research are grim. As national bodies control research funds, they assert the research priorities. Greene asserted her suspicion of deadly research which followed a political agenda, an agenda which is largely uninformed by the real world of teachers, students and their school communities, or at the very least is a program determined by an external agent which exploits the real world to achieve its ends. In contrast, the test, argued Greene (1978), for arts curriculum and arts research:

> is in the aesthetic experiences we can make possible, the privileged moment through which we can enable our students to live. There must be attending; there must be noticing, at once, there must be a reflective turning back to the stream of consciousness — the stream that contains our perceptions, our reflections, yes, and our ideas. Clearly, this end-in-view cannot be predetermined. I am arguing for self-reflectiveness, however, and new disclosures, as I am arguing for critical reflection at a moment of stasis and crystallised habits. If the uniqueness of the artistic-aesthetic can be reaffirmed, if we can consider futuring as we combat immersion, old either/ors may disappear. We may make possible a pluralism of visions, a multiplicity of realities. We may enable those we teach to rebel. (p. 182)

I am fond of this quote and regularly cite it with my students. I am fond of it because it resonates with my own understanding of the primary flaws in much arts education research which I read, research which is often conducted solely by university employees, that has an implied lack of faith in the voices and abilities of classroom practitioners, and which is pitched at an academic or bureaucratic audience. I am also fond of the quote because it is unnerving. For those curriculum officers who preach the new common and sterile language of conformity, Greene reminds us that this language fundamentally can deny the rebellious possibilities to which the arts aspire. The arts represent different, non-conventional and thereby potentially threatening images of reality. A common language thwarts threat or danger, it constrains possibility, and only makes the predictable occur within a probable outcome.

Just as much educational practice has become sanitized by a conforming view which puts teachers in the role of consumers educational research promotes a common belief that scholarly investigations fall outside of the province of teachers. We see this in the many counterpoints that exist: researchers and teachers, scholars and practitioners, academics and artists, generators and moderators. Is it any wonder that the educational experiences provided for our young continue to promote lifeless curriculum when teachers must constantly recycle the packages which others have generated? Would it be too much to have hoped that we might see a more engaging artistic-aesthetic curriculum where teachers and students attend together to the issues and questions that they have generated?

If we take a close look at what has happened recently in curriculum reform, what do we notice? In England, dance and drama have been eviscerated from a core arts entitlement, in the US there is voluntary curriculum in arts education which emphasizes standards and what every young American should know and be able to do, and in Australia the multi-million dollar attempt to formulate a national arts curriculum with eight learning level outcomes has a spurious future although there are many who have committed themselves to keeping it alive. In each case, a political agenda formulates the context in which an arts education curriculum either does or does not exist.

Greene's *streams of consciousness*, if they can occur, are framed by a dictated educational imperative which directs a course of action. The pedagogical climate is constructed by a conventional scientific paradigm which promotes outcomes, controls behaviour, and permits individual reflective turning within foreseen categories and codes. Greene's view that artistic-aesthetic rendering pushes the boundaries of experience, and opens up new ways of looking at the world and engaging with an experienced reality, is hopelessly struggling within a worldview which pays lipservice to imagination and which rewards those whose work is developed within prefigured criteria.

Just as opportunities for self-reflexiveness are gradually being denied to students and their teachers, there are growing signs that research in arts education is distorting the artistic-aesthetic curriculum. Governmental bodies or those commissioned by them determine the human competencies which they believe fit the required skill for business and technology. National research priorities are tailored to the exploration of these competencies, and the arts, we are told, if they are to maintain any status, must be presented as effective service agents when achieving a government agenda. Teachers, then, are the subject of research, the focal point by which their work will determine if the national agenda is to be achieved. 'They become the serving functionaries', argues Abbs (1994, p. 6), 'not of the life of culture and intellect, but of either the state or the free market.'

It is within this context that a crisis in researching the artistic-aesthetic curriculum is occurring. If a central aspect of arts education is the new light that is shed on a moment or event, or a different understanding provoked by the work and its non-conventional mode of rendering experience, how can teachers take risks with their students and thereby honour the artistry encountered? If arts works are about the possible worlds we can enter and the virtual realities exposed, how can research probe and liberate? How can students ever rebel when a fixed reality is the political vision, and a context-free outcome is the educational imperative? In other words, how can arts education research ever achieve its artistic-aesthetic mandate within a climate of scientism?

Re-thinking Research in an Era of Neo-Positivism

A recurring myth prevalent in educational research and which constantly denies Greene's pluralism of visions is that neo-positivism provides the secure framework upon which curriculum action must flow. Neo-positivism, a phrase which characterized the dominant epistemology informing contemporary understandings of research, has its derivative roots in the work of the nineteenth-century French philosopher, Auguste Comte. Comte argued that of the three stages that human thought progressed — theological, metaphysical, and the scientific or positivist stage — it was the latter which could only demonstrate truth (Kincheloe, 1991, p. 48). *A priori* reasoning or deductive modes of thought, where causes and effects exist, depend on sense or observed data rather than the intuitive or felt experience. We know what we see, and often what we see is only valid if it can be counted.

This mode of thought had its earlier roots in Descartes and Newton who asserted that knowledge must have no doubt, that truth exists in the objective and verifiable world. Such thinking saw a split between the mind and body. 'The way to inquire was to break reality down into small pieces', elaborates Courtney (1987, p. 17), 'and re-arrange those parts in their logical order.' The machine metaphor became a powerful image of human thought. Just as a machine consists of intricate parts that can be systematically linked, controlled and operated, so the mind existed as a separate unit within the body. This unit could be instructed, trained and tested.

Although many positivists were to accept that the basic premise upon which Comte's system of understanding was formulated had major flaws, and that many of the leading proponents of positivism were to claim that it was wrong, there are still clear signs that the tenets of positivism, what Kincheloe (1991, p. 49) characterizes as neo-positivism, inform current understandings of education and the research which will probe these understandings, especially within arts education.

Two examples from drama education highlight the immediate influence of positivism, and represent the neo-positivist trends in contemporary thought. The first comes from the opening paragraph of a text which proposes a *modular syllabus* which should be the hallmark of drama curriculum:

> Theory, and the challenge it implicitly presents to empiricism and 'common sense', is viewed, like ideology, with some suspicion by a culture traditionally disposed to favour practical ways of doing things. For years the drama-in-education community has been conventionally

instrumental in just this way, generally preferring to discuss and progress working methods rather than to worry too much about their theoretical or ideological implications. However, simply to ignore the existence of theory in the conduct of human affairs is to render ourselves powerless in the first instance to interpret events and then to influence them. Formulating theories is the way we make sense of our experience by giving ourselves meaningful structures within which it may be explained. (Hornbrook, 1989, p. 3)[1]

One feature of the above paragraph is that theory can exist and perhaps should exist outside of practice. There is an expressed belief in the power of theory to direct and to inform classroom work, and that this power has been ignored by drama educators, rendering the community of drama educators powerless. Like Descartes and his separation of mind from body, the above author asserts a separation of theory from practice. The authoritative basis which should inform the workings of the human mind must come from the theoretician. In this instance, the practitioners are not the authorities because they have seemingly avoided a theoretical framework. The theoreticians become those who are removed from the workplace.

We see the ramifications of this attitude when governmental decisions are made concerning the successful tenderers for national curriculum and standards documents. In the US, for instance, the school practitioners were 'the one group that seemed underrepresented' in the process of writing the *National Standards for Arts Education* (Hoffa, 1994, p. 17). Why is it that the voices of teachers do not dominate or feature widely in the design of these documents? Why is it that of the thirty-two names listed as committee members of the *Standards* only three, two high-school teachers and one principal of an elementary school, could be considered direct representatives of the predominant sites where these standards will be achieved (Consortium of National Arts Education Associations, 1994, p. 139)? Could a reason be that authorities do not believe teachers are capable of generating the conceptual framework of curriculum? Why are the practitioners relegated into the role of moderating the curriculum or standards which outside agents, the theorists, construct?

A study by Deborah Britzman (1991) highlights the flawed premise on which the separation of theory from practice hinged. In her study of teacher education programs and how student teachers learn in them, she discovered that the foundations and sources of theory lie in teachers' practice. Educational theorizing, she claimed, is situated within 'the lived lives of teachers, in the values, beliefs, and deep convictions enacted in practice, in the social context that encloses such practice, and in the social relationships that enliven the teaching and learning encounter' (1991, p. 50). The field setting becomes the site wherein understandings are shaped, and bases for curriculum action developed, in other words, the field is the direct site of theorizing. The irrelevancy of much academic theory to field settings, Britzman found, has led to a widespread hostility that many classroom practitioners have to the world of academia, a hostility that does not diminish over time. Teachers are forever reminded that they cannot generate their own power source, that they cannot tender for national educational initiatives, that they are merely the servants within a curriculum or standards game of others' making.

The drama education example confirms Britzman's thesis. Teachers who discuss working methods for dealing with immediate curricula happenings are construed as acting in opposition to scholarly and disciplined inquiry. Readers familiar with the field of drama education may be surprised that the example dismisses or ignores numerous works prior to its publication that explore theory. *Towards a Theory of Drama in Education* (Bolton, 1979), *Drama as Context* (Heathcote, 1980), *Children and Drama* (McCaslin, 1981), *Dorothy Heathcote: Collected Writings on Education and Drama* (Johnson and O'Neill, 1984), *Drama, Language and Learning* (Schaffner, Little and Felton, 1984), *Making Sense of Drama* (Neelands, 1984), *Time for Drama* (Burgess and Gaudry, 1985), *Drama Words* (Booth, 1987), and, *Teaching Drama* (Morgan and Saxton, 1987) are just a few texts which would have been available to the author at that time. Readers must induce that the theoretical frameworks provided in these books, allied to practice as they are, have no academic legitimacy in a neo-positivist culture which distrusts the understanding of teachers, their students and their school communities.

The second example develops upon the first. In this short extract, the outcomes of educational practice in the arts are highlighted and applauded. A recurring distrust of current pedagogy is emphasized and a statement as to how practice can be improved is asserted:

> In brief, educational drama has been culturally provincial. It now needs to widen its range and open itself fully to the whole circle of theatre. It needs to bring a wealth of philosophical conception from the long European tradition to its reformulations; not only the mandatory Brecht and Boal but also Aristotle's *Poetics*, Nietzsche's *The Birth of Tragedy* and the formulations of, say, Strindberg, Lorca, T.S. Eliot, Arthur Miller, Jonathan Miller and a hundred others. Students of drama, at whatever level, need more technical terms, more abstract concepts, more awareness of names, movements, genres. (Abbs, 1994, p. 135)[2]

Readers unfamiliar with the field of drama education will be able still to identify the tenor of this passage, reminiscent as it is of E.D. Hirsch's (1987) *Cultural Literacy*. The author's idea of a drama curriculum is one grounded in a long Anglo-European tradition of theatre, and predominantly, it seems, a theoretical grounding in the works of men. Technical competence is allied to a content knowledge base of names, movements and genres; a knowledge base, we assume, which is documented in books that students will read or in which they will be instructed. Knowledge exists in the outside world, it can be taught, tested and measured. The author seems firmly convinced of what is required, what is needed, to make a curriculum less culturally provincial. Students need to be trained, and teachers must train them, but that training must conform to a preconceived, rather than evolving, Eurocentric version of truth.

Students are the beneficiaries of a delivered and mechanical curriculum, not a constructed or negotiated one. There is an assumption that this delivered artistic-aesthetic curriculum will prepare a better and more dutiful workforce, and through implication solve political and economic dilemmas, and, we assume, decrease national foreign debt, balance the trade deficits, and promote a *culturally non-provincial* society. Again I am reminded of Britzman's (1991) research which indicated that there is not 'one monolithic culture that communicates unitary meanings'. To reduce a curriculum to a cultural set of recycled facts, events or happenings, denies the life experiences of teachers, students and their school communities. 'Within any given culture', found Britzman (1991), 'there exists a multiplicity of realities — both given and possible — that form competing ideologies, discourses, and the discursive practices that are made available because of them' (p. 57). There is a de-humanizing process at work, it seems to me, when curriculum advocates ignore the truth that people construct and experience curriculum on a daily basis.

The neo-positivism contained within both extracts and their implications for research in drama and arts education are worrying. While the above authors would claim that they are arts educators, they peculiarly draw on scientific principles — the foundation of neo-positivism — when launching their attack on current practice. My concern here is that research in drama and arts education is disfigured when it pursues a neo-positivist agenda, an agenda which is blind to contemporary understandings of the arts and how we research them. While current writers in drama and arts education promote neo-positivism as the foundational principle upon which knowledge is understood, they are reducing the arts to a measurable cohort of scientific experiences. I am drawing on the four key themes of neo-positivism as outlined by Kincheloe (1991, pp. 50–1) when making this case. These themes are: scientism, the positivist conception of science, the doctrine of scientific politics, and value freedom.

Scientism

Scientism has had a profound effect on the research act and continues to be promoted as significant in the arts. In this -ism the knower is independent from the known, objectivity is more valued than subjectivity, phenomenon is best understood when it is reduced to its constituent parts. In the two drama examples, we see a clinical analysis of curriculum which seemingly refutes the life experiences of all its players, preferring to promote a unitary or self-evident definition of content. The human *context* of lived experience is presented, at best, as secondary but most often as an irrelevancy to this definition.

What is ignored by those who preach this method of scientism is that students cannot simply be construed as learners or receivers. Students, as most good teachers would be aware, enter classrooms already knowledgeable about their world. They come from particular cultural and ethnic communities and have their own evolving physiological, emotional, social and sexual outlook. Curriculum content is mediated by the students' understanding of themselves and their place in the world. In the above extracts on drama education, there is a confirmed belief that children's meaning-making can be divided into discrete propositional stages in isolation from the students' world experiences.

Cartesian dualism which divided the internal world of sensation from an objective world of known truths (Kincheloe, 1991, p. 27) is reinforced by such an outcome-driven educational program. While a student's ability to recycle the names, movements and genres within a theatrical canon may indicate little about the student's comprehension of, or transaction with, an art experience, this prowess becomes the important determinant when measuring knowledge. As Jerome Bruner (1979, p. 74) reminds us, though, art as a form of knowing operates under a vision of multiplicity rather than a form of unification, 'For in the experience of art, we connect by a grammar of metaphor, one that defies the rational methods of the linguist and the psychologist.' That grammar of metaphor cannot be contained within a fixed vision of theory, facts and phenomena. The grammar of metaphor requires a liberation of self, an ability to transcend the world of familiar truths and enter an imaginary maze of possibilities. However, when the metaphor and the experience of that metaphor becomes secondary to its grammatical composition, it's unclear how an arts education entitlement can be fully achieved.

To reduce one's experience of literature, drama, dance, music or art, to a singular truth or to its grammatical components — for example, that Brecht introduced Epic Theatre, or that a European tradition of music should be central to curriculum, or that periods of art history can be taught in bite-size units — fails to engage us fully with the metaphor. 'What is lost in such translations', continues Bruner (1979, p. 74), 'is the very fullness of the connection produced by the experience of art itself.' While an understanding of Brecht, European developments, and criticism and aesthetics, may support our experience, it shouldn't predetermine it, although the frequency in which students resort to guides on how to read literature demonstrates the dangers of predetermination. When experience is construed only in terms of identifiable and reducible parts, the possibilities open to people as they interact with arts works are diminished.

The Positivist Conception of Science

In this theme, explanation and prediction of observable events are the mainstay. What cannot be rationally or scientifically articulated has no truth. Some years ago I tracked the pervasiveness of this conception within many research projects, especially those in drama education (Taylor, 1990, 1992). Here, the standard empirical model is pursued at all costs. Control groups are established, treatment groups offer counterbalance, statistical measurements become the popular advocacy tool for determining validity. In these studies, we learn little of the learning processes experienced by the treatment group but rather are provided with convoluted statistical analyses of the learning. Apparently my concerns regarding this model have not been heard as studies of the neo-positivistic kind continue to be conducted with great frequency.

An example from the US *Youth Theatre Journal* highlights the major features of this model. In an investigation which aimed to test the impact of creative drama on the social health of emotionally disturbed children, Buege (1993) grounded her research design in the principles of neo-positivism. When studying the effect of 'reverse mainstreaming' on the social health of fourth-grade children, a process where 'nonhandicapped children are deliberately placed into classrooms of handicapped children' (Buege, 1993, p. 19), some peculiar assumptions and categorizations are made. Her hypothesis was that creative drama, a controlled set of role-play activities with predetermined outcomes, would improve the self-concept of emotionally disturbed (ED) children. Little indication though is given as to what an ED child might look like, how self-concept is gauged, or why a researcher would want to analyse numerically the attitudes of non-ED children towards ED children. It is assumed that these points are obvious and known ones.

We see here an attempt to reduce a dynamic and lived experience of creative drama to a sequence of controllable and containable units, although one wonders how you can control or contain such an enactive encounter as creative drama? Buege's hypothesis concerning the effect of creative drama on self-concept would be *tested* by having the treatment or experiment group participate in 32 half-hour weekly sessions which involved creative drama. Within this experimental group, 'seven emotionally disturbed children (aged 6 to 8; mean age 7.4) participated with one fourth-grade class of 24 normal students (mean age 9.2). Another fourth-grade class of 23 students (mean age 9.0) served as a comparison group' (Buege, 1993, p. 19).

Rigour, it seems, comes from matching or pairing groups and attempting to control scientifically the learning which will occur. In this instance, a standard inventory on a scale of 1 (low) to 5 (high) is cited to analyse 'observed individual and group behaviours in concentration, imagination, nonverbal expression, verbal expression, evaluation and critical analysis, cooperative interaction, and attitude toward self and others' (Buege, 1993, p. 20). From these seeming observations, charts of annual growth for each student were prepared and the results analysed. One wonders how annual growth can be charted in this way? or, how researchers know when they're observing 'behaviour' like imagination, nonverbal expression, and attitude toward self and others? A paragraph from the result analysis is particularly intriguing:

The self-concepts of ED students increased from an average pretest score of 46.14 to an average posttest score of 58.71. [Any *t* scores less

> than 40 indicate low self-concept.] The calculated mean difference or
> effect size of 12.57 (SD = 8.04), t (6), $p < .006$) confirmed significant
> differences, in spite of the fact that two students may have inflated
> their scores to fulfill their need to appear socially acceptable. (Buege,
> 1993, p. 20)

Despite the emphasis on testing, measurement, and standard statistical analysis, the data's findings may be substantially skewed because of students' perceptions that certain responses in this study would be more 'socially acceptable'.
Student participants, or research *subjects* as they are often referred to in neo-
positivist studies, are quite adept, it seems, at predicting the answer or observation that they believe is required by the researchers. However, given this
limitation, the researcher proves her hypothesis, perhaps unsurprisingly, and
confirms her belief that creative drama can be usefully inducted into a curriculum which examines social health.

This example is but one of the many studies in drama education which
pursue a positivist conception of science (Taylor, 1993, 1995). While some
may dismiss the foolhardy attempt to manage research in this manner, the
implications for curriculum reform are pervasive. In England, for example, the
growing fascination with *modular syllabi* is geared towards listing the skills
and abilities which all members of a given age group should achieve. One
advocate of this model, for instance, promotes his own positivist conception
of science by identifying the skills children should demonstrate:

> ... by the age of 11 in drama most students should be able to make
> and take part in improvised scenes and act out convincing characters.
> They should also have developed sufficient physical flexibility to enable
> them to adapt voice and movement in a controlled manner to the
> characters they play ... At 11, most students in drama should be able
> to expand scenarios into simple dramatic scripts (in English, playscripts
> are specifically mentioned as an example of an appropriate activity for
> students working to level 5). By the time they leave the primary school,
> all students should know how to polish their work for presentation
> and should have become accustomed to the disciplines of rehearsal
> and to the process of refining plays in the light of audience response.
> (Hornbrook, 1991, p. 134)

If the above advocate were to research children's learning in drama, he would
no doubt find little fault in Buege's neo-positivist design. Children's ability, it
seems, can be quantitatively isolated, observed, and assessed. Within this
conception, there is an assumption that these criteria can be clearly pictured.
For instance, teachers are expected to identify easily the criterion of 'sufficient
physical flexibility' at age 11, and can note what primary children's ability
to 'polish their work for presentation' looks like. There is an assumption that

such behaviour can be observed and measured, but it would take little time to expose the flaws in this naive belief. Experienced teachers would know that a polished presentation for one primary child might be quite different from another's. Notions of *polish* in presentation would depend on each child's own context, and knowledge of and involvement with drama. Within primary and elementary schools there is little tradition of classroom drama anyway, so one wonders how children will achieve the flexibility and polish required of an 11-year-old?

Furthermore, within this model, one assumes that if teachers are not able to maintain this proficiency in their students, if they cannot bring their 11-year-olds to a state of 'sufficient physical flexibility' they are inevitably incapable of conducting their duties satisfactorily. The positivist conception of science, emphasizing unitary definitions of achievement, can police whether standards are being achieved. Attainment not only measures children's ability, then, but their teacher's capacity to get the children to the specified competency.

I remain unconvinced that outcomes and measures like those described above naturally fit within an artistic-aesthetic curriculum. There is a danger in predetermining curriculum content, in prescripting the required outcomes, in programming the skills and attainment, in wanting to control and be controlled. There is a danger in promoting a neo-positivist view of research which promotes technical modes of inquiry when describing artistic processes. There is a danger, in other words, of the arts becoming fundamentally linear and developmental symbol systems whose role is seen in utilitarian terms. Within this context, control and experimental groups only serve the modular syllabus. If this is the new world order, if the truth of the arts can be only justified in technical terms, in isolated performative acts, then we forget the transformatory capacity of the artform to release us into new forms of experiencing, new modes of rendering. Do we, as Greene fears (1989, p. 221), want to produce a generation of students who are incapable of seeing, hearing, and attending to the possibilities of arts works, but who are adept at intellectualizing over them?

Just as there is nothing more deadly than the skilled artist who has little to communicate but an armoury of skills, there is a corrupted ethos in motion which has arts educators seeking meaning and research in a sequential curriculum rather than an emergent one. If we agree with Greene that the arts are about risk-taking, about rebellion, about reflective turning, about the confrontation of senses, about the moving of people into the imaginary realm of possibility and the fostering of a human freedom, it is hard to see how the controls of neo-positivism will permit that release. 'I cannot conceive of imposing an aesthetic experience on a student,' asserts Greene (1989), 'of manipulating him/her into having one, anymore than I can conceive of having an aesthetic experience in a state of bland, uninformed receptivity' (p. 217). The neo-positivist conception of science is powered by imposition, an imposition which fails to include the meaning-making of those who should most benefit from it, the children and their teachers.

The Doctrine of Scientific Politics

Within this doctrine, advocacy statements only have legitimacy if they are presented in terms that the empiricists understand. If we return to Comte's claim that it is in the scientific or positivist realm that truth can be known, then that which deals with uncertainty or ambiguity cannot be tolerated. Metaphysical questions, dealing as they do with the abstract, the philosophical, the spiritual, and the imaginary do not stand convincingly in a neo-positivist world which demands concrete outcomes and reachable targets.

The arts, located often as they are within metaphysical and contradictory realities, are betrayed when their proponents demand fixed truths and appeal for neo-positivist research. An instance of such a betrayal is when process drama, a negotiated fictional encounter where theatre forms are used by classroom participants to explore the human condition, is dismissed because empirical designs, like those advocated by Buege, are not pursued. A number of critics have raised concerns with process drama (see Fletcher, 1995, pp. 29–30; Hoepper, 1995, p. 109; Varney, 1991). For example, a process drama with Canadian 5-year-olds where a teacher, working from a folktale about the migration of young Chinese men to North America, is criticized because it does not fit neatly within a neo-positivist curriculum. In this drama, the teacher, David Booth, assumed the role of a ship's captain looking for volunteers for the long voyage from China. The folktale became a pretext for him and the primary children to open up, through dramatic exploration, the harshness of journeying, of discovery, and of being taken from one's homeland.

As Booth (1994, p. 77) describes the children's encounter with drama, as he takes the reader through the observations that their regular teachers were making of the work, and how the artform seemed to permit the children 'to hypothesise, to identify with and clarify what is happening both in the story, in the drama and in . . . [their] life,' one commentator frowns, dismissing the author's observations and analysis of the leader's and students' work as lacking scholarship:

> . . . researchers must establish the actual *purpose* of process drama and determine how *effective* it is in achieving that purpose. It is by no means obvious to most people that the slim — at times invisible — outcomes of these experimental encounters are worth the hours of role-playing that precede them. Curriculum time is valuable, and the question has to be asked whether students might not as effectively achieve what often seem excessively modest goals in less convoluted ways. It is hard to refute, for example, the suggestion that David Booth's 10 year olds [sic] might equally well *discover the heart of a story* (whatever that is) by reading one. (Hornbrook, 1995, p. 86)

What is odd about this criticism is the dismissal of the observations that the children's teachers were making about the work, and especially about how the drama seemed to release specific students into the role-play. Booth painstakingly cites the teachers' logbooks when recapturing the story-drama session. One teacher, for example, comments on a shy and reluctant boy, Frank, who seemed incapable of engaging with the work until this teacher adopted a different role stance in the dramatic encounter. 'Frank slowly but surely entered the drama as I played a shy role,' observes this teacher. 'I found that by acting more timid than he,' she continues, 'I both empowered him and pulled him into the drama' (Booth, 1994, p. 76). She then proceeds to comment on concrete moments where changes in her student's actions were demonstrated. This teacher seems to be learning a great deal about process drama, its structure and potential within the curriculum for providing students with comprehensive experiences. Her ongoing and systematic attempt to investigate a teaching encounter, in other words her classroom research, has led to new insights into the potential of process drama as a powerful symbol system.

This description of a learning process reveals something of the complexity of a dynamic artistic-aesthetic encounter, but its power lies too in how the teacher was looking at and responding to the event, through the eyes of her reserved student, Frank. Why is it that the stories of classroom teachers at work with their kids are savagely discounted by those outside of the practical classroom context? Why can't outcomes be framed by practising teachers in terms of what students appear to be actually doing within a given moment? Can purposefulness and effectiveness only be construed in propositional terms? If we return to the earlier attainment targets of 'sufficient physical flexibility' and polished work, would it not be more beneficial to examine these criteria within a real and living context? In Frank's case, while both criteria seem evident, does it not seem narrow-minded to reject his work on the grounds that the outcomes were not predetermined but rather evolved?

Value Freedom

The fourth theme of neo-positivism which has assumed a potency with arts educators in recent times is that emotions should be removed from the research act. This argument is based on the premise that objectivity, a principal tenet of neo-positivism, ensures that the data is untainted or polluted by human interference. In Buege's (1993) study, for example, the fact that 'two teachers served as participant-observers and ethnographic auditors' (p. 19) evidently makes her findings more valid, although I fear there is a contradiction in terms with her phrase *ethnographic auditor*, implying as it does that an ethnographic account only has value if it is externally evaluated.

The argument for objectivity is cherished by those interested in quantitative measures. Numbers speak more truthfully than words, as Kincheloe (1991) explains:

> Positivists argue that the only way to avoid mistakes is through the application of a rigorous research methodology, i.e., one that follows a strict set of objective procedures which separate the researcher from

that being researched. In order to be meaningful, the argument goes, social inquiry must be rigorous. Indeed, positivists see the pursuit of rigor as the most effective means to validation. The basis of rigorous research is, of course, quantification. Unambiguous and precise, rigorous quantitative research reduces subjective influences and minimises the ways in which information might be interpreted. (p. 129)

In process drama research, for example, Booth's documentation of his own teaching, despite the presence of numerous participant-observers who kept logs, makes his account less objective and therefore more fallible, or at least that seems to be the thrust of the cited criticism. If another person were to research Booth's classroom, the findings, we are led to believe, would be more trustworthy. Buege's design which emphasizes scientific control and statistical measurement is apparently a more valid research paradigm because the researcher is value-free. The fact that Buege (1993, p. 20) discovered that 'two students may have inflated their scores to fulfill their need to appear socially acceptable' does not make the study less objective in her mind. The implications of this latter claim are damning though of her design, suggesting as they do that testing students does not result in reliable findings.

The myths in the claim for objectivity are becoming clearer. Objectivity has no greater hold on an external evaluator than it does on a classroom teacher. The critical point is that every attempt is made by each researcher to ensure the trustworthiness of the findings. Trustworthiness in interpretive-based design has been traditionally supported by ensuring that the researcher's observations are credible or believable ones. As we read Booth's account of the process drama class, for instance, as we encounter the log entries of the participating teachers, as we read the multiple accounts of the children's actions, the observations appear to be trustworthy, and are certainly no less so than an external evaluator's inventory of the number of times an *emotionally disturbed* fourth-grader displays imagination and nonverbal expression (Buege, 1993, p. 20). Just because one researcher keeps a checklist with a scale of 1 to 5, while another pursues thick description of an event does not make the former more credible, although I would like to think that the latter is a far more human-centred account.

Classroom teachers can be just as objective as they observe their kids at work, and are probably more likely to be so given that they are familiar with the personal histories of the children, a familiarity which external evaluators would not have. For instance, the teacher working with the reserved boy Frank, knowing his shyness, assumed a particular persona to draw the child into the process drama. The teacher's knowledge of Frank, a knowledge built up over some time and as a result of personal objective data, would have her in an informed position to select a strategy, perhaps even more informed than an assessor who knew little about him. Objective readings or the ability to understand the semiology of the classroom community is what good teachers do on a daily basis.

Value freedom does not lead to good teaching practice nor does it ensure good research. How is it possible for researchers to be free of their value system no matter what research design they are pursuing? For instance, for all of the previously cited criticism of Booth's process drama it is clear that what motivates our critic's resistance is his own value system or proclivity toward a particular mode of drama activity. When we know that he was an actor and director and would much prefer to watch children putting on formal productions rather than engaged in dramatic playing activity with their teacher, readers can better understand and respond to his argument. Most critics of process drama seem to have a similar proclivity.[3] We are all shaped by our values, by our experiences and by the specific influences on our lives. The following description of a school production, for instance, appears to have been a critical incident for our cited critic:

> . . . over two hundred children from all parts of a large comprehens-
> ive had researched, written and performed a play with songs, about
> their locality and its old mining tradition. Almost all their parents, and
> many of their grandparents, had been involved in one way or another,
> as had the school's music and art departments, the latter to the extent
> of structuring lessons around projects associated with the show. In the
> hall, on a first night packed with mums and dads and grannies and
> aunties and babies and dogs, as well as with children and their teachers,
> the atmosphere was electric. Anyone who has experienced the massive
> outpouring of energy and enthusiasm harnessed by a successful com-
> munity play of this kind will know what rich and unforgettable festivals
> they can be. (Hornbrook, 1989, p. 137)

Although no supporting narratives of these observations are presented, the reader must take the above *Father Knows Best* description on trust, the description is value-loaded rather than value-free. I wonder, though, whether such conventional ideas of family and play are the common experiences of teachers, especially in socio-economically challenged environments where there is often no extended family of 'mums and dads and grannies and aunties and babies and dogs'? What does this loaded information tell us about our critic and the kinds of school experiences he has had and values? The context shapes the meaning, and the context is rich with emotion and passion, to the point where the author would like to see that blissful moment or perceived effect in the school replicated, and his *modular syllabus* would be, he later states, the cause of that effect (Hornbrook, 1989, p. 138).

But the cause–effect argument cannot be the *modus operandi* of drama and arts education research. It would be a difficult and frustrating thing for a drama teacher to replicate the 'outpouring of energy and enthusiasm' present within that school community. Such energy and enthusiasm is powered by the context, the physical, psychological and cultural situation that the community found themselves in at that time, and which they may never experience again.

That experience is no different from the one that 5-year-old Frank and his teacher encountered, who at a moment in time found that through the process drama they could transcend the boundaries of their real existence and discover some new mode of being within the imaginary world.

How then do we describe the experience of students as they engage in the artistic-aesthetic curriculum? How do teachers investigate learning in the arts? What are the factors which impact upon the successful negotiation of an artistic-aesthetic curriculum? How can we research teaching in drama and arts education? These are the questions we must now look to given the era of neo-positivism documented in the above four themes.

Paradigms and Possibilities

The following chapters present a variety of ways of viewing research in drama and arts education, and propose frameworks through which knowledge might be gained. These frameworks are likened to paradigms, or holding-forms, which contain ideas about how reality in drama and arts education can be defined, investigated and reported on. Research questions often suggest the paradigms investigators might look to for design support. In general educational research literature, there has been a growing interest in research paradigms (Maykut and Morehouse, 1994). Guba (1990), for instance, has identified four of them: positivist, postpositivist, critical theory and constructivist. Each paradigm is governed by its own belief about the character and design of human understanding. The positivist and postpositivist paradigms, for example, emerge within the neo-positivist context discussed above, and are interested in the kinds of truths best demonstrated through quantitative research methods. Critical theory and constructivism, however, pose different questions about truth, power, and understanding, and share an interest in qualitative ways of configuring human experience, an interest pursued by many of the authors in this book.

Although these four paradigms seemed an attractive and neat way of organizing investigative modes, and could have been an appropriate structure to follow here, in my view there are too many overlaps in these categories. My concern is that discrete divisions might lead to separated rather than dialogical renderings of research paradigms. For instance, while critical theorists may be driven by interrogating the ownership of power, constructivists, too, might well find themselves questioning familiar ways of seeing the world as they recapture the apprehendable realities within their various field settings. As is noted by Saldaña and Wright in Chapter 7 in this volume, there should be no either/ors in research design, as often qualitative inquirers wish to quantify their observations, and vice versa.

Guba with Lincoln recognize the fragile nature of their four paradigms. In the *Handbook of Qualitative Research* they note that 'no final agreements have been reached even among . . . [each paradigm's] proponents about their definitions, meanings or implications' (Guba and Lincoln, 1994, p. 109). So, if the authorities are not in agreement about what characterizes research paradigms, then beginning investigators should feel comfortable with the complexity and multi-dimensionality posed when they embark upon selecting the methodology which will help them investigate their research question(s).

Rather than subdivide research paradigms into discrete *how to* sections which present tidy and non-refutable solutions to matters of design, this book is divided into two parts, each focusing on complex and challenging questions which might face those interested in inquiry into drama and arts education. Part One, *Paradigms*, identifies some of the major trends in research design and highlights the basic belief systems of researchers. These belief systems shape how studies are constructed, and demonstrate how researchers' values can influence matters of data collection and analysis.

Chapter 1 sets the scene by grounding investigative work firmly in the hands of the practitioner. Classroom-based inquiry, where teachers activate themselves, their students, and their wider school communities in a range of investigatory endeavour, what I liken to reflective practitioner design, celebrates the power of individuals and their mentors as they generate their own knowledge within their own field settings. Sharon Grady in Chapter 2 relates this work to critical theorizing and offers a wealth of theoretical lenses which inform research activity. Grady examines these theories within the context of theatre-in-education companies which tour schools and promote their own value-laden belief systems.

In Chapter 3, John Carroll shares Grady's interest in studies which represent multiple ways of viewing and construing the world. Carroll's interest in postmodernist literature and its commitment to grounded realities demonstrates his concern with case-study methodology. Research design, argues Carroll, is a political statement which identifies what is and is not cherished by the researcher. Chapter 4 by Brian Edmiston and Jeff Wilhelm takes us back to the classroom and provides an account, a case, of how teachers and their students can co-create a research community. Edmiston reveals how phenomenological, ethnographic and action research approaches, and the questions they pose, can release this community into fruitful and illuminating discoveries.

In Chapters 5 and 6, Lowell Swortzell and Angela O'Brien, respectively, remind us that belief systems are constructed out of the historical frameworks in which people find themselves. They open up the exciting world of inquiry into the past, present and future, and reveal how historically situated truths can be best represented and misrepresented.

The concluding Chapter 7 in this part, by Johnny Saldaña and Lin Wright, cautions us not to be too eager to dismiss research design which aims to quantify human experience. Saldaña and Wright examine the character of experimental design and how it interacts with other research approaches. Any research paradigm, they argue, is informed by human construction, even those which are driven by numerical and statistical configurations.

Readers interested in simplistic solutions to complex issues may not necessarily find them in these Part 1 contributions. As Guba and Lincoln (1994) have asserted, research paradigms,

... are all inventions of the human mind and hence subject to human error. No construction is or can be incontrovertibly right; advocates of any particular construction must rely on *persuasiveness* and *utility* rather than *proof* in arguing their position. (p. 108)

Such persuasiveness and utility is a feature of Part 2, *Possibilities*. In this section, four individuals share their own research journeys, their own investigative forays, their own understanding of what research can be and where it might lead drama and arts educators. Cecily O'Neill, Chapter 8, unlocks the exciting possibilities of theory and metaphor and how both have informed the practice of artists and artistry over many years. O'Neill describes her expedition into related disciplines as she inquires into the complexity of drama education; she does so, conscious of how this journey informs her own evolving conceptual framework.

In response to O'Neill, John O'Toole in Chapter 9 muses on how arts works contain the life histories of the people who construct them. O'Toole's interest in personal voice, and how scholarship in art can be rendered and made accessible to the wider educational community is a theme shared by other contributors to this volume. In Chapter 10, Jonothan Neelands reflects on how research and researchers seemed foreign in his previous employment life as a classroom teacher. Now, in his university post and as a full-time member of the conventional research community, he canvasses some of the challenges he faces as a drama researcher.

Margot Ely, in the concluding Chapter 12, allies many of these challenges to research presentation. How can investigative findings be communicated in a way which does justice to the form and which honours the researcher's voice? Ely's interest in novelistic accounts of human affairs, in playscripts, vignettes and pastiche as a medium for representing our research experiences, will appeal to the many arts educators concerned with the constraining distortions evident when they're expected to present data in standard dissertation style, a predetermined written form which can conflict with how artists make sense of and portray their world's truths.

Finally, a concluding afterword statement by Gavin Bolton reminds us of the complexities and ethics involved with research activity, and that the term, research, should not be used loosely to describe any investigative approach utilized in education. While many drama and arts educators might comfort themselves that they are naturally engaged in scholarly activity, Bolton cautions them of the flaws that could be contained in this naive attitude.

This book is an introduction to research paradigms and the possibilities that they offer us in drama and arts education. The ideas presented here offer support for those contemplating, beginning or even continuing research in drama and arts education. The task will be now for the readers of this volume to engage further in the dialogue suggested by the enclosed authors so that the field can continue to unfathom its decisive features and, in the process, contribute further to knowledge, advancement and advocacy.

Notes

1   David Hornbrook (1989, p. 3) was critical of the drama practice documented by the British educators Dorothy Heathcote (1980) and Gavin Bolton (1979). This practice, now widely referred to as process drama (O'Neill, 1995), is powered by teachers and students jointly enacting a fictional world as they explore the human condition. The basic thrust of Hornbrook's criticism of process drama seems to lie in the belief that negotiated and structured improvisational activity in schools denies students access to a critical theatre heritage. In response, Heathcote and Bolton (1995) have asserted that dramatic artistry can occur in process, and that a study of criticism and aesthetics should not be seen in opposition to the lived experience of process drama.

2   Peter Abbs (1994, p. 135), series editor of the Falmer Press Library on Aesthetic Education, has argued that process drama cannot be construed as an aesthetic activity because the artistic products are not clear in a neo-positivistic sense. Whereas Abbs' model separates the art object from its spectator, Heathcote and Bolton assume a constructivist stance where meanings and theories are generated in action and through a specific context. Within Abbs' model of an aesthetic field, conventional propositional outcomes appear to be emphasized over the ongoing understandings and meaning-making of the participants.

3   See Judith Ackroyd (1995) for a most convincing critique of the motives and values of those critical of process drama. As Ackroyd argues, it is ironical that such critics rarely present their own classroom practice for public scrutiny, being more interested to build their academic positions through a hostile and uninformed dismissal of those working with student participants in the field. Equally of interest is the critics' populist penchant for citing postmodernist and feminist theories for theoretical support which results in a mischievously distorted analysis, Ackroyd (1995) suggests, laden with 'obfuscatory language' and where readers strain 'to hear even the whisper of a child' (p. 6).

The use of feminist authors, rather than classroom participants, to help *theorize* about the perceived masculinist and phallocentric themes of process drama teachers is significant. For instance, the cited work of David Booth is apparently politically incorrect because it is informed by legends and cultures which are driven by journeys, quests, adventures, and the search for an indigenous identity, a search which some theorists believe should not be the subject of educational practice (see Nicholson, 1995). While it is not the place of this book to critique flawed and censored understandings of selected feminist theory as they apply in process drama, the point is well made that classroom practitioners, again, are seen in opposition to the theorists or researchers. Interesting, too, is the important growing literature in non-feminist studies, such as that found in gay and lesbian education (see Epstein, 1994; Harbeck, 1992; Misson, 1995), which provide a counterpoint to those who privilege a theoretical stance and which has been surprisingly ignored by those advocating a solely *gendered* position.

References

Abbs, P. (1994) *The Educational Imperative: A Defence of Socratic and Aesthetic Learning*, London, Falmer Press.

Ackroyd, J. (1995) 'But tell me, where do the children play: A response to Helen Nicholson', *DRAMA: One Forum Many Voices* (The Journal of National Drama, England), **3**(2), pp. 2–8.

Bolton, G. (1979) *Towards a Theory of Drama in Education*, London, Longman.

Booth, D. (1987) *Drama Words*, Toronto, Language Study Centre.

Booth, D. (1994) 'Entering the story cave', *NADIE Journal* (A publication of the National Association for Drama in Education, Brisbane, Australia), **18**(2), pp. 67–78.

Britzman, D. (1991) *Practice Makes Practice: A Critical Study of Learning to Teach*, Albany, State University of New York Press.

Bruner, J. (1979) *On Knowing: Essays for the Left Hand*, Cambridge, Harvard University Press.

Buege, C. (1993) 'The effect of mainstreaming on attitude and self-concept using creative drama and social skills training', *Youth Theatre Journal* (A publication of the American Alliance for Theatre and Education, USA), **7**(3), pp. 19–22.

Burgess, R. and Gaudry, P. (1985) *Time for Drama*, Milton Keynes, Open University Press.

Consortium of National Arts Education Associations (1994) *National Standards for Arts Education*, Reston: VA, Music Educators National Conference.

Courtney, R. (1987) *The Quest: Research and Inquiry in Arts Education*, Lanham, University Press of America.

Epstein, D. (ed.) (1994) *Challenging Lesbian and Gay Inequalities in Education*, Milton Keynes, Open University Press.

Fletcher, H. (1995) 'A response to arts education colloquium', in Taylor, P. (ed.) *Pretext and Storydrama: The Artistry of Cecily O'Neill and David Booth*, Brisbane, National Association for Drama in Education.

Greene, M. (1978) 'The artistic-aesthetic and curriculum', in Greene, M. (ed.) *Landscapes of Learning*, New York, Teachers College Press, pp. 168–84.

Greene, M. (1989) 'Art worlds in schools', in Abbs, P. (ed.) *The Symbolic Order*, London, Falmer Press, pp. 213–24.

Guba, E.G. (ed.) (1990) *The Paradigm Dialog*, Newbury Park, Sage.

Guba, E.G. and Lincoln, Y.S. (1994) 'Competing paradigms in qualitative research', in Denzin, N.K. and Lincoln, Y.S. (eds) *Handbook of Qualitative Research*, Thousand Oaks, Sage.

Harbeck, K. (ed.) (1992) *Coming out of the Classroom Closet: Gay and Lesbian Students, Teachers, and Curricula*, New York, The Haworth Press.

Heathcote, D. (1980) *Drama as Context*, Aberdeen, National Association for the Teaching of English.

Heathcote, D. and Bolton, G. (1995) *Drama for Learning: Dorothy Heathcote's Mantle of the Expert Approach to Education*, Portsmouth, Heinemann.

Hirsch, E.D. (1987) *Cultural Literacy: What Every American Needs to Know*, Boston, Houghton.

Hoepper, C. (1995) 'A review of "pre-text and storydrama"', in *NADIE Journal*, **19**(1), pp. 109–10.

Hoffa, H. (1994) 'National standards: The whys and what fors', *Arts Education Policy Review*, **96**(2), pp. 16–25.

Hornbrook, D. (1989) *Education and Dramatic Art*, Oxford, Basil Blackwell.

Hornbrook, D. (1991) *Education in Drama: Casting the Dramatic Curriculum*, London, Falmer Press.

Hornbrook, D. (1995) 'Mr Gargery's challenge-reflections on *NADIE Journal*: International research issue', *NADIE Journal* (A publication of the National Association for Drama in Education, Brisbane, Australia), **19**(1), pp. 79–88.

JOHNSON, L. and O'NEILL, C. (eds) (1984) *Dorothy Heathcote: Collected Writings on Education and Drama*, London, Hutchinson.

KINCHELOE, J.L. (1991) *Teachers as Researchers: Qualitative Inquiry as a Path to Empowerment*, London, Falmer Press.

MAYKUT, P. and MOREHOUSE, R. (1994) *Beginning Qualitative Research: A Philosophical and Practical Guide*, London, Falmer Press.

MCCASLIN, N. (1981) *Children and Drama*, 2nd edn, New York, Longman.

MISSON, R. (1995) 'Dangerous lessons: Sexuality issues in the English classroom', *English in Australia*, **112**, pp. 25–32.

MORGAN, N. and SAXTON, J. (1987) *Teaching Drama: A Mind of Many Wonders*, London, Hutchinson.

NEELANDS, J. (1984) *Making Sense of Drama*, Oxford, Heinemann.

NICHOLSON, H. (1995) 'Drama education, gender and identity', *Forum of Education* (A publication of the Faculty of Education, The University of Sydney), **50**(2), pp. 28–37.

O'NEILL, C. (1995) *Drama Worlds: A Framework for Process Drama*, Portsmouth, Heinemann.

SCHAFFNER, M., LITTLE, G. and FELTON, H. (1984) *Drama, Language and Learning*, NADIE Papers No. 1, Hobart, National Association for Drama in Education.

TAYLOR, P. (1990) 'Thoughts on narrative, positivism and ethnography,' *NADIE Journal*, **14**(2), pp. 2–5.

TAYLOR, P. (1992) 'Our adventure of experiencing: Drama structure and action research in a grade seven social studies classroom.' Unpublished Doctoral Dissertation, New York University (University Microfilms International, Ann Arbor, Number 9237780).

TAYLOR, P. (1993) 'Research design in educational drama', *DRAMA: One Forum Many Voices* (A publication of National Drama, Newcastle Upon Tyne, England), **1**(2), pp. 16–21.

TAYLOR, P. (1995) 'Our adventure of experiencing: Reflective practice and drama research', *Youth Theatre Journal*, **9**, pp. 31–52.

VARNEY, D. (1991) 'Drama education: A re-staging', *NADIE Journal*, **15**(3), pp. 17–22.

Part One

Paradigms

1 Doing Reflective Practitioner Research in Arts Education

Philip Taylor

Prologue: Millennium Approaches

In 'Millennium Approaches', Part One of Tony Kushner's epic two-part play *Angels in America* (1992), the audience is thrust into a hypercritical vortex where honour is fleeting, a brutal disease savages young lives, and betrayal guides human action. Kushner has a 1980s middle-America myopically seeking guidance from a detestable breed of self-serving individuals who are motivated by guilt, lust, or their own need for self-aggrandizement. The young, ambitious and closeted gay Mormon Republican, Joe Pitt, who aspires for a Washington appointment demonstrates this breed. 'I think things are starting to change in the world,' Joe says to his alienated and drug-dependent wife Harper, appealing that she share in his dream. 'For the good,' he continues:

> Change for the good. America has rediscovered itself. Its sacred position among nations. And people aren't ashamed of that like they used to be. This is a great thing. The truth restored. Law restored. That's what President Reagan's done, Harper. He says, 'Truth exists and can be spoken proudly.' And the country responds to him. We become better. More good. I need to be a part of that, I need something big to lift me up. I mean six years ago the world seemed in decline, horrible, hopeless, full of unsolvable problems and crime and confusion and hunger and . . . (Kushner, 1992, p. 15)

But Harper knows better. The world for her is becoming a more frightening and lurid denizen every day where the environment's decay is mirrored in the gradual breakdown of humanist values. Harper's disconnectness from the planet is no more evident that in her growing estrangement from Joe, an estrangement which plunges her into chemical addiction and provokes a rapid retreat into a hallucinatory maelstrom.

Angels in America has been an extraordinary success for its playwright, playing to packed houses in London, San Francisco, New York and Sydney, as well as being the recipient of numerous theatre awards, including the Pulitizer Prize for Drama. While dealing with gay themes, perhaps it is more the human struggle to find meaning in a nonsensical world which has contributed to the play's following among an eclectic audience? Perhaps Kushner's harsh depiction of the corrupt establishment resonates with a universal understanding of how power destroys life and soul?

As I write these words, I contemplate the desperately confusing times that we live in. Every day seems to bring a continual parade of government inquiries into political misdemeanours where ministers and senators are accused of misleading the public. I am reminded of the frequent abuses of power and privilege which can have responsible citizens physically and sexually harass those they employ. While I watch the TV images of beguiling politicians with their contracts for a better society, and hear the moral majority and Christian Coalition who preach their homily of containment and self-control, I see the Pro-Choice lobby under attack, the National Endowment for the Arts fading, and minorities of every kind continually suppressed and struggling to speak, let alone be heard. I go into classrooms where kids come to school hungry because there isn't any cash or time at home to feed them. I see teachers who receive little moral support, who work with class sizes of thirty-five plus, and who are often the first ones attacked by parents and politicians when economic times are tough. I watch from my window and see a homeless man in Brisbane, a city known as the most livable in Australia, approach a teenage skateboard rider for a few coins and being told to 'Fuck Off!' And I do all of this being reminded of *Angels in America* and Joe's belief that 'Truth exists and can be spoken proudly.'

The politicians would have us believe that there is such a truth but my experience tells me otherwise. Truths are constructed from within the circumstances in which people find themselves, and just as those circumstances may change at any given time, so might the truths. In 1987, for example, when I began my graduate study, I was told that the only way I could investigate classroom drama was to establish an experimental study with two groups, a control and treatment group. The control group would not participate in drama but the treatment group would. Both groups would have the same test at the beginning and at the end of the experiment, usually a written test, and the results would be graded and then tabulated. Believing in this truth, I was quite prepared to launch myself into the experiment until it was later suggested to me by Professor Margot Ely, who became a supervisor of my doctoral work and who is also a contributor to this volume, that learning and children could not be controlled in this way. 'Surely your background in drama, Phil,' she asserted, 'would tell you that human activity is multi-dimensional and complex. How could you ever hope to study an aesthetic moment by drawing on a conventional scientific instrument?'

And, so, I date that time, 1987, as a point where I learned that there was more than one truth in research design. I learned that not only could I describe rather than measure learning processes of students but I could also describe my own learning processes as a teacher. I learned that there was a strong tradition of teacher research in education, especially in the social sciences and humanities. I discovered the power of qualitative and interpretive-based research design, became very excited by ethnography, and began what I hope will be a lifelong interest in what I describe as reflective practitioner research. And while there are many Joe's out there who inhabit university offices as well as government ones, I constantly remind myself that while I do this work they still need to be told that there are many truths in research design which can be proudly spoken of.

The Reflective Practitioner Researcher

So what is reflective practitioner research, and, how can this design access the multiplicity of visions and permit the multiplicity of truths that I am interested in? Often when people hear the term *reflective practitioner research* they think of intense introspective activity, or navel-gazing as one colleague of mine recently suggested, a more inward thinking approach toward research methodology. While I would agree that the stance of the reflective practitioner requires the ability to scrutinize the immediate context, there is the unfortunate connotation that navel-gazing implies being lost in oneself, or removed from the group. I don't see myself as a navel-gazer. On the contrary, the reflective practitioner stance demands a discovery of self, a recognition of how one interacts with others, and how others read and are read by this interaction. It is a stance peculiarly neglected by drama and arts education researchers. This is so perhaps because of various misconceptions and concerns about how the stance interacts with ongoing and comprehensive inquiry, or perhaps because of the discipline that it involves. However, it will be a central argument in this chapter that for arts educators to ignore reflective practitioner design is to remain ignorant to the kind of artistic processes which are the lifeblood of our work.

The work of Chris Argyris and Donald Schön (1974) at the Massachusetts Institute of Technology has been invaluable in my understanding of the reflective practitioner, especially in their recognition that professional competence is linked to an ability to try out ideas on-line and to understand how these trials might lead to improvement within the workplace context. In his book *The Reflective Practitioner*, Schön (1983) examines five professions — engineering, architecture, management, psychotherapy, and town planning — to show how professionals go about solving the questions, dilemmas and problems which they encounter on a daily basis. Although he does not specifically examine arts education, Schön draws on artistic processes, notably improvisational modes of inquiry, as vital to the ongoing and sustained competence of professional development.

In brief, Schön claims that the language of the bureaucrats and the technicians, which is housed in the positivist and neo-positivist world of technical rationality, is not immediately translatable to situations of daily practice. When dealing with the immediate challenges that professionals encounter, they not only draw on an intuitive knowledge base as a way for dealing with these challenges, what Schön refers to as knowing-in-action, but they utilize reflection-in-action as a means for directing their own and others' behaviour. This immediate process of reflection is characterized by a complex internal dialogue which requires prompt decisions about what the practitioner is seeing and how that seeing should influence behaviour:

> When someone reflects-in-action, he [sic] becomes a researcher in the practice context. He is not dependent on the categories of established theory and technique, but constructs a new theory of the unique case. His inquiry is not limited to a deliberation about means which depends on a prior agreement about ends. He does not keep means and ends separate, but defines them interactively as he frames a problematic situation. He does not separate thinking from doing, ratiocinating his way to a decision which he must later convert to action. Because his experimenting is a kind of action, implementation is built into his inquiry. This reflection-in-action can proceed, even in situations of uncertainty or uniqueness, because it is not bound by the dichotomies of Technical Rationality. (Schön, 1983, pp. 68–9)

Rather than pursuing other people's idea of truth, like Joe does with President Reagan's idea in *Angels in America*, reflective practitioners interrogate the character of their own truths. Although there are aspects of Schön's model which don't translate easily into the artistic-aesthetic curriculum — for instance, his weighted emphasis on problem-solving and experimental inquiry tend to defy the interpretive features of the paradigm often required in arts education research — his text does highlight one of the principal means through which arts educators operate, i.e., through their reflection-in-action, or their reflective conversation with the situation (1983, p. 268).

I am drawing an important distinction here between reflection-in-action and reflection-on-action. Readers might be familiar with the kind of action research models or the approaches to teacher research as inspired by the work of Lawrence Stenhouse (1975) in England. These models have been quite popular in educational research given that they empower teachers to take control over their own classrooms. However, there is a significant difference I would like to make between the action research model and that informed by reflective practice. Whereas action researchers tend to emphasize evaluation, rather than ongoing reflection, as a culminating activity, i.e., one plans, one acts, one evaluates, then one plans again, reflective practitioner researchers are concerned with documenting and understanding the tacit and known knowledge base which enables reflection-in-action to occur. What leads teachers to make on-the-spot decisions with their classes? How do educators know what course of action to assume within a challenging circumstance? How do teachers' interventions in a pedagogical moment impact upon the learning? These are the kind of questions which reflective practitioner researchers ask.

For arts educators, there is an attractiveness in reflective practitioner design because it honours the intuitive and emergent processes that inform artistic meaning-making. It seems to me that at the heart of the artistic act is a willingness by both the arts' makers and spectators, to transcend the boundaries of fixed realities and to enter virtual ones. Now, I would argue that the ability to transcend and to enter occurs in part because the makers and watchers engage immediately with the situation, and allow that situation to work upon them.

The opening of Stephen Sondheim's musical *Sunday in the Park with George* is a classic illustration of the decisive features of reflective practice and will help illuminate how reflective practitioner approaches are informed by artistry. As the curtain rises on a stark white space, the audience is greeted by Georges Seurat, the nineteenth-century French neo-impressionist. As this seated figure sits downstage with canvas and easel in front of him, a series of ascending arpeggios press the artist into motion. While playfully manipulating the tools of his craft, he verbalizes his understanding of significant form:

White: A blank page or canvas.
The challenge: bring order to the whole.
Through design.
Composition.
Tension.
Balance.
Light.
And harmony. (Sondheim and Lapine, 1984/91, pp. 17–18)

The images that he dabs and daubs begin to inhabit the world of the stage. Just as Seurat's white canvas is transformed into blocks of coloured patterns, the theatrical work is swept into motion. The artist's reflective conversation with himself, with the artwork, with the people and objects which inhabit that work, and with the audience, is what gives the craft its life. The artist's reflection-in-action brings into being the virtual world.

I am aware that this being is not simply powered by the creative energy which inhabits the **making** phases of artistic endeavour. Arts works are constructed through intense phases of reflection after an activity as well, and I do not want to be setting up oppositional modes of reflective activity. However, contained within the history of arts works, especially in the performing arts, is a recognition that their power rests on their lived experience. Many American dancers of Martha Graham's era, for instance, resisted and scorned the celluloid image, valuing the impression that a single performance would leave on their audience. Graham's dances were a reflection-in-action, they achieved the features of Schön's on-line exploration, a willingness to draw on and submit to one's breadth of worldly experiences when bringing form to an idea. 'Life today is nervous, sharp and zig-zag,' Graham once said. 'It often stops in mid air . . . It is what I want for my dances' (Graham in Gardner, 1993, p. 274).

While there were years of technique that went into Graham's dance, the aesthetic experience for the audience was generated not only by the skill but also by her structured spontaneity. Both dancer and spectator submit to the art work at the moment in which it is realized in form. For Graham and many other artists, reflection not only happens before and after the performed event, but informs the very event itself.

Little is known about the character of reflection-in-action. Most of us rarely have time to examine what factors lead to our own competent practice, we are too intent trying to implement or research others' versions of competence. We rarely see ourselves as the experts, as the ones who can know and reflect in action, yet without immediate and ongoing reflective activity it is difficult to see how any teaching or learning event would ever occur.

We are confounded constantly by notions of singular truth and authoritative ways of working. Perhaps artists like Graham contribute to this confusion given their emphasis on a firm skill base and grounding in the content bases of the discipline. 'The body must be tempered by hard, definite technique — the science of dance movement,' she claimed, 'and the mind enriched by experience.' Such statements imply that an artistic-aesthetic curriculum should comprise technique instruction only. However, if, as she believed, 'Nijinsky took thousands of leaps before the memorable one', (Graham in Gardner, 1993, p. 298) it seems that an analysis of the circumstances which created the *memorable one* would help us understand more completely how the dance works.

Likewise, arts educators' ability to investigate fully why they make the decisions they do, or how they reflect in action, might unravel the intricate and messy happenings which characterize a pedagogical moment. Indeed, many of the great leaders in our field are able to reflect in action and articulate how they reflect in action. In drama education, for example, there have been any number of eminent practitioners, such as Gavin Bolton and Cecily O'Neill, who have achieved recognition because they can identify cogently and artistically the decisive characteristics of sound pedagogy. How, I wonder, can we achieve this cogency and artistry within the regular world of classroom teachers? How can we enable teachers to understand and to articulate their own artistic-aesthetic curriculum? Reflective practitioner research, in my view, provides some assistance.

The Interventionist

Schön has argued that the emphasis on the expert is a damaging one to the sustained competence of professionals. He highlights difficulties in mainstream research activity when university academics, for example, enter schools as authoritative or expert figures. While those people might present exciting action research models, it is unclear how the reflective practice of those in the field will benefit from them. Schön distinguishes his idea of the *reflective contract* from the dominant *traditional contract* when developing professional competence:

In the Traditional Contract	*In the Reflective Contract*
I put myself in the professional's hands and in doing this I gain a sense of security based on faith	I join with the professional in making sense of my case, and in doing this I gain a sense of increased involvement and action
I have the comfort of being in good hands. I need only comply with his [sic] advice and all will be well	I can exercise some control over the situation. I am not wholly dependent on him [sic]; he is also dependent on information and action that only I can undertake
I am pleased to be served by the best person available	I am pleased to be able to test my judgements about his competence. I enjoy the excitement of discovery about his knowledge, about the phenomena of his practice, and about myself (Schön, 1983, p. 302)

In arts education we have inculcated a research culture which conforms to the traditional contract. For the most part, the researchers are not full-time employees of the sites in which they investigate, rather they are visitors who bring with them a bevy of ideas based on their recognized wisdom. Eisner (1985) has likened such approaches to 'educational commando raids' wherein external researchers enter classrooms for the briefest periods only to 'collect the data and to leave' quickly (p. 143). Outside experts often are employed by universities where job advancement is dependent on the research activity of its members, whereas the ongoing employment status of teachers in schools is tied into other criteria, notably their teaching and service.

The experts become the all-knowing interventionists, capable of managing, directing, and evaluating action. Interventionists have been common in action research models and are usually consultants, counsellors, facilitators and evaluators, who are co-opted by or who co-opt field settings to conduct research (Orton, 1994, p. 86). For the most part, teachers do not see themselves as able to perform the intervention role themselves, they look to an outsider, a stranger to the field, who will conduct this function.

While interventionists are incorporated within reflective practitioner design, Schön construes their role as a mentoring one, where the talents of all parties inform the research act. Power and control come from a sense of ownership, and the belief that each player can contribute important input to effective practice. Although I am not entirely convinced that teachers are incapable of performing the role of interventionist themselves, in other words, that they are incapable of pressing into their practice devices through which they can individually address their own questions, I do believe that Schön's reflective contract, where teachers collaborate with outside interventionists, can be an invaluable educative experience.

An Example of a Reflective Contract

Carl, an elementary school teacher from an inner-city school in a densely packed urban setting, was interested in how I, a college lecturer in drama education, could design jointly with him a series of classroom drama experiences which would explore the impact of chemicals on the environment. We decided that a useful approach might be to induct his grade five/six students (10–12-year-olds) into the role of investors and workers in a new factory to be named Enviro. This factory produced a number of chemical agents which would constitute cleaning fluids, including detergents and window-cleaning products. While the students worked on creating life in the factory, and imagined that they were performing such tasks as making bottles, designing labels, and testing the cleaning products, another smaller group would be encouraged to increase productivity by experimenting, secretively, with a new and dangerous toxic substance on animals.

In one lesson, a visiting teacher, John, would work with this smaller group in an adjoining room while Carl would help the other factory workers continue the production line. In our plan, this smaller group eventually would be hot-seated and interrogated about their secret experiment by the larger group. The aim of the lesson would be to raise the question, *Are Chemicals a Necessary Evil?* and challenge the students to consider what costs they would be prepared to endure when maintaining their company's productivity?

When the lesson was conducted the classroom dynamic was volatile. The 37 students demonstrated both lethargic and frenetic behaviour at numerous points. The small group in the adjoining room, a collection of highly energized boys, had difficulty focusing on the task which led to my decision to change the plan in action. No longer would this secret group report to the others about the secret experiment but they would demonstrate through four frozen images, or tableaux, the nature of their experiment. This change was driven by my observation that this particular group could not accomplish a sophisticated improvisation with the larger group, what was required was a held-up or displayed representation of their secret experiment. This display would not only help the smaller group focus on their experiment but neatly capture for the larger group the nature of the secret enterprise. I made this pedagogical decision without consulting Carl. After the lesson I knew that I would have to make clear to Carl why I spontaneously decided to transform the plan in action. We had developed a strong partnership and I was concerned that our relationship might have been jeopardized by my non-collaborative decision.

The transcript below begins with my question to Carl on how the larger group reacted when two of the experimenters from the smaller group returned after deciding not to proceed with animal testing. On the lefthand side are the actual words which we spoke during our reflective conversation, while on the right I isolate the features of the intervention and how it impacted upon our reflective practice.

Interview

Phil: Did the kids know why they came back in?

Carl: They might have thought they'd got the boot for mucking around, I don't know . . .

Phil: In a way they did.

Carl: Well, they probably did. They were disruptive and didn't want to join, so you can go back . . .

Phil: Yeah . . . and they were miffed by that.

Carl: Were they?

Phil: And ironically, when they went back in, the others decided[1] that they didn't want anything to do with animal testing and I thought, *Oh, well, John can deal with this*, and I went back inside, and by this stage the whole factory operation had come to a standstill . . . as John was struggling out there and you were struggling in there and I just stood in the middle thinking, *Oh, no!*

Carl: That was the stage yesterday when I thought, *Oh, God, will I just pull the plug on this and get them to sit down?* And that's when I said, *This is hard, work at it* . . . It must have been hard for you to stand back and not step in . . . was it or not?

Phil: It was hard to stand back and not step in but because I didn't know what was going on there . . . or why there was a hold up, I felt well I just can't step in . . . So, I felt kind of lost there.

Carl: I'm glad you did too, I think.

Phil: So, I didn't know what to do and then I just went outside, I think. And by this stage . . . John . . . the kids had decided on the rats.[2] They decided on the rats and then I thought well, we've got to have some way which this material is displayed to the other group to see how they respond to it. So then I layered in this thing of why don't you prepare four photographs?

Carl: Well, I had no idea that's how they were going to come back and present it to . . .

Phil: I don't think I had that in the plan.

Carl: No it wasn't in the . . . that's why when you came back and you've got these photographs . . . you were carrying a folder or something . . . I thought, that was quick, I didn't know about that one . . .

Phil: Well, I knew that it had to be held up and displayed and the way in which they were improvising it, they couldn't pull it

The Reflective Practitioner

Here I check with Carl whether the larger group of students that he was working with understood why two from the smaller group in another room would not be a party to animal testing. The *kids* in my question refers to the larger group.

Prior to this lesson I had assumed that this smaller group would be willing accomplices to the secret experiment. Here, I express surprise that some resisted it. I also share my frustration that the energy of the group was such that the visiting teacher, John, had trouble mobilizing the small group's interest. I share my vulnerability with Carl. The unpredictability of the lesson threw me off balance.

I could see that Carl was also frustrated. He was unable to have the students retain their concentration in the factory's production line.

Because I was observing two groups at work, Carl with the larger group and John with the smaller group, I was reluctant to assume an authoritative position when I observed Carl's frustration during the lesson.

My vulnerability as a teacher educator is being exposed again. Should I express this vulnerability to this classroom teacher who hopes to learn from me, the recognised expert, the way to proceed? Can mentors state openly that they feel lost?

I am struggling to explain to Carl my actions. I am explaining an intuitive process which I have developed over a number of years of off satisfactorily, in a committed way for an audience . . . in a sense they didn't have to improvise it because the critical thing here was how was this other group going to react when they got access to information that this group was getting involved in? Now, initially what was going to happen was that group was going to come back in and go to their own group.[3]

Carl: That's right . . .

Phil: . . . and break the news to them. And I thought that this movement needed to be frozen. We need to actually see in a concrete sense what is happening. And how do we do that? We do it through a photograph.

Carl: It's funny, that group that was chosen or they chose themselves in many ways because they had a lot of zeros on their application form . . . probably six or seven of them, then it dropped back to five . . . two dropping out[4] . . . Had I to choose them myself, they would probably have been the **last** of my choice given the fact that probably two or three of them are perpetual clowns in the group. So, it will be interesting to see how seriously they take this, whatever the next step is going to be, with their role going back to the group. I think a couple of them can do it pretty well but I have my doubts about how well. Two or three of that group will be able to go back and maintain some degree of seriousness . . .

Phil: So you thought John was going to be in for a difficult time with that group did you?

Carl: I did yes.

Phil: (Laughing) And he was.

Carl: They're a feisty bunch.

Phil: But they pulled it off.

Carl: They did. I was agreeably surprised with it.

Phil: They had to work on their photographs though. I had to constantly remind them that if they're rats we have to know that they're rats in the photographs. And in the end, we didn't know they were rats or not but we did know they were some kind of beasts. And we had to distinguish the adults from the rats . . . Maybe we might need to look at those photographs again to see what's happened to the adults? . . . Can you see why I did that? Why I changed that lesson at that point? In terms of photographs . . .

Carl: I think it was to focus the whole group's attention. It may have been the fact

drama teaching and am unsure whether Carl finds my explanation satisfactory.

Through the process of describing to Carl my decision I begin to understand how the alternate strategy was a far more effective one for helping the group focus.

The teacher's observation that the composition of the smaller group was one he would not have consciously chosen interests me. As an outsider I do not have access to this information about group dynamics and select those students who volunteered to be in the group. I have no sense of censoring their involvement.

I was determined to remind Carl that even though the plan was transformed because of the group composition and energy level, the tasks were still managed satisfactorily by the whole group, especially by the smaller group of boys.

I am reminded of my mentoring role. I do not want Carl to see me as the expert with the correct idea for strategy. He must have a role to play in the action if he is to continue using drama in the classroom.

that because John was having difficulty with that bunch out there, you may have jumped to a similar conclusion that I did, that those kids might not have been able to carry it off if you sent them back individually. Or it may have been the fact that you came into the factory and saw that the factory had broken down and wasn't operating very smoothly . . . to re-focus everyone's attention back onto this particular aspect . . .

Phil: Though when I came back in the second time the factory was working.

Carl: That's what took the hard work and that's when I sort of said, *Bugger it. I'll make this factory work.*

Phil: So it was your own bludgeoning.

Carl: Perseverance . . . in getting it to work . . . because I think I said that after the session, that was a battle and it just had to be worked through. It got there in the end and it functioned quite nicely.

Phil: It did . . . everything was connected.

I express my support for Carl's perseverance in struggling to maintain the factory line's productivity.

In my mentoring role, Carl and I unpack the processes which led to a change in the tasks. The seeming lack of teacher and student focus resulted in a different strategy that would hold the work up for all students to contemplate its implications: four tableaux of factory owners engaged in testing on rats. The reflective conversation probes the immediate pressures of classroom teaching and attempts to understand how teachers are made in the encounter. The transcript documents a subtle concern that expressions of vulnerability may undermine rather than build sound pedagogy.

The transcript reveals a willingness to interrogate practice and shows how Carl and myself position ourselves around this interrogation. Although I want Carl to be liberated, to express vulnerability, I am cautious that the work's improvisational challenges may stymie the teacher's willingness to experiment on-line. Carl is a beginner in classroom drama. The aim of the exercise is to build his confidence and preparedness to understand how structured improvisation interacts with curriculum learning. At the core of this approach, though, is that outcomes are discovered in process and that the leader is often a follower. In this sense, the work challenges central questions about schooling, curriculum, the role of teachers and students.

The challenges occur within a framework characterized by Schön's reflective contract. Carl attempts to understand my thinking while I articulate the qualities of my reflection-in-action. Security is not gained from faith in my expertise, but rather it is generated through a mutual agreement to be honest about what motivates action, and our understanding about the effectiveness of that action. Dependency is not encouraged in this contract, because dependency fails to liberate. While Carl is able to interrogate in a public sphere the action that was taken, we both gain professionally from the talk generated around a classroom event.

An Interpretive-based Paradigm

When engaged in this kind of reflective contract, where the individual voices and experiences of the participants are central to competency and effectiveness in the workplace, it is apparent that the mechanisms for collecting and analysing data are better sought from within a narrative tradition. Just as Eisner feared the Rambo-style educational commando raids which university employees seem to direct daily on schools, I fear the tightly conducted experiments which endeavour to document school experience through statistical measurements. 'Educational practice as it occurs in schools', concurs Eisner (1985), 'is an inordinately complicated affair filled with contingencies that are extremely difficult to predict, let alone control' (p. 104). The unpredictable nature of classrooms is documented in my example with Carl, where our planning had to be redesigned in the experience of its implementation. Unpredictability and uncertainty removes us from the world of singular truth, and plunges us into multiple realities and multiple visions. It is this multiplicity which is at the heart of reflective practitioner design. How, then, is this multiplicity best researched?

It will come as no surprise that reflective practitioner design most effectively yields insights into a specific teaching and learning encounter when ethnographic techniques are utilized. Ethnography's history is situated within cultural anthropology, and is exemplified in the work of field researchers like Franz Boas, Bronislaw Malinowski, Margaret Mead and Clifford Geertz, who would enter isolated communities and describe an aspect of cultural life. Their thick or rich descriptions would be grounded in a natural setting where the observed events would not be distorted by clinical measurements often pursued in a positivist or neo-positivist tradition. As ethnographers maintain that a primary feature of human social life is that individuals are continually interpreting and making sense of their world, any investigation of that world must relate these interpretations to the natural everyday situations in which people live. Ethnographers are interested in pursuing a qualitative research orientation which 'places individual actors at its centre' and focuses 'upon context, meaning, culture, history and biography' (Hitchcock and Hughes, 1995, p. 25).

In the arts, there are numerous examples of works which demonstrate interest in the power of ethnography to provide comprehensive insights into artistic processes. In drama, for example, Anthony Sher's (1985) *Year of the King* is a fascinating account of how Sher grew into the role of Richard III when he was rehearsing Shakespeare's play for the Royal Shakespeare Company. Sher's account assumes a reflective practitioner's style as he projects himself into the role, and shares with his readers the substance of his interventions during the rehearsal process. Peter Brook's (1987) *The Shifting Point* and Richard

Schechner's (1985) *Between Theatre and Anthropology* document these directors' growing interest in the theatre forms of non-western cultures, and especially their interest in describing the shared theatre beliefs, practices, and knowledge of particular and isolated communities. We can even see in the work of Constantin Stanislavski (1949/1987) at the Moscow Arts Theatre earlier this century a passion in case study and how the intensive description of a rehearsal process can reveal the skills of artists and artistry. 'Less is more' seems to be a tenet in this kind of work which probably accounts for the widespread use of case studies when presenting ethnographic accounts.

In drama education, studies which incorporate ethnographic techniques are becoming increasingly popular, especially in Australia where there is particular interest in this design (Donelan, 1995; McDonald, 1994; McLean, 1995; Mienczakowski, 1994; O'Mara, 1995). However, there is a danger that the term ethnography might be used too broadly as an attempt to define any study where fieldwork is utilized. Ethnography demands an understanding of how people think, feel, and act within their own naturalistic settings. And while many researchers adopt techniques of data collection and analysis used by ethnographers, the fact that their case studies are not capturing the complete lived experience of the participants prevents them from commanding the status of an ethnography (Ely, Anzul, Friedman, Garner and Steinmetz, 1991, p. 3; Martin, 1987, p. 20).

It would be difficult to discuss reflective practitioner research design, though, without paying homage to ethnography. Both are based on the same principle; that reality is multiple and shifting and that truths evolve and transform over time. Both are not so much interested in testing a preconceived hypothesis, but rather allow the data to generate a hypothesis. This latter distinction is a particularly important one. Just as Carl and I discovered that questions, dilemmas and uncertainties evolve in process, just as Georges Seurat in the Sondheim musical discovers the images through the experience of artistic-making, the design in reflective practitioner research must permit the focus of the inquiry to transform once the study has been launched.

Broad questions become those preferred. In my study with Carl, the guiding question, How might drama interact with the science curriculum in the elementary school? developed into, How can Carl manage drama given the curriculum constraints under which he operates? The questions in reflective practitioner design inevitably change once observations commence, as indeed they should if the researcher is to be open to the range of diverse interactions which inform an educational event. Other examples of broad guiding questions from studies which are the hallmark of this research design are:

- What characterizes my playmaking process as a playwright?
- How do my understandings of dance education interact with the experiences of grade six children? (Collins, 1995)
- How might an aesthetic framework operate in drama curriculum? (McLean, 1995)

- How can I describe teachers' and their students' work in drama education? (Donelan, 1995)
- What might reflective practice look like in my grade eight classroom? (O'Mara, 1995)
- What happens when I introduce process drama into the social studies curriculum? (Taylor, 1991)

In my experience, the broader the question, the less likely the reflective practitioner will pre-script a schedule of predetermined categories and codes through which data will be collected and analysed. The danger in such a pre-script is that it locks the researcher into testing hypotheses or researching problems, and thereby prevents the possibility to be open to the multiplicity of happenings and events which can occur in the field site.

I am aware that action research models can pivot on quite a different proposition than the one I am proposing in this chapter:

> Action Research begins with a problem in the practice of a person or group of persons. The problem normally appears as ineffectiveness: a practitioner does **X** with the intention of achieving **Y**. **Y** does not occur. **Non-Y** (what does occur) is unacceptable. The practitioner is thus faced with the dilemma of wanting to achieve **Y** but only knowing how to produce **non-Y**. (Orton, 1994, p. 86)

While I do not want to undermine the importance of teachers investigating problems within their classroom contexts, a difficulty in aligning these problems to ineffectiveness is that it can promote a simplistic cause-effect view of human experience. Testing hypotheses could prevent the researcher to be open to their generation. For example, in a study which aimed to examine how creative drama affected the quality of narrative writing in second- and third-graders in Utah, the investigators were constrained by their research design. The experimental constraints, we are told, produced a rigid inflexibility and, in certain instances, stifled students' interest. The fact that the children were presented with a series of exercises with predetermined outcomes which had to be completed within specific time limits, meant that the researchers' observations were locked into measuring one theory. 'These observations', they regretfully mused, 'suggest that drama might be a more successful planning activity under naturalist conditions' (Moore and Caldwell, 1990, p. 18). Their dependence on testing an hypothesis within conventional understandings of empirical design, distorted their ability to allow natural events to unfold around them.

Just as empirical studies may limit discovery, action research, committed to concrete solutions to immediate problems, could unintentionally promote a view that conflicts can be resolved, that truth can be found, and that life can be controlled. Perhaps it is the word 'problem' that is worrying me here. I suppose I am more interested in how research can explore possibilities, can raise an agenda rather than test a problem. In this respect, I agree with Maxine Greene (1989, p. 215) that if artists are for disclosing the extraordinary in the ordinary, then research into this disclosure should realize the troubling questions which arts works often raise. Just as Greene is interested in how artists transfigure the commonplace, I am keen to explore how reflective practitioners are reading their world, what decisions they make about importance and value, how they struggle with ambiguity and contradiction, and how they begin to ascertain the logical procedures through which they will collect, analyse and present that struggle. I am interested then in the human dimension present in reflective practitioner research, the questions this dimension implies for a study's design, the special kind of rigour faced by investigators, and how this rigour informs the artistic-aesthetic curriculum.

The Rigour and Artistry of Reflective Practitioner Design

A recurring myth that is often presented in design of this type is that the studies lack the hard-edge of reports informed by numerical renderings of human experience. Numbers, it seems, are more credible than descriptions of people and their work. Reflective practitioner design challenges this myth in two primary ways: the reflective practitioner is the principal instrument for mediating data; and, multiple perspectives on the event researched help crystallize the rigour, artistry and trustworthiness of the findings.

The Human Instrument

> At the beginning of our lesson I told Tortsov, the Director of our school and theatre, that I could comprehend with my mind the process of planting and training within myself the elements necessary to create character, but that it was still unclear to me how to achieve the building of that character in physical terms. Because, if you do not use your body, your voice, a manner of speaking, walking, moving, if you do not find a form of characterisation which corresponds to the image, you probably cannot convey to others its inner, living system. (Kostya, from Stanislavski, 1949/1987, p. 3)

In one of the most engaging accounts on the art of acting, *Building a Character*, Stanislavski demonstrates his understanding of art not by discretely listing the features of acting technique, but by presenting the diary of a fictitious student Kostya. Kostya's diary, a comprehensive record and novelistic account of the experiences of a group of actors with their Director Tortsov, enables Stanislavski to probe the world of characterization through the hearts and minds of a troupe of dedicated performers. The scope of Stanislavski's intent is beyond the focus of this chapter, however, a recurring theme of his work which relates to reflective practitioner design, is the centrality of the human instrument in the collection, analysis and presentation of data. Just as the actor explores the human condition and probes how the body can represent most powerfully that condition, reflective practitioners too draw on their own understanding of human affairs.

Reflective practitioners use their own instrument, themselves, to raise the questions of inquiry, to process how those questions will be investigated, and to consider how their emergent findings will impact upon their lifelong work. Like qualitative research design, there is a recognition that 'the field research process is as much concerned with the hopes, fears, frustrations and assumptions of the researchers' (Burgess, 1985, p. 2). My study with Carl, for example, could not have taken place unless he was receptive to the idea of incorporating process drama into this science curriculum. He agreed to proceed because he believed that this approach would be of benefit to him in the classroom. For instance, in the following excerpt from an interview I conducted with Carl, he discusses how some earlier work I did with his grade five/six students on the topic, Convict Settlement in Australia, influenced his understanding of drama and its power in the curriculum:

> *Carl*: Now, *that's* sort of putting drama into a social context rather than a personal growing within type thing. Putting it into some context it can relate to language development, problem solving situations, cooperative group activities . . . those sorts of things, very much in line with what I'm on about in the classroom. So when I first saw you do that work with them initially as the leader to them, I think I would see this is a pretty powerful tool you've got here and I've never seen it used in a way, I never thought drama could be done in a way to teach history, for instance. I never thought you could take a topic of settlement, early settlement in Australia and approach it from a dramatic point of view and I was staggered by what the kids came up with out of that, two . . . just two sessions.[5]

Carl's openness to process drama, a belief that drama will inform his teaching, prompted a reflective practitioner project. The study was not coerced or pressed by a foreign agent, he went after it himself.

Immediately, Carl's stance is different from those who research an externally imposed agenda. In Australia, for example, it is usually governmental bodies such as the Australian Research Council or the Department of Employment, Education and Training who list the research priorities. Applications for research funding have to be tailored to these priorities. Perhaps unsurprisingly these priorities usually fail to include reflective practitioner approaches. As one report on national research activity argued, the 'participants in educational processes' have been seen as 'objects for external researchers' who have not been 'agents in the research process itself' (National Board of Employment, Education and Training, 1992, p. 59). In other words, the work of teachers is the subject for external researchers. One can only surmise what deathly research papers might ensue if research priorities continue to be driven externally and thereby imposed upon the field.

Reflective practitioner design fundamentally resists the idea of an externally driven agenda. These studies tend to generate from within the school as a result of issues which teachers themselves formulate. Carl wanted to find out how drama could be incorporated into his science curriculum, he pursued his own agenda. Similarly, in another study conducted in a junior-high school in New York, I was interested to explore whether process drama would provide a group of Chinese-American students with a voice in their social studies curriculum (Taylor, 1995, 1992). For twelve months, I worked with a grade seven class and documented how process drama interacted with their curriculum learning. Both the Australian and US studies are mediated by the human dimension. They share the concerns of Kostya and his fellow actors in that the agenda is internally driven. In reflective practitioner design, our own work, our life experiences, become the vehicle for the exploration of a lived event.

Logbooks

If the human instrument is the principal medium for raising the agenda in reflective practitioner research, then the logbook is the place where that agenda is recorded. This habit is one informed from anthropology where field notes and their dedicated entry into logbooks become a pivotal feature in data collection and analysis. Diaries, journals or portfolios have had a long established tradition in artistic practices. Throughout time the artist's need to make sense of experience by thoroughly recording a relationship to an event or process has been integral to cultural expression. This artist's record is not only a written composite but can include a range of media.

I am reminded of the intricate designs which Rudolf Laban (Haynes, 1987) drew of his dances which enabled him to construct visual formulae of his technique; I see how haunting images of spidery webs and bottleneck toads drawn by Anthony Sher enabled him to understand the workings of Richard III's mind and provide a gateway into characterization; while Howard Gardner (1993) helps me understand how Martha Graham's creative life was powered by her conscientious and obsessive cataloguing which would occupy evenings of intensive activity. Graham is an especially good example of how logbooks can interact with reflective practice. 'Her heroine St. Denis', writes Gardner, 'had always scribbled down words, essays and poems, from which her dances had somehow emerged.' Readers can only speculate whether Graham's poetic imaginings would have danced on stage had she not embarked upon the Denis-inspired portfolio inquiry described in the following reflection:

I get the ideas going. Then I write down, I copy out of any books that stimulate me at the time many quotations and I keep it. And I put down the source. Then when it comes to the actual work I keep a complete record of the steps. I keep note of every dance I have. I don't have notations. I just put it down and know what the words mean, or what the movements mean and where you go and what you do and maybe an explanation here and there. (Graham, in Gardner, 1993, p. 299)

In each case — Graham, Sher and Laban — we see how the logbook becomes the tool for demonstrating the evolving understanding of particular phenomena.

Carl, too, used his log entries to record how process drama strategies were experienced by himself and his students. One entry reveals how he found great strength when he assumed for the first time a role, in this instance the role of a Health Inspector, within the process drama:

I think that the kids respond much better when they have a strong lead being given by the teacher or the person leading the group at the time. This element appears to be very important for the implementation of a quality drama program with children. It was during this session, when I took the role of the Health Inspector, that something seemed to occur to me from within. I had the confidence to take on this role in such a way that I was almost no longer their teacher, but a different person in their midst. I feel that this was the pivotal moment in the entire project for me and I was very excited by it. I was using a different tone in my voice, short sharp delivery of words in a somewhat harsh and aggressive manner. I was able to respond to questions and comments from the children without losing role. I could even discipline some in role. This was in direct contrast to my day to day teaching style.[6]

The dedication to log-keeping becomes a way for Carl to penetrate the character of his reflective practice and to understand how artistic processes informed his work. The logbook is his sourcebook, and recalls his evolving relationship to the drama activity. In the above instance, his reflective conversation helps him consider how the teacher-in-role strategy can be a powerful artistic tool for helping the leader and students confront aspects of their world. The discipline required in maintaining the logbook assists Carl in his contemplations of the value of a pedagogical strategy, and how that strategy might be effectively managed in the future.

There are no short cuts to keeping a logbook in this kind of research. As many leading qualitative researchers have written on this technique and its centrality to interpretive-based design I will not repeat this work here (Clandinin and Connelly, 1994; Ely *et al.*, 1991; Eisner, 1991; Hitchcock and Hughes, 1995;

Lincoln and Guba, 1985). However, in my experience those researchers who are unable to keep their logbook in a timely, comprehensive and ongoing manner are disadvantaged when they analyse and/or write up their data. It is difficult to record your observations of an educational event which occurred days, months, even years ago, let alone attempt to analyse those observations. The trick it seems is to follow Graham's lead and become passionate about the study and want to put it on the public record where it can be scrutinized and where it can direct, hopefully, further action.

The Art of Crystallization and Trustworthiness

Developing multiple perspectives on the event(s) being examined have permitted reflective practitioner researchers to develop confidence in the trustworthiness of their findings. There is always the fear in this kind of inquiry that researchers might misread participants' responses and actions, and pursue illogical stances based on skewed interpretations. Just as the logbook can become a place where reflective practitioners can probe the character of the field setting and their own relationship to it, other strategies can be adopted to check out whether a viewpoint has currency or is shared by others. While not wanting to deny the importance of following individual hunches, which seem to characterize reflection-in-action, if reflective practitioner researchers are to honour multiplicity, then means have to be found which permit all those involved in the investigative process to have a voice.

In the past, I, like other qualitative researchers, have used the term triangulation to describe best the process of confirming the believability of observations (Taylor, 1992). Triangulation suggested to me the ability of researchers to understand or corroborate what happened at a given point of time, to examine what led to a particular behaviour or what accounted for a specific action or reaction. Surveyors often divide an area into triangles as they map the accuracy of a recorded angle or measure the dimensions of a fixed point (Lincoln and Guba, 1985, p. 305). However, in earlier drafts of this chapter both Donald Schön and Margot Ely alerted me to the contradictory nature of my use of this term, especially in my confusing implication that triangulation implied certainty and commitment to a known position or truth. While triangulation may well serve geometry, they argued, it constrains the multiplicity and complexity of human experience that I am promoting here. 'We do not read as much for accuracy (accuracy is the easiest to check, i.e. how many kids were in the group) as we do for a multiplicity of views,' writes Ely. 'So we work in support groups, with our participants, with ourselves to check our "readings," to solicit other possible readings, to hone our insights and findings, and to gain the needed distance, and so to work for credibility.'[7]

Ely directed me to Richardson (1994) who likens the process of rendering truths and trustworthiness in the postmodern era to a crystallizing of ideas,

Crystals are prisms that reflect externalities and refract within themselves, creating different colors, patterns, arrays, casting off in different directions. What we see depends upon our angle of repose. Not triangulation, crystallisation. In postmodernist mixed-genre texts, we have moved from plane geometry to light theory, where light can be both waves and particles. (p. 522)

Like Ely, Richardson rejects positivist and neo-positivist ideas of truth, validity and falsification, and confirms the importance of struggle, ambiguity and contradiction, all noted features of the reflective practitioners' journey.

Crystallisation, without losing structure, de-constructs the traditional idea of validity (we feel how there is no single truth, we see how texts validate themselves); and crystallisation provides us with a deepened, complex, thoroughly partial, understanding of the topic. Paradoxically, we know more and doubt what we know. (1994, p. 522)

The metaphor of crystallization works well in reflective practitioner design. It works well because it beautifully captures how our perspectives are shaped by 'our angle of repose'. The techniques we adopt to investigate our practice will inform our evolving perspectives. In qualitative inquiry, these techniques can include interviews, student journals, audio-visual resources, peer support groups, and negative cases (Ely *et al.*, pp. 156–66).

Each technique provides an opportunity for reflective practitioner researchers to gain some distance from the work being explored, distance enables a possible new perspective on a familiar event, a rethinking of an ingrained belief. Distance makes the familiar strange, it decentres the principal investigator from the lived event and provides a valuable opportunity to hear other voices, see new faces, while building a comprehensive understanding of the one event.

Defamiliarization is not a foreign concept for arts educators. Crystallization seems to operate on the same principle. Artists are forever seeking a new curve on a familiar event, a different way to manipulate the form to express or demonstrate an idea. In the theatre, there have been many playwrights and directors, such as Antonin Artaud, Harold Pinter, and Samuel Beckett, who have worked against convention, exploring unique relationships between form and content. We could liken their work to reflective practice where the artists set the agenda, and deliberately inquire into an aspect of their craft.

The great theatre genius, Bertolt Brecht, achieves archetypal status as a reflective practitioner as he sought for distancing devices which would assist both actors and spectators to understand the truths contained within his drama. There has been much written on Brecht's idea of an Epic Theatre and his various attempts to discover through the dramatic art form ways of detaching the audience from the performance. Brecht was critical of orthodox theatre which presented simplistic and saccharine solutions to life's problems and which required a hallucinated participation of the spectators. His early work, especially with the Berliner Ensemble in the 1920s, saw a growing commitment to exposing the machinery of the theatre to an audience so that they would not submit or lose themselves within the piece:

> Give us some light on the stage, electrician. How can we
> Playwrights and actors put forward
> Our view of the world in half-darkness. The dim twilight
> Induces sleep. But we need the spectators'
> Wakeful, even watchfulness. Let them
> Do their dreaming in the light. The short night-time
> We now and then require can be shown by moons
> Or lamps, likewise our playing
> Can make clear what time of day it is
> Whenever needed . . . (Willet, 1977, p. 161)

Arts education is filled with workers who share Brecht's concern and dream for methods which can activate the spectators' contemplative powers. These alert states, what Greene (1978, p. 161) has referred to as participants' wide-awakeness, are shared by reflective practitioners as they search for a variety of techniques to hone their observations. Two popular methods used in interpretive-based design are interviews and journals and to these I now turn to illustrate briefly how they can be employed as significant crystallizing devices.

Interviews

In reflective practitioner research this method is particularly useful as it can reveal how the participants within the study, usually the students, are interpreting the work. Interviews permit the researchers to follow up hunches, to probe complexity, and to understand why certain behaviours were demonstrated. In my study with Carl, for example, it was important to examine how the grade five and six students were reading process drama and what value, if any, they saw it playing in the curriculum. By getting into the students' heads, we could develop another perspective on the work. By sharing our own observations or our *angles of repose* with another, by injecting another insight or slant on the one event, we come closer to, and develop confidence in, the trustworthiness of our findings.

In some instances, these interviews can be quite revealing, as in the following case where three of Carl's grade five and six students provided invaluable assistance in the planning of our sessions. This interview occurred following the session with Carl discussed earlier in this chapter. On the lefthand side are the students' responses to my questions while on the right, a description of how these responses influenced the reflective practice:

The Interview

Phil: What arrests your attention now? What are you interested by so far in the work that you might want to explore further?

Jimmy: Somebody's leaked to the newspaper and then people come in to check us out and we have to cover it up.

Sharon: And all spies hiding in the factory just take their pictures and stuff.

Dean: And we've got to be very, very careful and we have to . . . some people have to stop work to keep the building under control and make sure nobody's doing anything wrong and there's a big panic going on because people are not sure what's going on because there are so many rumours going around.

Jimmy: And maybe the police or someone . . . or the RSPCA[8] has paid one of the workers to spy on the plant and stuff and find out what's going on and how it's going on and none of the workers really know who it is except for that one person . . . It's a bit like Musical Detective . . .

Dean: And you can play that game where you um . . . where everybody gets a rumour and whispers it in someone else's ear and they all pass rumours around so that it would be sort of be like what is actually happening . . . because like if say on the news, somebody's going to bomb [the school's suburb] and then people . . .

Sharon: . . . will go into panic . . .

Dean: . . . yeah . . . some person who listened to some radio show or something and find out that it's the Americans and so they tell someone else, *Look I heard this I think it's the Americans*, and then somebody else will come up and say, *Listen it's not the Americans . . . it's the people from Iceland . . .*

Phil: Yes, good ideas. So what would you do with those people who have decided to leave the factory?

Dean: Well they could play along.

Jimmy: They could shut up.

Sharon: And I'd like to do more on like families and long-term implications.

Phil: Long-term implications?

Sharon: Yes.

The Reflective Practitioner

I take a gamble and assume that these students have been interested in the work. The breadth of ideas that they offer for future planning seems to confirm this interest and challenges me to incorporate their thinking into the process drama.

Jimmy has identified a key element in process drama, the idea that people concealing information can lead to satisfying work. Sharon provides a concrete strategy, members of the class could create frozen images, or tableaux, of what was really happening in the factory. Dean develops her idea. I am reminded of how kids build on each other's work, and the importance of collaborative learning.

Again, these students have a wonderful armoury of strategies and techniques which can demonstrate what the process drama is about. The students are becoming important co-leaders as they suggest ideas for future action. Why should teachers feel burdened with having to do all the planning themselves?

Dean returns to Sharon's earlier idea and suggests that the class create rumours to be circulated.

Given that some students during the process drama had decided to leave the factory, and not be a party to animal testing, I challenge Sharon, Dean and Jimmy on how the teacher might manage their decision. Again, though, the students surprise me with their ideas, especially Sharon who suggests that it might be valuable to examine the impact of this decision on the worker's family and the long-term implications.

A number of studies in drama education are now documenting the classroom work from the student's as well as the teacher's perspective (McLean, 1995; O'Mara, 1995). It would be fair to say that such documentation has been rare in the past, where the emphases of writing on classroom practices have been through the teacher's or leader's eyes. Readers have had to put their faith in the author of these studies and assume the teacher's observations are credible ones. Just as Brecht feared the overwhelming appeal to emotion prevalent in conventional theatre forms, reflective practitioner research should avoid skewed observations which might ensue from one perspective. Interviewing students or other members of the reflective community is a time-consuming process and one that I am unable to do justice to here. I would argue though that reflective practitioner researchers in arts education need to develop strong interviewing skills and consider the variety of questioning techniques that have informed interpretive-based design (Fontana and Frey, 1994; Lofland and Lofland, 1984; Minichiello, Aroni, Timewell and Alexander, 1991).

Journals

Beyond the standard journal which is often used in drama classrooms to help students record their *angle of repose*, in reflective practitioner design these journals can be more dynamically utilized to provide insights into what students are thinking. I know that journals are often used in haphazard ways in the classroom, as places where students make notes or address the teacher's questions. When used in this instrumental fashion, they become nothing more than checks on task completion, an intrusive evaluation tool which only serves the teacher's need for behavioural control.

In reflective practitioner research, journals can become powerful devices for providing another perspective on the work. Like the interview, they can invite students to expose their evolving relationship. In my study with Chinese-American seventh-graders, for example, I encouraged the kids to keep their own journals after I shared with them my own logbook. I told them that as my log consisted of my perceptions of what occurred in class, it would be helpful if I could read their written perceptions too. My observations, I admitted, could be quite different from theirs. Any matter of interest, or uninterest for that matter, could be written in their journal. Students could write on a voluntary basis: they were not co-opted into writing the journal. The journal would not be graded.

During the course of this study, I discovered an important journal strategy which seemed to release the students into responding to classroom activities in non-threatening ways. This strategy which I call the Guided Case Study, and which has been written about elsewhere (Taylor, 1993), developed as a result of my frustration in finding out how a class of grade seven students was responding to process drama. While the students seemed to enjoy writing the letters, the petitions, the advertisements and other tasks which informed our drama work, having them critique the quality of teaching and learning was a different matter. Responses tended to be quite glib and pedestrian. Experienced drama teachers will not be surprised by this comment. Journals tend to become deathly documents in classrooms, which inhibit rather than liberate.

In my attempt to find a liberating means for releasing the students to share in their journal their ideas on drama, how drama can be structured, and what stance the teacher and students should assume in the classroom work, I asked myself, What would happen if the students were presented with a fictional situation which mirrored the kind of experiences they were having in the drama sessions? Just as these seventh-graders had little experience of classroom drama, what might they say in role to a fictitious teacher, Mr Gibbs, as he struggled to introduce drama in the curriculum? The quality of the responses which emerged from this strategy were surprisingly rich.

I propose to examine two guided case study situations with which Albert, a 13-year-old Chinese-American student was presented. I will include his responses to those situations and my reflective analysis of them as, in my view, they illuminate how the reflective practitioner researcher can stumble across significant devices for describing teaching and learning processes. I intend to isolate the main features of Albert's written reflections in his role as the principal of Mr Gibbs' school. His written responses which follow are intact and I include copies of his original work. These copies were written in pencil by Albert and are difficult to read in places. I have not modified or amended Albert's expression or grammar. The names given to Albert and his classmates are pseudonyms which is standard ethical procedure in interpretive-informed research.

Situation 1

Mr Gibbs is a grade seven social studies teacher. Each year he has to include the American War of Independence in the curriculum. He likes to teach by having the students read from the textbook and then complete short answer and multiple choice questions. He always ends his study with a chapter test. Although he sometimes conducts group discussions, Mr Gibbs finds that it is always the same students answering the questions. He believes this is because many are shy and would prefer to write in their notebooks. Mr Gibbs is about to teach a unit of work on Boston in the late 1700s.

Imagine that you are the new principal of the school in which Mr Gibbs works. You have seen his style of teaching previous units of work and you would like to make some suggestions on how he might approach his Boston study.

Albert's response

Mr Gibbs, I value highly acting out scenes from the chapter, especially making them understanding what's going on, not just words. Make the students able to picture it and interpret it correctly. Do a short session of acting, and a person reading from the textbook as a narrator. Be sure that the students interpret the chapter as concepts (#1 blah, blah, #2 blah, blah, #3 blah, blah) or as a story (First, blah, afterword, blah, finally, blah). I think that a classroom should have a lighter touch and atmosphere, and to get people to be more open, center attention on them, let them know that it is not a yes/no question, but a question of his/her opinion.

I think this is why many students don't like to talk, they know they can get away with it. I think a chapter is easier to understand as a story than as facts so that tests will be easier for them. I think a short session of writing will help because the writing will calm them and also give them a chance to interpret. School is too much work and not enough action.

I think my suggestion of play, story, giving shy students more attention and getting not-so-shy students to support, and writing may not seem to work at the beginning, but as time goes, the people will gradually accept and work by the new activities. I think the test should be the same.

Final suggestion — relate incident to something we understand.

Figure 1.1: Albert's writing on Situation 1

Mr Gibbs, I value highly acting out scenes from the chapter, especially making them understanding what's going on, not just words. Make the students able to picture it and interpret it correctly. Do a short session of acting, and a person reading from the textbook as a narrator. Be sure that the students interpret the chapter as concepts (#1 blah, blah, #2 blah, blah, #3 blah, blah) or as a story (First, blah, afterward, blah, finally, blah).

I think that a classroom should have a lighter touch and atmosphere, and to get people to be more open, center attention on them, let them know that it is

a yes/no question but a question of his/her opinion. I think this is why many students don't like to talk, they know they can get away with it. I think a chapter is easier to understand as a story than as facts

so that tests will be easier for them. I think a short session of writing will help because the writing will calm them and also give them a chance to interpret. School is too much work and not enough action.

I think my suggestions of play, story, giving shy students more attention and getting not-so-shy students to support, and writing may not seem to work at the beginning, but as time goes, the people will gradually accept and work by the new activities. I think the test should be the same.

Final suggestion - relate incident to something we understand.

My reflective analysis

The Mr Gibbs scenario in Situation 1 developed from my observation that at Albert's school students seemed to be taught in a traditional manner. I would frequently note classrooms based on Freire's (1970) 'banking' concept of education, 'in which the scope of action allowed to the students extends only as far as receiving, filing, and storing the deposits' of the teacher (p. 58). Frequently, the students would describe classes preoccupied with notebooks, copying from the board, and listening to teacher talk about the textbook.

The Gibbs' situation and Albert's response confirms the dreary scholastic routine which Albert and his classmates experienced. What is interesting though is Albert's understanding that certain teaching strategies such as questions which require a yes or no response limit students' ability to interpret the work. He recognizes the power of conceptual thinking and how the construct of stories can help deepen and extend students' reflections on the social studies curriculum. Albert implies that a curriculum rooted in discourse, dialogue, action and interaction should serve as a classroom model. In this respect, he was sharing a view with educational theorists who have emphasized a shift from the mastery of information to the growth of skills and intelligences that help students become 'learners who can approach knowledge in a variety of ways and struggle with the contradictions' (Verhovek, 1991, section B, p. 4). The Gibbs' scenario is providing me with insight into what Albert understands by effective curriculum management.

Situation 2

Mr Gibbs has tried to incorporate the principal's suggestions into his Boston study. However, all has not gone well. Gibbs makes an appointment to conference with the principal. 'I thought it might be interesting if the students assumed the role of journalists working for the Boston Gazette *in the 1770s,' he says to the principal. 'I enacted the role of Benjamin Edes, an editor with anti-Royalist sympathies. In the role of Edes, I proceeded to inform the journalists that I was concerned about the imminent arrival of many British soldiers. I was hoping the students, in their role of journalist, would suggest how the* Gazette *might influence public opinion to resist the soldiers' arrival. But the class seemed confused by my role as they did not speak. They blankly looked at me and remained unresponsive. I kept commenting about how hard it was living in Boston but each attempt was met with silence or a disturbing giggle. I don't know why I bothered. Where do I go from here?'*

Albert's response

I think it didn't work because they weren't into it. I presume you just told them they were journalists, but that is not getting deep enough. For example, you might list occupations such as head journalist, editorial

---

journalist, mail journalist, celebrity interviewer journalist, behind the head-line journalist, and all kinds of crazy things, and ask them from each field (mail journalist) what type of mail was received this week. Give them time to think of answers, to prepare, to *shine*!! Oh yes, you were still the teacher when you tried to talk and influence them to talk. Figure it this way, be either the boss of the paper or a hard working journalist too. If I were you, I might change my role of Ben Edes, and let someone take over. Make sure that the students are comfortable with the replacement, like the replacement has no enemies or is funny and can handle it. I will become a new staff member that needs to be taught about how each field works (Mr X, how does the town feel about lobsters, I new at the editorial and need info). I also would not get too close to the person because then they will be scared and not think well. Don't stand too far because then they will feel that the answer doesn't matter and not give a good answer. Stand at a reasonable distance.

They didn't contribute because it was different and perhaps too unclear to work with. It was not easy for them to answer because they don't want to be different from the 'mob', or just shy. I think you should ask some people you know could answer so that other people can follow an example.

Figure 1.2: Albert's writing on Situation 2

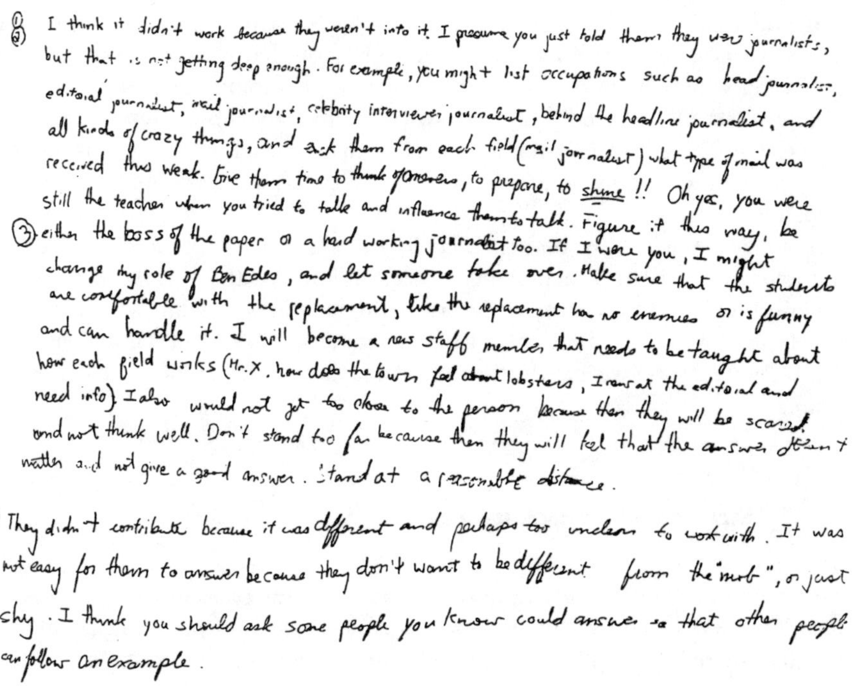

My reflective analysis

There was a close parallel between the above situation which Gibbs describes and an in-role drama I had attempted to negotiate with the students. I was interested to learn from my students how they read teacher-in-role and what circumstances assisted their active verbal participation. I deliberately layered into Gibbs' reflections his frustration with the students' silent responses. In my experience, it is not uncharacteristic for student groups to experience bafflement or uncertainty when the teacher assumes a role in the students' dramatic play. However, before this guided case study with Albert, I had never attempted to follow up consciously the possible explanation for such student response.

Albert's acute and insightful perceptions on teacher role-play transformed my approach toward this strategy. His observations on the relationship between the leader's clarity in specifying the task and the depth of student involvement should be a lesson to all those interested in incorporating teacher in role in the classroom. Albert aligns quality of participant response to the teacher's ability to provide a richly coloured scaffold. 'Getting deep enough', he urges, demands assisting the students' storying possibilities. This assistance, he offers, may involve allowing students to assume leadership roles and drawing on the skills of students who are willing to participate.

Albert is also aware that students' engagement is tied into their comfort threshold. I remembered how I would often walk around the classroom and attempt to engage students with the role-play. But, in Albert's mind, this tactic can potentially backfire as shy students 'will be scared and not think well'. Teacher role-play, therefore, may need to be coupled with a human relations posturing which encourages student participation. Simply assuming a role and asking for students' feedback will not promote a dynamic interaction.

Cecily O'Neill (1989) reminds us that when teachers assume roles they must invite the student watchers, 'to respond actively, to join in, to oppose or transform what is happening' (p. 535). However, as Albert reminds us and her, this invitation will only be accepted if the situation is of sufficient motivating interest for them. Teachers need to experiment with different status levels and find the ways and means of constructing avenues through which students can travel down and gain entry to an imaginary world. The Gibbs' situation and Albert's response has further informed my understanding of classroom drama.

Streams of Consciousness

These comprehensive descriptions at interviewing participants and finding insightful ways of using their journals demonstrate the methodical attempts pursued by reflective practitioner researchers as they aim for crystallization and work for meaning-making. The more avenues of inquiry reflective practitioners can tap into, the more perspectives sought, the more likely their conclusions can be read as credible ones.

There is an undeniable rigour in this design as the investigator penetrates the decisive features of an educational event. It seems ludicrous to argue that this rigour is less than would be found in other paradigms, such as conventional empirical design, where numbers seem to speak more powerfully than do words. Because reflective practitioner researchers often raise more questions than solutions, critics should not downgrade the meticulous concern with detail which is faced by those pursuing this design. Perhaps we even need to re-think our use of the word 'rigour' given its freezing and austere connotations. Rigour does seem to be a word much loved by the neo-positivities. See Taylor, 1996, for a further discussion on this point.[9]

I've only focused on two data collection methods here, ignoring the application of audio-visual resources and the widespread use of computer technology which can be employed in this paradigm (Richards and Richards, 1994; Tesch, 1990). Readers must uncover the variety of techniques and strategies open to them and be prepared to discover their own as I did with the guided case study. These discoveries, though, must still be cognizant of our students' rights and the need to have their identity protected. The days of entering schools and describing the work of teachers, students and the wider educational community without written permission are long gone. Such agreement usually entails consent from all relevant parties, including primary caregivers in the case of minors, as to how the observations are going to be analysed and presented. Participants within reflective practitioner research should have the power to say no to a proposed inquiry, and be provided with opportunities to respond positively and negatively to any description of their work before it enters the public arena.

But we should not let these necessary clearances and matters of ethics stifle our reflective journey. Indeed, they should liberate reflective practitioners into engaging the wider educative community in their investigations. The more who have ownership, the more change is possible. It seems to me that there is a complete freedom when our motives are shared, our hopes revealed, and our frustrations explored. Educational research in arts education has too long been contained within the hands of the few, a select coterie of researchers, the same faces who present at conferences, and the same names who apply dutifully for national competitive research grants. Surely this closed shop and monopolistic routine cannot be healthy for the future of arts education research. The field is too small anyway to be controlled by a dutiful band of attendants. As Maxine Greene (1978) reminds us:

So many of us today confine ourselves to right angles. We function in the narrowest of specialities; we lead one-dimensional lives. We accommodate ourselves so easily to the demands of the technological society — to time schedules, charts, programs, techniques — that we lose touch with our own streams of consciousness, our inner time. (pp. 198–9)

Reflective practitioner research can put us back in touch with our streams of consciousness. For, in this design, we can listen to our kids and to our teachers, and work with them as colleagues, perhaps seeing for the first time the classroom from Albert's eyes, or understanding the curriculum implications that Carl will face as he continues to implement process drama. Reflective practitioners can remove the stifling shackles of expertise in education and revise conventional understandings of authority. They can interrogate the truths that they daily confront and imagine what is possible in education, what is not possible, and what might be.

I cannot think of a more valuable investigative approach in arts education than the challenges presented by reflective practitioner design. The beneficiaries are not only the small coterie of scholars who write for refereed journals, but the participants, and all the players, within the educational act itself.

Epilogue: Perestroika

In Act Five of the second part of Tony Kushner's *Angels in America*, 'Perestroika', Harper makes her decision to leave Joe. Like other characters in the drama, she has realized that it is more sensible to break with custom, to escape from the hypocrisy, retreat from the deceit and from the shallow truths which seemed to govern human behaviour. 'Maybe lost is best,' she comments to her estranged husband. 'Get lost, Joe. Go exploring,' are her final words to him. For Harper, loneliness is a terrifying prospect but in the end it is seen as a more soothing alternative than the emotional confusion presented in a world wracked by duplicity.

As I think of Harper, and as I try and articulate the importance of reflective practitioner research, I cannot help but recall the haunting images she raises from her plane's window seat, en route to the west coast:

Night flight to San Francisco. Chase the moon across America.

God! It's been years since I was on a plane!

When we hit thirty-five thousand feet, we'll have reached the tropopause. The great belt of calm air. As close as I'll ever get to the ozone.

I dreamed we were there. The plane leapt the tropopause, the safe air and attained the outer rim, the ozone, which was ragged and torn, patches of it threadbare as old cheesecloth, and that was frightening . . .

But I saw something I could only see, because of my astonishing ability to see such things:

Souls were rising, from the earth far below, souls of the dead, of people who had perished, from famine, from war, from the plague, and they floated up, like skydivers in reverse, limbs all akimbo, wheeling and spinning. And the souls of these departed joined hands, clasped ankles, and formed a web, a great net of souls, and the souls were three-atom oxygen molecules, of the stuff of ozone, and the outer rim absorbed them, and was repaired.

Nothing's lost forever. In this world, there is a kind of painful process. Longing for what we've left behind, and dreaming ahead.

At least I think that's so. (Kushner, 1994, p. 96)

The images of the souls acting as a buffer, a kind of ghostly latex protection for the living, reminds me of the many ironies that exist in this world, the irony that can have people finding meaning in a desolate place, the irony of a recurring belief, a hope, that people are fundamentally good in light of a global destruction. Arts works, such as Kushner's play, work best for me when they highlight those unsettling ironies, and capture the condition of the troubled human spirit 'longing for what we've left behind' and dreaming for a future. The most compelling arts experiences, as Suzanne Langer (1953) reminds us, are always in a state of becoming.

Like Harper, reflective practitioner researchers are never certain of what the future will bring, what discoveries we will make, what troubling questions will occur for us as we listen, watch, interact and hear. Pain and discomfort seem to go with the design as we chase the moon, and pursue a guiding light in arts education which will illuminate in some clearer way how the artistic-aesthetic curriculum can be developed and better understood. And while our reflective practitioner journey may be wheeling and spinning like the entanglement of souls, Harper sees, in the end, there is comfort that our journey is a human and humane one, for while we search for meaning within our own field settings, while we reach out in the hope of connecting with our kids, we participate in the struggle of inquiry, a struggle which has been shared by many teachers and artists over time. By participating in this struggle, we join and honour all those reflective practitioners who have preceded and who will follow us. We too join hands, clasp ankles, and form a net, a network of folk dedicated to a journey of becoming which will raise the streams of consciousness to which an artistic-aesthetic curriculum aspires.

At least, I think that's so.

Notes

1   *Others* refers to the remaining members of the small group who were in an adjoining room with the visiting teacher, John.
2   In other words, the smaller group would test the chemical on rats only.
3   Members from the smaller group were to return to established factory groupings and explain that animal testing was proposed for Enviro. This strategy, as I discuss, was aborted.

4 Refers to the smaller group in the adjoining room who were the main investors in the factory, Enviro. In a previous session, the main investors had indicated on their job application forms how much money they would invest in the operation.

5 These extracts are taken from interviews I conducted with Carl in October 1994. The interview is characterized by stops and starts, and with Carl thinking through ideas. The three dots (. . .) interspersed in the transcript represent pauses.

6 Carl's unpublished log, page 10.

7 Unpublished correspondence with author, October, 1995.

8 In Australia, the acronym RSPCA stands for Royal Society for the Prevention of Cruelty to Animals.

9 Although the 'habit of rigorous, systematic reflection' has been used to define research activity in drama education (see Editorial, 1996, Research in Drama Education, p. 6), 1 sometimes wonder how appropriate this quantitative characteristic is when describing fundamental processes surrounding the artistic-aesthetic curriculum?

References

Argyris, C. and Schön, D. (1974) *Theory in Practice: Increasing Professional Effectiveness*, San Francisco, Jossey-Bass.

Bolton, G. (1985) 'Changes in thinking about drama in education', *Theory into Practice*, **XXIV**(3), pp. 151–7.

Brook, P. (1987) *The Shifting Point*, New York, Harper and Row.

Burgess, R. (1985) *Field Methods in the Study of Education*, London, Falmer Press.

Clandinin, D. and Connelly, F. (1994) 'Personal experience methods', in Denzin, N. and Lincoln, Y. (eds) *Handbook of Qualitative Research*, Thousand Oaks, Sage, pp. 413–27.

Collins, M. (1995) 'The articulation and creation of power relationships in a primary dance education setting.' Unpublished Master's Thesis, The University of Melbourne.

Donelan, K. (1995) 'The teacher, the students and the drama classroom: An ethnographic study.' Unpublished Master's Thesis, The University of Melbourne.

Editorial (1996) *Research in Drama Education*, **I**(1), pp. 5–10.

Eisner, E. (1985) *The Art of Educational Evaluation*, London, Falmer Press.

Eisner, E. (1991) *The Enlightened Eye: Qualitative Inquiry and the Enchantment of Educational Practice*, New York, Macmillan.

Ely, M., Anzul, M., Friedman, T., Garner, D. and Steinmetz, A.M. (1991) *Doing Qualitative Research: Circles within Circles*, London, Falmer Press.

Fontana, A. and Frey, J. (1994) 'Interviewing: The art of science', in Denzin, N. and Lincoln, Y. (eds) *Handbook of Qualitative Research*, Thousand Oaks, Sage, pp. 361–76.

Freire, P. (1970) *Pedagogy of the Oppressed*, New York, Continuum.

Gardner, H. (1993) *Creating Minds: An Anatomy of Creativity Seen through the Lives of Freud, Einstein, Picasso, Stravinsky, Eliot, Graham and Gandhi*, New York, Basic Books.

Greene, M. (1978) *Landscapes of Learning*, New York, Teachers College Press.

Greene, M. (1989) 'Art worlds in schools', in Abbs, P. (ed.) *The Symbolic Order*, London, Falmer Press.

Haynes, A. (1987) 'The dynamic image: Changing perspectives in dance education', in Abbs, P. (ed.) *Living Powers: The Arts in Education*, London, Falmer Press.

HITCHCOCK, G. and HUGHES, D. (1995) *Research and the Teacher*, 2nd edition, London, Routledge.

KUSHNER, T. (1992) *Angels in America: A Gay Fantasia on National Themes*, Part One: 'Millennium Approaches', London, Royal National Theatre and Nick Hern Books.

KUSHNER, T. (1994) *Angels in America: A Gay Fantasia on National Themes*, Part Two: 'Perestroika', London, Royal National Theatre and Nick Hern Books.

LANGER, S. (1953) *Feeling and Form*, New York, Scribner.

LINCOLN, Y. and GUBA, E. (1985) *Naturalistic Inquiry*, Newbury Park, Sage.

LOFLAND, J. and LOFLAND, L. (1984) *Analysing Social Settings: A Guide to Qualitative Observation and Analysis*, Belmont, Wadsworth.

MARTIN, N. (1987) 'On the move', in GOSWAMI, S. and STILLMAN, P. (eds) *Reclaiming the Classroom*, Portsmouth, Heinemann, pp. 20–7.

MAY, A. (1996) 'Playwrighting: A process of thinking, learning and shaping'. Unpublished Master's thesis, the University of Melbourne.

McDONALD, J. (1994) 'The impact of the educational setting on the aesthetic dimension in the drama classroom', *NADIE Journal: International Research Issue*, **18**(2), pp. 5–13.

McLEAN, J. (1995) 'An aesthetic framework in drama.' Unpublished Master's Thesis, The University of Melbourne.

MIENCZAKOWSKI, J. (1994) 'Reading and writing research', *NADIE Journal: International Research Issue*, (A Publication of the National Association for Drama in Education, Australia), **18**(2), pp. 45–54.

MINICHIELLO, V., ARONI, R., TIMEWELL, E. and ALEXANDER, L. (1991) *In-Depth Interviewing*, Melbourne, Longman.

MOORE, B. and CALDWELL, H. (1990) 'The art of planning: Drama as a rehearsal for writing in the primary grades', *Youth Theatre Journal*, **4**(3), pp. 13–20.

NATIONAL BOARD OF EMPLOYMENT, EDUCATION and TRAINING (1992) *Educational Research in Australia*, Canberra, Australian Government Publishing Service.

O'MARA, J. (1995) 'From Venus to Victoria.' Unpublished Master's Project, The University of Melbourne.

O'NEILL, C. (1989) 'Dialogue and drama: The transformation of events, ideas and teachers', *Language Arts*, **66**(5), pp. 528–40.

ORTON, J. (1994) 'Action research and reflective practice: An approach to research for drama educators', *NADIE Journal: International Research Issue*, (A publication of the National Association for Drama in Education, Australia), **18**(2), pp. 85–96.

RICHARDS, T. and RICHARDS, R. (1994) 'Using computers in qualitative research', in DENZIN, N. and LINCOLN, Y. (eds) *Handbook of Qualitative Research*, Thousand Oaks, Sage, pp. 445–62.

RICHARDSON, L. (1994) 'Writing: A method of inquiry', in DENZIN, N. and LINCOLN, Y. (eds) *Handbook of Qualitative Research*, Thousand Oaks, Sage, pp. 516–29.

SCHECHNER, R. (1985) *Between Theatre and Anthropology*, Philadelphia, University of Pennsylvania Press.

SHER, A. (1985) *Year of the King*, London, Methuen.

SCHÖN, D. (1983) *The Reflective Practitioner: How Professionals Think in Action*, New York, Basic Books.

SONDHEIM, S. and LAPINE, B. (1984) *Sunday in the Park with George*, New York, Applause.

STANISLAVSKI, C. (1949/1987) *Building a Character*, New York, Methuen.

STENHOUSE, L. (1975) *Introduction to Curriculum Research and Development*, London, Heinemann.

Taylor, P. (1991) 'Playing with form', *NADIE Journal*, (A publication of the National Association for Drama in Education, Australia), **15**(3), pp. 3–12.

Taylor, P. (1992) 'Our adventure of experiencing: Drama structure and action research in the grade seven social studies classroom.' Unpublished Doctoral Dissertation, New York University.

Taylor, P. (1993) 'Reflecting in the third person and the guided case study', in Michaels, W. (ed.) *Drama in Education: The State of the Art*, Vol. 2, Leichhardt, Educational Drama Association NSW, pp. 89–102.

Taylor, P. (1995) 'Our adventure of experiencing: Reflective practice and drama research', *Youth Theatre Journal*, **9**, pp. 31–52.

Taylor, P. (1996) 'Resisting research myths', *Drama: One Forum Many Voices* (The Journal of National Drama, England), **4**(2).

Tesch, R. (1990) *Qualitative Research: Analysis Types and Software Tools*, London, Falmer Press.

Verhovek, S.H. (1991, June 21) 'Plan to emphasize minority cultures ignites a debate', *The New York Times*, Section B, p. 4.

Willet, J. (1977) *The Theatre of Bertolt Brecht: A Study from Eight Aspects*, London, Methuen.

2 Toward the Practice of Theory in Practice

Sharon Grady

Like other fields of theatre practice such as acting (Zarrilli, 1995) and directing (Whitmore, 1994) contemporary critical theories including semiotics, feminism, and poststructuralism are beginning to affect profoundly the field of educational drama and theatre (Grady, 1992; Nicholson, 1993; Fletcher, 1995; Merriman, 1995). In this chapter, I examine the complex relationship between contemporary critical theories, practical work, and research designs in our field. Further, the ways in which these theories are applied depend on the sets of commonplace assumptions drama/theatre practitioners or researchers bring to their work. These paradigmatic ways of seeing or doing filter the various theoretical lenses we might choose to employ and will necessarily effect our practice and research. My present concern is with how these theories and assumptions affect our research activity and its outcomes.

What is Theory?

What is theory? Unfortunately, some see contemporary theory with a capital 'T', think it only refers to new critical theories each with its own specialist discourse, and see such theories with their own dauntingly dense ideas as useless to their practice. In this view, 'Theory' is confused or conflated with 'jargon'. Terry Eagleton (1990, p. 35) explains, however, that jargon is simply language which is not familiar. A group of plumbers, for example, would be just as mystified by our special terminology of practice such as 'teacher-in-role', 'hot-seating', and 'depictions' as I/we would be by the language used to describe the intimate workings of a sewer system. Like other kinds of language or skill acquisition, these specialist discourses become familiar through exposure, use, and practice.

Eagleton (1990) further suggests that a statement as deceptively simple as 'I've just put the cat out' is based in theoretical propositions that reflect 'controvertible statements about the nature of the world' (p. 24). Although this basic sort of theorizing keeps 'theory' in the background, it is predicated on assumptions about the world. We are constantly theorizing about how the world works and then revising our theories as we learn and reflect. In this view, the act of theorizing is not foreign to us. We do it all the time invisibly, unintentionally. In this sense, as Eagleton (1990) asserts, 'all social life is in some sense theoretical' (p. 24). There is a 'theory' or particular way of seeing the world implicit even in our most commonplace sets of assumptions.

Contemporary critical theories are *self-consciously* reflexive ways of viewing the world and what we do in it. Each might be thought of as a special lens which allows us to examine the world in a particular way, asking certain questions of what we see or do and *how* we see it or do it. For example, feminist theatre critic Gayle Austin (1990) clearly articulates that 'a feminist approach to anything means paying attention to women' (p. 1). For Austin, applying feminist theories to theatrical playtexts allows the opportunity to focus attention on 'when women appear as characters and noticing when they do not' (p. 1). Further, this lens can not only expose the gendered construction of characters but can be widened to include some of the 'invisible' mechanisms behind those constructions.

The use of various critical theories allows us to *intentionally* place our attention and bring assumptions to the foreground instead of keeping them in the background. What differentiates a critical theory from a commonplace set of assumptions is the degree of reflexivity involved. Theory and theorizing 'happens' whether one is paying attention or not. As my colleague, Charlotte Canning, tells her students, you can participate in what is going on from either informed and examined positions or from uninformed, unexamined ones. In this view, even if we wish to remain 'outside' theory and therefore 'innocent' of the implications of examining our commonplace working assumptions, we cannot do so.

As shown in Figure 2.1, there are a variety of useful theories available to us, both within the immediate purview of our field as well as from other fields. Theories with a more cultural base include critical social theories such as the various feminism(s) and Marxism(s); more literary-based theories include semiotics and attention to reception and reader-response theory; more educationally oriented theories include critical pedagogy with attention to transformative theory and dialogism; more psychologically based theories including the psychoanalytical theories of Freud and Lacan; and more theatrical or aesthetic theories such as those put forward by Piscator, Brecht, and Boal. While certainly not an exhaustive list, it is beyond the scope of this present chapter to examine all these theoretical lenses in great depth. However, identifying a range of lenses can begin to suggest the multitude of ways we might focus our attention in our research activity and practice. This focus can help us ask more complex and provocative research questions. Readers should note that the figures I include in this chapter should be viewed not in terms of absolutes, but rather as one way of viewing the relationship between theoretical lenses, filtering paradigmatic sets of assumptions, and methodological tools through which we see and interpret the world, our work, and our practice.

Figure 2.1:   Useful theoretical lenses for drama/theatre in education

Theoretical Lenses

More *Cultural*
* Critical social theory
   * feminism(s)
   * Marxism(s)

More *Literary*
* Critical literary theory
   * semiotics
   * reader-response theory
   * reception theory

More *Educational*
* Critical pedagogy
   * transformative theory
   * dialogic theory

More *Psychological*
* Psychoanalytic theory
   * Freud
   * Lacan

More *Theatrical*
* Politics of Performance
   * Piscator
   * Brecht
   * Boal

Research as an Active, Reflexive Process

It is evident in this present volume that once a research question has been identified there are many research methodologies available to us. As Figure 2.2 shows, research activity can be more historical dealing with primary sources, secondary sources; more literary with focus on the text; more quantitative with surveys, pre-tests, and post-tests; more qualitative with descriptive, ethnographic, action, and reflective work; and, as we have seen recently, more artistic with role-play, image work, drawing, puppetry, storytelling, and actual performance (ranging from solo to full production). Employing a variety of practical methods as additional research tools or as research destination points in their own right can provide a tangible way of illustrating the connectedness between theory and practice.

Ideally, research should be a process symbiotically linked to our practice, thinking, and reflections on both. Sometimes our focus may be on analysis, at other times on practice, but there should always exist a dialectical relationship between theorizing and practice. In this view, theory *is* a practice, and good practice is theorized. As Dorrine Kondo (1990) explains:

> Theory lies in enactment and in writing strategies, not simply in the citation and analysis of canonical texts. (p. 304)

Figure 2.2: *The range of research activity for drama/theatre in education*

The Range of Research Activity

More Historical
    * primary sources
    * secondary sources

More Literary
    * textual

More Quantitative
    * surveys
    * pre-test/post-test

More Qualitative
    * descriptive
    * ethnographic
    * action research
    * reflective

More Artistic
    * roleplay
    * image work
    * drawing
    * puppet work
    * storytelling
    * performance-oriented
        —solo
        —TIE
        —full production

> [. . . T]he real challenge is to enact our theoretical messages, thereby displacing a theoretical/empirical opposition. (p. 43)

Unfortunately, too often this is not the way research in our field is conducted. How do we consciously enable or disable the reflexive process of theorizing in our work? How do we responsibly account for our own theoretical under-pinnings? How do we teach others to do this difficult work?

The Power of Paradigms

When I first started teaching graduate students about research design, I thought I could simply present a 'palette' of theories and a 'palette' of methods from which they could mix and match according to the kinds of questions they were asking. However, a student playwright helped me realize that a key ingredient was missing. Interested in the question of the playwrights' respons-ibility to the construction of gender in their work, my student wanted to focus his research activity on an analysis of several playtexts for young audiences. I revelled in his fascinating question and was quite eager to see where he would go with it. During an early draft, however, this rich question resulted in a rather simple head count of the number of female protagonists in plays for young people, an enumeration of role types (i.e., friends, side kicks, maids, and mothers), and the conclusion that there should be more 'meatier' or substantive roles for young women. I realized that I had failed my student by not stressing the importance of intervening and/or mediating paradigms as filters between theoretical lenses and research activity. A general theoretical lens had been identified, along with a research strategy — but the operative paradigm serving as a backdrop for the work limited the potential complexity of the inquiry and the nature of the questions asked.

To clarify, a paradigm 'is constituted by a set of beliefs which both enables and constrains research: a framework or scaffold which can underpin or support further work but which, of necessity, also excludes a range of possibilities' (Hawthorne, 1992, p. 126). In Kuhnian terms, paradigms change and/ or shift for good reasons — old structures don't tend to accommodate new information or new assumptions about phenomena. Egon Guba (1990) simplifies and states that a paradigm is 'a basic set of beliefs that guides action, whether of the everyday garden variety or action taken in connection with a disciplined inquiry' (p. 17). Guba (1990) characterizes the differences between paradigms according to their responses to three basic ontological, epistemological, and methodological questions:

1 Ontological: What is the nature of the 'knowable'? or, What is the nature of 'reality'?
2 Epistemological: What is the nature of the relationship between the knower (the inquirer) and the known (or knowable)?
3 Methodological: How should the inquirer go about finding out knowledge? (p. 18)

For our purposes, it is useful to consider how different paradigms perceive the nature, status, and locatability of the 'knowable' or 'truth'. As diagrammed in Figure 2.3, the question of 'truth' informs the degree to which an inquiry includes a variety of mediating factors affecting the phenomenon on which attention is placed.

Considering these paradigms as filters with a potential to cloud or clarify our theoretical lenses can be useful as a means through which to examine more closely our motivating assumptions. For example, my student's attention was on gender but his post-positivist filtering paradigm didn't allow for him to ask a more complex set of questions and therefore engage in a more substantive level of critique (see Figure 2.4, p. 65). A more poststructuralist approach, in which truth is seen to be multiple and material conditions are seen to have a profound effect on how experience is shaped, could have substantially changed his research design and methodology. Subsidiary questions concerning *why* women are so often ascribed stereotypical roles in plays for young audiences, or how the *sacredness of authorship* and the 'truth' of a work of art might effect gender construction in plays, or what *received understandings* about what plays 'sell' to a general audience (i.e., boys won't sit through a play

Figure 2.3: Theoretical lenses, filtering paradigms and research activity

Theoretical Lenses	Filtering Paradigms (What is the status of truth?)	Research Activity

More Cultural
* Critical social theory
   * feminism(s)
   * Marxism(s)
	* *Positivist*
	(There is an absolute truth.)
	
	* *Postpositivist*
	(Rigor can provide a reasonable
	  approximation of truth.)
		More Historical
		* primary sources
		* secondary sources
		
		More Literary
		* textual

More Literary
* Critical literary theory
   * semiotics
   * reader response theory
   * reception theory
	* *Structuralist*
	(Truth can be schematized.)
		More Quantitative
		* surveys
		* pre-test/post-test

More Educational
* Critical pedagogy
   * transformative theory
   * dialogic theory
	* *Utopian*
	(Truth lies in the oppressed outside
	  a normative structure.)
	
	* *Poststructural*
	(Truth is multiple and situated.)
		More Qualitative
		* descriptive
		* ethnographic
		* action research
		* reflective

More Psychological
* Psychoanalytic theory
   * Freud
   * Lacan
	* *Constructivist* (Guba)
	(Truth is multiple but how might we
	  reconstruct a deconstructed world?)
		More Artistic
		* role play
		* image work
		* drawing
		* puppet work
		* storytelling
		* performance-oriented
		   —solo
		   —TIE
		   —full production

More Theatrical
* Politics of Performance
   * Piscator
   * Brecht
   * Boal		

Figure 2.4: Research reconfiguration for student project on playwriting and gender, moving from postpositivist to poststructural paradigms

Theoretical Lens	Filtering Paradigm	Research Activity
Feminism	Postpositivist ↓ Poststructural	More Literary * textual

with a female protagonist) could have enriched this study, adding depth through contextualization.

Obviously some theories come with a good deal of 'paradigmatic baggage' and some are fluid enough to be read through several different filters and/or in tandem with other theories. This can be seen, for example, by fragmenting the general theoretical lens of 'feminism'. Feminist theatre critic Jill Dolan (1988) has articulated three different strands of political feminist thinking — liberal, radical, materialist — which can be seen as having relatively close allegiances to very different filtering paradigms.

Liberal feminism 'developed from liberal humanism, stressing women's parity with men, based on universal values' (Austin, 1990, p. 5). Working within the dominant system, Dolan (1988) asserts that women strive to 'create legislation that will promote parity between men and women' (p. 4). The system itself remains intact; effort is concentrated only on its effects. This point of view, in which the 'truth' of the existing system is not challenged but rather the issue of equity is the main concern, can be seen as having been shaped by a positivist position despite the attention on women.

Conversely, radical (or cultural) feminism is based on the 'reification of sexual difference based on absolute gender categories' (Dolan, 1988, p. 5). Austin (1990) asserts that 'cultural feminists stress that women are both different from and superior to men, often advocate expressing this fact through female forms of culture' (p. 5). By positing that the most important difference between women and men is their biology, the critique offers a kind of structuralist schematization of truth with an extensive scaffolding that 'explains' the phenomenon.

Materialist feminism 'deconstructs the mythic subject Woman to look at women as a class oppressed by material conditions and social relations' (Dolan, 1988, p. 10). Austin (1990, p. 5) notes that the materialist position gives prominent attention to questions of race, class, and sexual preference, which are largely absent in the first two. From this position, not only are the effects of patriarchy examined, but the reification of women is made problematic as are the inner workings of the apparatus, class, and state. Closely aligned with a poststructuralist view, gender is seen as a cultural construction with multiple meanings and, therefore, multiple truths.

Different paradigms have challenged how we focus various theoretical lenses just as different theories have challenged long-held paradigmatic stances. How does this translate into practice and research in our field?

Escaping Utopia

It is 10 November, 1991. A team of four university students are at Wingra Alternative School in Madison, Wisconsin doing a trial run of a theatre in education program, *Do You Know Me?*, with a central focus on the complicated processes of 'Americanization' and 'identity formation'. We firmly believe in the guiding principle behind theatre in education (TIE), a British-based combination of presentational theatre and participatory educational drama work: when the tools of theatre are focused on a significant curriculum topic, they can provide a profoundly effective way of engaging a classroom of students in active critical learning. As TIE 'actors', our job is to serve in the dual roles of actor and teacher, with planned breaks in the action of the 'play' to ask students questions, invite them to play in role in the next scene, or to even determine and play out possible consequences of actions.

With a setting typical of a junior high school during a break between classes, the following scene is enacted:

> David and his friend, Rasheda, a 15-year-old Uzbeki foreign exchange student, are walking toward their lockers. Sam, Rasheda's locker mate, stands with her back to them knowing they will be approaching any minute. Sam listens to her Walkman apparently oblivious to anyone else around. David and Rasheda repeatedly ask Sam to move, but she feigns that she can't hear them. Rasheda finally taps her on the shoulder. Sam wheels around, with mock surprise and anger. They ask Sam to move so they can get to the locker but Sam refuses and starts to insult Rasheda.
>
> 'She doesn't have any rights to anything here. She doesn't belong here. I do! She's not an American! She's just a smelly foreigner. Why doesn't she go back home?' Sam spits vehemently.
>
> David tries to defend Rasheda, who has backed away. Sam, feeling braver, starts name-calling and walks threateningly toward Rasheda who is terrified. David tries to step in to block her. Sam shouts: 'Look at her. She's such a loser!'
>
> 'Look who's talking!' counters David, now caught in the middle of the confrontation.

The action freezes and, as facilitator, I ask the group of twenty-five sixth-, seventh-, and eighth-graders who have been watching this scene unfold: 'What is bothering Sam about Rasheda? What did she mean by, "not American"? What is an American? What is Sam worried about losing? What is she really afraid of? Why might she feel so threatened by Rasheda?'

The student responses are alarmingly simple: 'You shouldn't treat foreigners that way.' 'You shouldn't call people names.' As actor/teachers we quickly ready ourselves for the next scene, all the while noting the mild panic seeping in among us. For all of our careful planning, we seemed to be four very eager 'would be' actor/teachers stuck in the middle of a predictable and rather simplistic TIE program. How had this happened? We believed theatre in education had the potential to help students grapple with large questions about the world. But it seemed to be failing us — or we were failing it. Rather than an interactive exploration of the rich complexities and contradictions of the 'Americanization' process we had hoped for, why had it turned into nothing more than a simple moral lesson — the equivalent of, 'Be nice to everyone and they'll be nice to you'?

I later realized that, in part, such simplistic moralizing was uncomfortably related to my previous work as a political theatre maker in which I often created and spouted didactic messages to the 'converted'. What emerged from my past was the comfort of a similar kind of easy moralizing which verges on propaganda, not the active grappling, wrestling, or struggling I was currently aiming at — but telling, spoonfeeding, injecting.

Emerging from this often reductionist past into my current position as a professional in the field of educational theatre, I find much of the work aimed at young people on the more simplistic side of the continuum and very little work focused on the complexities. I discovered the hard way that making manifestos, whether encouraging workers to unionize or children to examine what it means to be a 'good' citizen, doesn't get you very far without the critical engagement of your intended 'audience'. Pronouncement leads to closure of thought — not openness.

Sometimes couched in a positivist pursuit of the 'truth' of 'universal' values, or framed by a Utopian desire to correct the evils of injustice, it wasn't surprising that the response was so bland and unthoughtful. Our redevising process required us to refocus our work, which initially began with research and reading in materialist feminist concerns of identity politics, through the more appropriate poststructuralist filter. In our literalizing of theory and assumptions, the students were now implicated as part of the problem — 'That's what you'd do, isn't it?' we asked them directly; 'Rasheda's role' was passed ritually between and embodied by different cast members to call attention to her various constructions by others; outside forces (Immigration and Naturalization Service, economic realities) were more clearly spotlighted.

Although this research had a TIE program as its destination point, the impact of carefully choosing a theoretical lens and using it with an appropriate filtering paradigm made the work much more complex and engaging for us and our students (see Figure 2.5, p. 68). Identifying and escaping a Utopian set of assumptions and moving beyond simple solutions toward more complicated considerations provided the rich learning environment we had intended.

'To draw a carp . . .'

In a noisy secondary school drama hall a 'house warming party' is in full swing. Phyllis, an artist, has just moved into a loft and is busily

Figure 2.5: Research reconfiguration for 'Do You Know Me?', moving from a Utopian filter to a poststructural one

Theoretical Lens	Filtering Paradigm	Research Activity
Materialist Feminism		
	Utopian ↓ Poststructural	More Artistic * TIE

entertaining her friends — passing around imaginary drinks and making small talk. Soon people are dancing, including Phyllis and her new friend, Graham, who gradually becomes the focus of everyone's attention. They dance slowly — deliberately — enjoying the closeness of their bodies. Phyllis gently removes herself from his embrace and joins a group of students who have been watching them dance. Graham continues his self-possessed solo dance, not noticing Phyllis's absence.

'Oh, he's lovely!' she whispers to a group of 13-year-old girls who are now clustered around her. 'I think I'm gonna ask him to stay the night.' The girls giggle and watch closely as Phyllis reenters the scene and leads Graham to her bed. They slowly mime taking off their clothes as they prepare to embark on their first sexual encounter together. Some students snicker while others shuffle uncomfortably. Some chuckle when Phyllis finally asks Graham if he has any condoms. He doesn't. 'This is love,' he coos. 'This is passion!' 'You don't have any?' Phyllis asks incredulously, and then quickly adds, 'Well, that's alright. You can use mine. I've got loads!' Some students laugh out loud; others roll their eyes; a few others exchange embarrassed glances at a frowning teacher, who in turn darts a concerned look at a visiting district funder, who flashes a quick, uncomfortable smile then returns his gaze to his investment.

This complex set of interactions is from *Fighting For Our Lives*, a theatre in education program devised specifically for 13- and 14-year-olds by Pit Prop Theatre in the Greater Manchester district of northwestern England. During this two-day program of promenade performance and workshops about the world HIV/AIDS crisis, students were asked not only to watch but to engage actively in the process of meaning-making by interacting with characters and expressing their opinions. However, they were not the only ones making meaning of this event. Nervous teachers, uncertain funders and school administrators, as well as politically motivated company members all had a stake in how this event made, shaped, and evoked meanings. How can a researcher productively discuss the collision of meanings in a theatrical event of this kind?

In my ethnographic account of *Fighting for Our Lives*, I began dealing with this complex question of how can meaning and experience be made sense of not only in TIE work but in other forms of participatory drama work. While mining what Bruce McConachie (1989) calls the 'theatrical formation' that constituted this piece (including students, company members, teachers, funders, and administrators), I structured my written account as a series of displacements in which the 'truth' is always in question, given the 'dance of negotiation' played within and between the overlapping and interactive socio-cultural, economic and political contexts of the members of this formation. At the base of this study, then, is the idea that meaning-making is a situated, creative practice that is ideologically loaded and contextually nuanced.

In this study I used several overlapping theoretical templates in an approach typical of much work in cultural studies: materialist feminism with attention to social, political and economic setting of this cultural event; reader-response and reception theory with attention to what 'readers' do with 'texts'; neo-Marxist new historicism with attention to theatrical formations, culture, and economy of production. I combined these with several methodological templates: ethnography and ethnographic methods with a commitment to sharing the voices of those involved (via participant observation, interview) as well as historical and literary research as needed. The overall filtering paradigm of poststructuralism helped to ground the work and influenced the complexity of the questions asked. However, I moved between poststructuralism and what Egon Guba (1990) calls the 'constructivist' paradigm which:

> intends neither to predict or control the 'real' world nor to transform it but to reconstruct the 'world' at the only point at which it exists: in the minds of constructors. It is the mind that is to be transformed not the 'real world'. (p. 27)

While a deconstructive paradigm allows for substantive critique, it often leaves a vague sense of despair. How to redress that void is my ongoing project as I continue to struggle with refiguring my role as a qualitative researcher and practitioner.

This intertwining of subjectivity, context, and meaning is also present in media critic David Morley's (1992) evocative metaphor for qualitative and empirical approaches to research:

> To draw a carp, Chinese masters warn, it is not enough to know the animal's morphology, study its anatomy or understand the physiological functions of its existence. They tell us that it is also necessary to consider the reed against which the carp brushes each morning while seeking its nourishment, the oblong stone behind which it conceals itself, or the rippling of water when it springs toward the surface. These elements should in no way be treated as the fish's environment, the milieu in which it evolves or the natural background against which it can be drawn. *They belong to the carp itself*. . . The carp must be apprehended as a certain power to affect and be affected by the world. (p. 193, emphasis added)

Figure 2.6: Research design for 'Between Production and Reception' using multiple theoretical lenses filtered between constructivist and poststructural paradigms

Theoretical Lens	Filtering Paradigm	Research Activity
Materialist Feminism		
Neo-Marxism	Poststructural ↑↓	More Qualitative * ethnography * reflective practice
Reception Theory	Constructivist	

After seeing *Fighting for Our Lives*, one student told me that the only thing she remembered about the program was the 'bed scene' (described above) and talked about how her boyfriend was pressuring her to have sex. 'I want to make sure that I'm a bit older before I even have anything. He's like, dirty sometimes. I don't like that.' This student's personal life experiences with her boyfriend were part of what made her experience of *Fighting for Our Lives*, if crudely, 'belong to the carp itself'. Each position (company member, student participant, teacher, and funder) has a 'certain power to affect and be affected by the world', and *Fighting for Our Lives* was, like all cultural formations, a practice through which these 'worlds' were constituted for these particular positionalities. That it is ultimately impossible to separate the foreground from the background, an 'informant' from her milieu, the 'event' from its 'surroundings', challenges many of the ways in which those of us in educational theatre have conducted our research and have placed our attention (see Figure 2.6).

Implications

David Morley (1992) points out that our understanding of cultural events 'should be premised on the integration of environment and action in the ways we think about it and research it' (p. 183). I submit that by engaging in practice and research from informed positions, that is, through careful examinations of our own and others' paradigmatic assumptions, we can actively choose challenging theoretical and methodological tools that allow us to focus and attend to the complexities of the practice of theory in practice.

References

AUSTIN, G. (1990) *Feminist Theories for Dramatic Criticism*, Ann Arbor, University of Michigan Press.

DOLAN, J. (1988) *The Feminist Spectator as Critic*, Ann Arbor, University of Michigan Press.

EAGLETON, T. (1990) *The Significance of Theory*, Oxford, Blackwell.

FLETCHER, H. (1995) 'Ethics and equity: A cautionary tale.' International Drama/Theatre and Education (IDEA) conference paper presentation, Brisbane, Australia (July).

GRADY, S. (1992) 'A postmodern challenge: Universal truths need not apply', *Theatre*, **13**(2), pp. 15–20.

GRADY, S. (1995) '"Misplaced concreteness": [Re]searching for meaning-making', *Youth Theatre Journal*, **9**, pp. 1–13.

GUBA, E. (1990) *The Paradigm Dialog*, Newbury Park, Sage Publications.

HAWTHORNE, J. (1992) *A Concise Glossary of Contemporary Literary Theory*, London, Edward Arnold.

KONDO, D. (1990) *Crafting Selves*, Chicago, University of Chicago Press.

McCONACHIE, B.A. (1989) 'Reading context into performance: Theatrical formations and social history', *Journal of Dramatic Theory and Criticism*, (Spring) **3**(2), pp. 229–37.

MERRIMAN, V. (1995) 'Making difference: Drama, dialogue and identity.' IDEA conference paper presentation, Brisbane, Australia, July.

MORLEY, D. (1992) *Television Audiences and Cultural Studies*, London, Routledge.

NICHOLSON, H. (1993) 'Postmodernism and educational drama', *Drama*, **2**(1), pp. 18–21.

NICHOLSON, H. (1995) 'Performative acts: Drama, education and gender', *NADIE Journal*, **19**(1), pp. 27–38.

WHITMORE, J. (1994) *Directing Postmodern Theater*, Ann Arbor, University of Michigan Press.

ZARRILLI, P. (1995) *Acting Reconsidered*, London, Routledge.

3 Escaping the Information Abattoir: Critical and Transformative Research in Drama Classrooms

John Carroll

The problem with data is that it's dead. We should bring it back to life by thinking through all the relationships it participates in. (Agre, 1994, p. 94)

This chapter examines another way of researching drama that tries to avoid cutting up the creative processes of drama and research into cling-wrapped packages of dead experience. To understand what can be studied in drama, how it can be classified, and in what contexts it could be analysed, we need to unpack some current notions of the research process.

The framed role-shifted interactions of drama in education allow drama researchers to consider some alternative possibilities about what constitutes valid research in this area of the arts. In the past, drama was often thought too difficult for qualitative research and so analysis was mainly confined to the level of personal anecdote or narrative. Alternatively, quantitative research reduced drama to dead survey statistics that omitted from its results the human and artistic interactions that gave the drama value in the first place.

However, one form of research that seems to be particularly useful for retaining the immediacy and life of drama is that of critical theory. Critical theory is a useful research approach because it shares some of the concerns of classroom drama practitioners. In a sociological sense, drama can be seen as a deliberately structured activity. That is, an activity which is bracketed off from the usual world of everyday classroom interaction by the art process. The communication strategies, the interactions and the negotiation of power used within the drama are seen as valuable areas of investigation. The framed nature of drama encourages analysis in terms of dramatic structure and agency expressed through enactment. These issues of structure and agency are also the central focus of critical and transformative research.

Because drama occurs in a negotiated reality it throws the taken-for-granted structural limitations of the school social context into high relief. It is this social context of education, the institutionalized group nature of the encounter between teachers and students, that constitutes the reality of day-to-day classroom teaching that drama illuminates. As Foucault (1972) makes clear,

> ... what is an education system after all if not a ritualisation of the word; if not a qualification of some fixing of notes for speakers, if not the constitution of a (diffuse) doctrinal group; if not a distribution and an appropriation of discourse with all its learning and its powers. (p. 227)

This view of education encourages the drama researcher to interpret the institutional nature of power and authority by viewing it through the lens of alternatively framed dramatic realities. It also highlights the creative awareness of students as they construct meanings within the institutional framework of schools.

Drama emphasizes this agency of the participants by renegotiating the relationships of power that exist within the school environment. It does this through its deliberately framed and role-shifted form. It is this dramatic 'penalty-free' examination of structure and agency that focuses the questions critical researchers ask. These questions concern the contested sites of power and authority that constitute the social context of the educational system and serve as the conceptual orientation of critical theory. So the critical researcher in drama focuses on the intensely social and constructed nature of reality within the school environment and the inequalities, relationships, and social structures that make this up. The 'orientating theory' (Whyte, 1984) of the critical researcher becomes part of the dialogue of the research process. This has been described as, 'consisting of concerns about inequality and the relationships of human activity, culture and social and political structures' (Carspecken and Apple, 1992, p. 511).

Critical and transformative theory, then, is a research model that deals with interpersonal relationships, role, power and context. These issues are also close to the centre of drama in education work. Previous drama research (Carroll, 1988) has shown that the use of interpersonal power within drama became extremely important if the role-shifted discourse enabled students to take control of the situation through their dramatic enactment.

The transformative elements of this process require the researcher to be engaged in the process of attitude change, emancipation and collaboration. The research process deliberately refutes the dichotomy of researcher and researched by classifying all those involved in the drama process as researchers. Ultimately this form of research is seen as an attempt to understand and change social reality (Lather, 1992, p. 87).

A further way to see the difference between critical and transformative research and other forms of research is to consider it in terms of its overall paradigm, its methodology and the range of methods it uses. Following Sarantakos (1993, p. 30), these theoretical distinctions should help clarify the ways in which critical theory operates.

John Carroll

Research Paradigms

In simple terms, a *paradigm* is a world view, a set of propositions that explains how the complexity of the world is perceived by the researcher. It tells them, 'what is important, what is legitimate, what is reasonable' (Patton, 1990, p. 37). A *methodology* is a framework that provides guidelines about how research is done. The paradigm or world view is translated into a research language that shows how drama can be explained and studied. *Method* refers to the practical techniques used by the drama researcher to gather data.

This three part division of the research process is useful because it helps explain the metaphors that lie behind the notions of research and especially the metaphors of critical research. In the past, the metaphor operating for drama teachers who saw drama only as performance was that of an outside assessor, an audience member, and ultimately a critic. It located the observer in a god-like position outside the action of the drama. However, within the field of drama in education the development of teacher-in-role strategies has allowed different metaphors to emerge for the teacher and the researcher. In drama, as in any form of human communication, it is now accepted that there is no omniscient vantage point from which all things are visible (Sless, 1986, p. 38).

In drama, the teacher and students are engaged in constructing as well as experiencing the dramatic frame, they are involved in what Augusto Boal (1981; 1995, pp. 42–4) calls *metaxis*. This dual position of holding two points of view in mind simultaneously demands a new sort of research question. The drama researcher has to ask, What is my relationship with the subjects of my research and where am I standing to conduct it? The metaphor for the researcher in drama is more like someone who is part of a group of travelling players, figures moving in a landscape. The image of the travelling players in Bergman's film *The Seventh Seal* is a particularly strong picture that comes to mind for me. We can see only what is before us and must imagine what is hidden from view; our position in the landscape gives each of us a singular view though we share a common set of conditions within the drama frame (Sless, 1986, p. 39).

This metaphor helps clarify the subjective positioning of the researcher within drama and places this form of research clearly within what has been called the critical theory paradigm. Before we go on to examine the methodology and methods used in this sort of research it would be useful to compare it with the two other main paradigms used in research. Of course, there are many forms of critical theory that use alternative theoretical lenses to give different perspectives on the research questions that are raised. These range from a variety of feminist perspectives through postmodernist, semiotic, literary, psychoanalytical and theatrical forms. See Sharon Grady's account in Chapter 2 of this volume for a further discussion of this paradigm. All of them in some way draw on the general field of critical theory for their methodologies and methods. However, for simplicity only the three generally agreed on paradigms are used to distinguish critical theory from more traditional forms.

Table 3.1:   Research paradigms

Paradigm	Positivism	Interpretivism	Critical Theory
Nature of reality	Objective	Subjective	Social
Purpose of research	Explain and predict	Interpret and understand	Disclose and empower
Research perspectives	Survey	Naturalistic	Transformative
Methodology	Experimental	Ethnographic	Case study
Focus	Comprehension	Interpretation	Exploration
Methods	Quantitative Statistical	Qualitative Descriptive	Dialectical Grounded

Table 3.1 illustrates the three most common conceptions of research. Each is based on the world view or 'orientating theory' that informs it. We will be concentrating on the area of critical research as it is here that drama and the notions of transformation that are inherent within it are most effective. As already noted, in the past it used to be that the metaphor for the researcher was of someone standing outside the research process. Positivism saw research in an instrumental way, as a tool for discovering knowledge that existed 'out there' and that by the application of the right research methods the researcher would discover it.

Interpretivism developed as a paradigm as researchers came to understand that knowledge was socially created. What became important in such a subjective metaphor was not so much the observable social actions of individuals but rather the subjective meanings attached to such actions. The task of the researcher was to interpret and understand the meanings that were operating within the group being researched.

This paradigm shift still left researchers outside the process they were observing and metaphorically still in an omniscient position in relation to the subjects of the research. The key characteristic of this view of research is description. Many of the methodological problems encountered in this form of research involve the degree to which the researcher 'goes native' by adopting a subjective stance in relation to the research subjects. It is often thought that this subjectivity compromises the objective description and theory building that is being attempted.

More recently, critical theory has been seen as another way of approaching research in drama. This is because the politics of research are now a contested area and the social dimension of the power relationships operating within research have become clearer. As Foucault (1980) sees it, 'power is crucial in the construction of reality, language, meanings and the rituals of truth' (p. 133). For many researchers, and especially drama researchers, it is no longer a matter of seeing the choice as one between positivism or interpretivism because both paradigms can be seen as modes of power/knowledge that position ultimate control out of the hands of the participants in the research.

The critical theory paradigm claims that reality is neither objective as claimed by positivism nor subjective as claimed by interpretivism but a complex combination of both perspectives. Subjective meanings are important and reality is created by people operating in social structures but objective relationships also cannot be denied to exist. Reality is seen as a state of tension and contradiction resulting from the conflicts between the presentation of what 'appears to be', and an underlying reality which may be based on illusion and exploitation.

The purpose of critical research in drama is to get below the surface of social relations and disclose the myths and rituals of social relationships (Lather, 1992, p. 87). By using drama methodology, critical and transformative research attempts to understand and modify social reality. In drama research the participants are knowing subjects within their cultural context and they can construct dramatic narratives about the world drawn from their personal experience and imagination. What is required is a form of research analysis that takes this into account. As Westwood (1991) says about the research perspective of critical theory, 'Research projects in the transformative mode have to offer those involved not simply a voice but a speaking position through the narrative mode. This avoids the use of subjects as cases or as examples of fragmented beings' (p. 83). This model of research fits clearly into the notion of transformation that is at the heart of drama in education.

When involved in drama, participants use transformation to generate learning in two related ways. First, it is used where experience and knowledge are transformed through representation into action. Second, it is used to transform knowledge through the creation of dramatic symbol. Eco (1976) calls this process 'transmediation' (p. 7). This ability to transform experience enables dramatic role to function in the classroom. An identification through role creation and a representation of this into action allows the complex transformation of the self into role to occur. Dorothy Heathcote defines this as '. . . a complexity to do with the varying ways in which we function in different social situations under so many different kinds of authority and power' (Heathcote in Robinson, 1980, p. 12). Because drama is so centrally concerned with transformation it is uniquely positioned to deal with a further level of transformation in the area of research.

A shift to a transformative research methodology will enable the students to be engaged actively with the researcher in an exploration of the relationship between power and knowledge. The values surrounding our research efforts should be made explicit for the participants in a way that opens it up for them to become engaged in the enterprise of knowledge generation. As Deshler and Selener (1991) say, 'what we decide to research and the way we conduct our research is a political statement about who and what is important to us' (p. 9).

The methodology of critical theory and the transformational perspectives of drama research is a way of theory building and is grounded in the interpretation of actual data of the drama but it differs from other ethnographic forms in that it is a more narrowly focused inquiry. Participants in drama research work together in a dialectical way. This is the process of constantly moving between concepts and data as well as between society and the concrete interactions of the drama. It is a process that begins with an initial concept to be investigated by the researcher. This focus concept along with any subsidiary ones is considered in terms of connections and reflections regarding surface appearances and the real situation that may underlie it. The researcher forms opinions about the issues within the drama and thus new concepts are generated. These new concepts are developed and re-examined and a tentative theory is inductively derived from the study of the drama interaction.

The Case Study

The overall methodology for critical research in drama is grounded in the natural setting of the drama activity. While all drama in education and especially role-based work can be seen on one level as a non-real-life situation, once 'the willing suspension of disbelief' is accomplished it proceeds 'as if' the activity at hand was the setting the drama frame had established. That is, the framing devices of drama allow the participants to respond with authenticity to the dramatic world that has been established. The research methodology that most clearly fits these special conditions of drama is that of the case study.

Case study fits because drama, by its very nature as a negotiated group art form, is a non-reproducible experience. The participants within a drama in education session or series of sessions create a unique set of social relationships that becomes a single unit of experience capable of analysis and study. Because of the complexity of the interactions, the whole creative sequence needs to be studied and not just aspects of variables within it. These characteristics are also aspects of a case study methodology (Hartfield, 1982) and provide a close fit for drama researchers to follow. The case study honours the agency of the participants and sees them as experts not just a source of data for analysis. This is also a central tenet of critical research. To summarize, a case study can be seen as, '. . . an empirical inquiry that investigates a contemporary phenomenon within its real-life context when the boundaries between phenomenon and context are not clearly evident; and in which multiple sources of evidence are used' (Yin, 1991, p. 23).

The case study is useful when, as is usual in drama, the researcher is interested in, and deeply involved in, the structures, processes and outcomes of a project. This is especially so when the researcher is operating inside the group using dramatic role conventions (Neelands, 1991, p. 5) that help frame the constructed world of the drama. Case study methodology is capable of examining in an open and flexible manner the social action of drama in its negotiated and framed setting. It is also able to interpret the nature of power structures and the interaction of the participants within them.

There are four main criteria which distinguish this case study methodology as described by Lamnek (quoted in Sarantakos, 1993, p. 261):

- *Openness*: there is no restriction that could limit the action of the researcher or direct the research into predetermined goals or paths of action.
- *Communicativity*: case studies perceive reality as emerging in interaction between the actors [sic]. Action and communication constitute reality.
- *Naturalism*: the researcher studies relations in their natural stage, not as artificially constructed models.
- *Interpretativity*: social reality is defined as 'interpreted' reality and not objective reality.

These four criteria fit drama research because the interpreted reality of the drama frame becomes the meaningful and significant everyday reality of the research process. Because of the high level of artistic content and complexity involved in improvisation it is usual that sampling is by single case study that is developed over time. So time series analysis, pattern matching and explanation building are useful methods of data analysis (Yin, 1991, p. 70). However, the most powerful method of data analysis for critical research is that of grounded theory.

Grounded Theory Method

If the case study provides a methodology for critical research in drama then grounded theory is the method by which this is done. It takes the form of a qualitative inductive analysis that studies the drama under investigation as an autonomous research unit with its own structures, boundaries, and history. Therefore, the qualitative interaction evident in case study methodology and grounded theory method are closely linked. This linking of case study methodology and grounded theory method occurs because of the researchers unique immersion in the social settings of the drama and the requirement for an intersubjective understanding between researchers and participants. This research method was developed by Glaser and Strauss (1967) and is *grounded* because it relates to and emerges out of the empirical phenomena it represents. As Strauss and Corbin (1990) put it,

A grounded theory is one that is inductively derived from the study of the phenomenon it represents. That is, it is discovered, developed, and provisionally verified through systematic data collection and analysis of data pertaining to that phenomenon. Therefore, data collection, analysis, and theory stand in reciprocal relationship with each other. One does not begin with a theory, then prove it. Rather, one begins with an area of study and what is relevant to that area is allowed to emerge. (p. 23)

In terms of critical theory and drama this implies that a case study will encompass a complete drama experience that exists as an autonomous area of work and that the drama methods used in the research will develop from the material. This can vary from a single lesson to a series of linked drama experiences that move from improvisation through to performance. In essence, this drama research method is concerned with the meanings and power relationships within the drama experience. Creativity is also seen as central in the development of grounded theory method. When used in drama, the procedures of this method force the researcher to break through assumption and to create new order within the drama frame. It differs from more open ethnographic description in that data is conceptually grouped and arranged in categories. These concepts are then coded by means of statements of relationship. It is unusual in descriptive studies for interpretation of data to take place on this scale.

To return to Table 3.1, the nature of reality considered in terms of grounded theory method is similar in concept to that of the dramatist. Reality is seen as socially constructed and represented through enactment. The researchers in drama work within the context of the constructed world of the drama. They attempt to approach the product of the framed experiences in an unprejudiced manner at the same time as they are engaged in forming and shaping the drama experience.

Being grounded in the interactions of the drama experience, the method takes as a central element the primary experience of the participants. The concepts that flow from this connection to everyday experience are developed as categories. These have conceptual power because they are able to arrange systematically otherwise complex and fragmented interactions. However, these categories are not static constructs. As new knowledge is acquired so new categories are developed. In line with drama theory the development of concepts is seen as a constantly changing process not a pre-existing structure.

Tentative theories about the relationships that evolve within the drama process are developed and then refined and tested in a continuous unending cycle. This involves the processes of:

Induction — the development of a temporary statement that identifies the area of drama to be studied.
Deduction — the deriving of implication from involvement within the drama process.
Verification — testing the validity of these implications within the drama framework.
(Sarantakos, 1993, p. 70)

So the research questions for grounded theory are oriented towards action and process in the same way as much drama in education work. This orientation makes the methodology a very useful tool and complements the collaborative developmental aims of drama research.

Grounded Theory Research Procedures

To return to the main elements within the grounded theory method, the following procedures need to be followed when carrying out this kind of research. The steps within the method are closely interrelated and may, in some cases, be employed simultaneously depending on the type of drama activity being investigated. These procedures are set out in detail within *Basics of Qualitative Research* (Strauss and Corbin, 1990), however, the following notes apply more specifically to using the method within a drama context.

Procedures

- Developing a concept-indicator model. Within the negotiated drama frame the empirical indicators of enactment and dialogue are observed and described through interview, text documentation or audio-visual recordings. The information becomes an indicator for a concept which the researcher is developing about the drama. This is an initial and temporary position which is modified as data is collected.
- Data collection. This involves asking questions from within the drama as well as outside of it. The collection of data from the drama is coded through the use of theoretical memos and continues until no new information is available.
- Coding. This is a process of asking questions about categories and their relationships within the drama. Coding helps to discover categories and subcategories which are named and further processed. Coding is initially open which allows further refinement and reinterpretation. Once codes are verified, selective coding concentrates on coding key categories. Strauss (1991, pp. 122–3) sets out the following basic rules for coding:

  - One should not paraphrase sentences but discover and name genuine categories.
  - One should set categories as directed by the coding paradigm (i.e., in reference to conditions, strategies, and consequences).
  - One should set categories in relationship with subcategories, one by one.
  - One should always relate to data and refer adequately to them.
  - One should underline, which makes sorting easier.
  - Categories and subcategories must be interrelated.
  - Unrelated categories must either become related or eliminated.

- Key categories. This process of discovering and naming categories within the drama allows the researcher to deal with interaction strategies and the consequences of enactment. By discovering key categories, the researcher can go on to theoretical sampling and data collection which may lead to the development of a theory.
- Theoretical sampling. This is the sampling of further data on the basis of concepts that have proven theoretical relevance to the evolving theory within the drama context. The central concern is with the representativeness of concepts rather than in more traditional paradigms with the representativeness of the sample.
- Comparison. Constant comparison is a central tool of analysis, as new knowledge is acquired so new concepts are developed that have conceptual density.
- Saturation and integration of theory. Analyses and comparisons continue until all available information is derived from the drama case study. When additional information does not achieve a change in existing data, saturation is considered to have been reached and the process of analysis is complete.
- Theoretical memos. Memos are written by the researcher in drama at all stages of the procedures. They are essential procedures which enable the drama researcher to keep an ongoing record of the analytic process. They are central to the validity of the research process and are expected to follow certain rules (Strauss, 1991), the most important one being that data and memos should be kept separate.

The whole procedure is aimed at organizing the thoughts and experiences of the researcher and participants as they accumulate them throughout the drama case study.

It is clear that this form of analysis is able to handle the layered complexity of role interaction and provide insights into this dramatically structured source of non-numerical data. Grounded theory provides the method that can handle such complex sources of role-derived information without oversimplifying or losing its complexity and content. However, on the surface it can appear to be a complex method that requires highly disciplined and well-trained researchers to carry it through to completion. What is required is some assistance for the researcher that will deal with the complexity of this sort of information. Fortunately, there are now available computer-aided software packages that allow the researcher to categorize and classify the information in a way that is compatible with Strauss and Corbin's (1990) techniques.

Computer-aided Analysis

There are an increasing range of computer software packages that are capable of coding and retrieving qualitative research information. They include *The*

Ethnograph, Qual Pro, Textbase Alpha, TAP, and *Hyper Qual* (Tesch, 1991) as well as *NUDIST* which stands for Non-mathematical Unstructured Data Information Searching Indexing and Theorising. This Australian computer software package (Richards and Richards, 1994) is particularly well suited to grounded theory. It differs from many of the code and retrieve packages in that it is able to assist in grounded theory building, within the complex layers of drama interaction. It helps the grounded theory method user to:

- manage, explore and search the research texts, whether they are transcriptions, documents or audio visual recordings.
- manage and explore ideas about the data.
- link ideas and construct theories about the data.
- generate reports. (Richards and Richards, 1994)

The value of such computer-aided grounded theory research is that,

> First, the emerging categories can be explored and cumulatively built up without losing any of these links to the data. Second, memos about theory can be stored and linked to the data. Third, the index can be flexible and have the ability to change rapidly to adapt to emerging categories. Finally, the system supports the inclusion of all data in an infinitely flexible system. (Richards and Richards, 1991, p. 274)

Of course, the interpreting and thinking is still done by the researcher. The computer software is not capable of making conceptual decisions. The really hard work of deciding what is important data within the drama is still firmly part of the critical research process. However, paradoxically it is this use of computer-based research method that encourages the philosophical paradigm shift to critical and transformative research. Instead of research being seen only as data manipulation, independent of the life of the subject, a more sophisticated view can now be accommodated. This view sees research knowledge as a relationship that exists between and among people in particular times and contexts. This encourages the notion of transformative research that enables the participants (subjects) to engage actively with the researcher in an exploration of the relationship between power and knowledge. Critical and transformative research honours the 'emotional literacy' (Carroll, 1995) of its subjects and allows the agency of the participants to be present in the research. It also allows the power structures within the relationships, including the position of the teacher/researcher to be negotiated. This approach to the ethics of fieldwork is linked to the notion that drama research can be seen as a collaborative conversation about learning and inquiry that should in some way allow for personal transformation through the medium of the art form of drama.

Conclusion

This exploration of research into drama has taken us from the paradigm of critical theory through to the methodology of the case study and on to methods of computer-aided grounded theory. This is only one path among many within the wider field of critical theory. However, this path does provide one answer to the call for more rigorous research techniques in the field of drama. More importantly, because of the role-shifted nature of drama, the areas of discussion concerning power and inequality are radically widened. This widening of the discourse occurs because the drama framework protects the participants while freeing them to voice opinions within dramatic role that would not normally be available to them. In earlier research (Carroll, 1988) it was shown that by changing the parameters of what can be seen as legitimate knowledge, drama allows the participants the freedom to transform and explore the issues of human concern and intellectual inquiry that the constraints of the centrally controlled classroom denies them.

The researcher and the participants within the research process can take the initiatives, protected by role conventions, that allow them to venture outside the bounds of socially controlled knowledge. They are able, because of the drama research process, to construct new ways to explore drama and hopefully can empower themselves in the process.

References

AGRE, P. (1994) 'Living data', *Wired*, **2.11**, November, pp. 94–6.

BOAL, A. (1981) *Theatre de LíOpprime*, Numero 5, Ceditade An 03.

BOAL, A. (1995) *The Rainbow of Desire*, London, Routledge.

CARROLL, J. (1988) 'Terra incognita: Mapping drama talk', *NADIE Journal*, **12**(2).

CARROLL, J. (1995) 'Video lives: Dramatic role and emotional literacy.' Paper presented at the International Drama/Theatre and Education (IDEA '95) Conference, Brisbane.

CARSPECKEN, P. and APPLE, M. (1992) 'Critical qualitative research: Theory, methodology, and practice', in LE COMPTE, M., MILLROY, W. and PREISSLE, J. (eds) *The Handbook of Qualitative Research in Education*, San Diego, Academic Press, pp. 508–53.

DESHLER, D. and SELENER, D. (1991) 'Transformative research: In search of a definition', *Convergence*, **XXIV**(3), pp. 9–21.

ECO, U. (1976) *A Theory of Semiotics*, Bloomington, Indiana University Press.

FOUCAULT, M. (1972) *The Archaeology of Knowledge*, Trans from the French by A.M. Sheridan Smith (First published in 1969 by Gallinard), New York, Pantheon.

FOUCAULT, M. (1980) 'Truth and power', in GORDON, C. (ed.) *Power/Knowledge: Selected Interviews and Other Writings, 1972–1977*, New York, Pantheon Books, pp. 109–33.

GLASER, B.G. and STRAUSS, A.L. (1967) *The Discovery of Grounded Theory: Strategies for Qualitative Research*, Chicago, Aldine.

HARTFIELD, G. (1982) *Workbook of Sociology*, Stuttgart, Kroener.

LATHER, P. (1992) 'Critical frames in educational research: Feminist and post-structural perspectives', *Theory into Practice*, **XXXI**(2), pp. 87–99.

Neelands, J. (1991) *Structuring Drama Work*, Cambridge, Cambridge University Press.

Patton, M. (1990) *Qualitative Evaluation and Research Methods*, Newbury Park, Sage Publications.

Richards, L. and Richards, T. (1991) 'Computing in qualitative analysis: A healthy development', *Qualitative Health Research*, **1**(2), pp. 234–62.

Richards, T. and Richards, L. (1994) *Qualitative Data Analysis Solutions for Research Professionals* (*NUDIST* program manual), Victoria, Qualitative Solutions and Research Pty Ltd.

Robinson, K. (ed.) (1980) *Exploring Theatre and Education*, London, Heinemann.

Sarantakos, S. (1993) *Social Research*, Melbourne, Macmillan.

Sless, D. (1986) *In Search of Semiotics*, London, Croom Helm.

Strauss, A.L. (1991) *Grundlagen Qualitativer Sozialforschung, Datenanalyse und Theoriebildung in der Empirischen Sozialforschung*, Munich, Wilhelm Fink Verlag.

Strauss, A.L. and Corbin, J. (1990) *Basics of Qualitative Research*, Newbury Park, Sage Publications.

Tesch, R. (1991) 'Software for qualitative researchers: Analysis needs and program capabilities', in Fielding, N. and Lee, R. (eds) *Using Computers in Qualitative Research*, London, Sage Publications, pp. 16–37.

Westwood, S. (1991) 'Power/knowledge: The politics of transformative research', in *Convergence*, **XXIV**(3), pp. 79–85.

Whyte, W.F. (1984) *Learning from the Field: A Guide from Experience*, Beverley Hills, Sage Publications.

Yin, R.K. (1991) *Case Study Research Design and Methods*, Newbury Park, Sage Publications.

4 Playing in Different Keys: Research Notes for Action Researchers and Reflective Drama Practitioners

Brian Edmiston and Jeffrey Wilhelm

Introduction

How can I improve my drama teaching? Though we may not recognize it as such, this is a research question that could lead a teacher to conduct classroom-based or action research. Action research is qualitative inquiry through which teachers can research their own practice. They focus on 'some aspect of their practice in order to find out more about it, and eventually to act in ways they see as better or more effective' (Oberg and McCutcheon, 1987, p. 117). When we question an aspect of our practice, reflect on events from one day and subsequently change our plans for the next day, we are informally researching our teaching. Action research formalizes this process and enables us to become more systematic and rigorous in our analysis of our teaching. We become better teachers because we understand how our actions affect the classroom context.

Reflection by practitioners is central to the process of conducting action research in the classroom. If we pay close attention to the broad *questions* students ask they can provide us, as action researchers, with *bass* keys upon which we can improvise with students. In our view, listening carefully to determine what puzzles students enables us to shape work around *their* concerns and explore ideas *with* them. In doing so, we can become more reflective and thus more competent drama practitioners.

The Classroom Context

Recently there has been a resurgence of interest in 'inquiry-based' education where students work together on research projects (Short, Harste and Burke, 1996). Jeff Wilhelm's rural middle school classroom for 12- and 13-year-old students was organized along the principles of an inquiry-based curriculum. He frequently had his students work together on projects. He endorsed the principles of student-motivated cooperative thematic study where students pursued their questions. He encouraged students to regard teachers as one of many resources in the classroom rather than as the authority on all knowledge.

As students extended their studies, he mentored them as they gathered, analysed, and presented their data.

The students were concluding three-week team research projects, which were part of a unit on Civil Rights, when Brian Edmiston came into the school to work through drama with self-selected small groups of two to four students. Earlier in the year at different times, Brian and Jeff had led whole group sessions and the students were comfortable with using drama in the classroom. Over two days Brian led thirty students in seven different small groups in one or two forty minute process drama sessions.

Each small group of two to four students had read books, and interviewed relatives as informants or watched videos about their topic. They then formulated questions which guided their reading, writing and talk about their particular topic. For example, four boys in what we refer to as the 'Hank Aaron group' were interested in the life of this African-American baseball star of the 1950s. One of their questions was 'How did Hank Aaron get to be so great at baseball?' They had collected and recorded all the information about him that they thought was relevant.

Each group had also begun to prepare for their final presentations which were to be shared with the whole class. Students used either computer hypermedia or videotapes of themselves for their presentations. Many had written first drafts of their scripts or presentations, but had indicated dissatisfaction with their questions, their findings, or with how they were framing and understanding their topic. For example, the Hank Aaron group had written scripts of scenes which they were planning to videotape. The scenes were to inform their classmates about what they considered important about Aaron's life. However, three of the four boys in the Hank Aaron group said the scripts were 'boring'. The scripts were dramatized reports of facts — for example, that Hank and his brother would hit bottle caps with broom handles. So when Jeff told his classes that Brian was interested in working through drama to help them explore their topics in more depth, there was a host of volunteer groups.

In each drama session, the students were encouraged to continue to think and position themselves as researchers who were exploring questions. Jeff had helped each group agree on guiding questions for their research. On meeting each group, Brian identified and clarified a question which the group had been considering and which they were interested in exploring through drama. These became each group's initial research question for the drama session. Jeff later worked with each group as they re-thought their questions in preparation for their end-of-year presentations.

Knowing their initial research questions, Brian planned drama activities and agreed with each group on a beginning encounter. In the fictional context of the drama, the students adopted the position of various 'informants' — people who could provide significant information about the topic. For example, in the Hank Aaron group, the students adopted the perspectives of Hank Aaron, his family, and the baseball players in the Negro and Major Leagues. As the students participated in drama worlds they explored their questions from the viewpoints of various additional informants as well as from the perspective of researchers.

Teacher Play and Experimentation as Reflection-in-Action

Schön (1987, pp. 68–79) argues that reflective practitioners recognize that they 'play games' within situations and 'experiment' as they reflect in action. He identifies three interrelated ways of playing and experimenting as we act: exploration, hypothesis testing and move testing. All three approaches provide us with ways in which we may elicit and clarify students' questions. Knowing which playful/experimental approach we use makes us more reflective.

- Exploration. When we are open to whatever consequences follow, then our actions probe and explore.
- Hypothesis testing. When we act assuming a particular broad way of viewing a situation, then we test out a hypothesis.
- Move testing. When we have an end in mind as we act, then we test different moves to achieve that end.

Exploration

We explore with students as we try to find out what questions interest them. Discussion and open-ended fictional encounters in drama can generate questions as we ask, What interests you? What questions do you have? or What were you wondering about when we imagined we were in that place? As such, exploration is not only a network of possible questions which a group might ask but it is also our safety-net as we work with students — we can always stop what we are doing and ask the students for their feedback. We also explore as we pay attention to the questions which seem to be raised for students as we and they interact in drama. We can share, then, our observations with the students or reflect and ask the students to share their thoughts. As we explore implications we enable students to move beyond their initial, and often limiting, questions.

In a brief discussion, the Hank Aaron group agreed that they wanted to explore the question, How did Hank Aaron get to be so great at baseball? Though their understanding of his 'greatness' changed during and after their two sessions of drama, the group remained committed to exploring this question and many sub-questions over several weeks of work in the library, in class and at home. Their interactions led to more questions about why he was so 'great'. For example, the students wanted to explore what life was like for Hank Aaron in the locker-room, at home, and at practice. They wanted to know, What did Hank Aaron have to do off the ballfield to become great?

Hypothesis Testing

Extrapolating from students' core questions leads us to form a hypothesis about an implicit and tacitly agreed-upon view of the field they are researching. Our broad drama structuring can then be seen as a way of testing that hypothesis with the students. Schön (1987) notes that a hypothesis-testing experiment is like 'a game with the situation in which [the practitioner] seeks to make the situation conform to his hypothesis but remains open to the possibility that it will not' (p. 75). The hypothesis may or may not be confirmed in practice.

After initially talking with the Hank Aaron group, Brian (who was unfamiliar with Aaron's life and accomplishments) hypothesized that for these boys the story of Hank Aaron was one of individual struggle to become a skillful player. He began by having the students swing an imaginary baseball bat and asked them if they were Hank where might they be? One boy replied, 'Playing in the Negro League.' He talked to the boys and realized that they had not read or thought about race as a relevant factor in considering his 'greatness'. Brian's hypothesis of how the students viewed Hank Aaron's life needed to be substantially revised to include their blindness to race as an issue. This shift in perspective necessitated a change of plan so that attitudes to race could be examined, especially how Hank Aaron might have been regarded and treated by other players in his original Negro League team and in his new team when he first joined the Major League.

Move Testing

Having identified a question in which the students are interested, we can experiment with different 'moves'. We can, in effect, ask ourselves, Given this question, what activities, interactions and encounters do I think will have the desired effect of exploring this question? If we find that one move is not working we can try a different move though still with the same purpose of exploring the question in which the students seem interested. With the Hank Aaron group, at one point Brian wanted the students to reflect on the significance of Hank Aaron's first public appearance in the Major League. He asked the students to share their inner thoughts, but when one resisted and seemed embarrassed, he switched to have the students talk to each other in pairs.

As we make choices and structure a session we will explore and test hypotheses and moves, often at the same time. Knowing that we can explore, test a hypothesis or test a move gives a center to our plans, our evaluations and, most importantly, a metacognitive awareness to our teaching.

Student Researcher and Informant Stances

If students are exploring questions through drama they will need to stop 'playing' with a question and think about what has been 'played'. As they interact, the students will be constructing new understandings which may clarify some ideas yet problematize others. Our interventions can influence this process when we direct the students' attention toward making or interpreting the fictional world.

Another way to think about teacher intervention is to see it as facilitating shifts between students imagining they are informants and critiquing as researchers. The student stances of informant and researcher parallel the perspectives of participants in and spectators on the events of any drama session. As spectators, students reflect on and interpret their experiences in the drama. If, as they reflect on their experiences, the students consider how their research question is being explored and 'answered' then, we argue, they adopt a researcher stance.

The students will shift between the stances of researchers and informants as the drama progresses. They will often do so without our intervention when they slip in and out of role, interact as if they are other people, or talk as themselves. However, if we are aware of the significance of switching between these stances, we can intervene at one moment in order to structure their interactions as various participants/informants and at another moment to ask for their interpretations as spectators/researchers.

An example from the end of the first Hank Aaron session illustrates how we can intervene when it 'feels' appropriate to enable the students to shift back and forth between being informants and researchers. All four boys were informants as they imagined and spoke the sort of racist remarks Hank heard behind his back in the locker room. When Brian asked the boys how they thought Hank would have felt, they switched into researcher mode. One boy said that he would have wanted to hit them, another said he couldn't because it would have made matters worse. A third boy, Mike, said he would have walked out and gone home. He wanted to represent Hank and they all returned to informant mode. Three repeated the racist slurs as Mike listened without expression and then made a move to leave. Brian stepped forward to whisper, 'Do you want to be remembered as a quitter? How will you explain this to your grandchildren?' He was asking the group to reflect as researchers on the meaning of such an action.

Different Research Modes

No matter what questions students are interested in exploring they will imagine that they are informants and reflect on their experiences as researchers. However, different student questions have different 'ends-in-view'. Different questions suggest different 'moves' to test out with the students; different bass keys in which to improvise with them.

Educational researchers have a host of research modes for the exploration of different questions. To return to the metaphor of musical keys, working in each mode is like playing in a different key. Before the drama, groups were

Brian Edmiston and Jeffrey Wilhelm

Table 4.1: Modes of research

Mode	Question	End-in-View
Empirical research	What are the objective facts?	Decontextualized information
Phenomenology	What are the lived experiences of particular people?	Contextualized personal individual meanings
Ethnography	What are the patterns of experience for people in general?	Contextualized shared social/cultural meanings
Action research	What am I doing? What can I do to achieve my goal?	How action changes contexts and people

in effect mostly playing in quantitative and empirical research keys. Their end-in-view was the objective accumulation of facts and information. They had not been playing in qualitative research keys. For example, the Hank Aaron group were mostly detached observers of the events of his life and they read books for factual information which they recorded in lists and notes. They were interested in the names of people he had played with, the number of home runs he had hit, and the different clubs he had played for. The moves which Jeff made, enabled the students to achieve their end-in-view. He helped them find books, locate information and record details.

By the time Brian came to work with the students, the Hank Aaron group, like most of the others, seemed to have largely exhausted this approach — they were 'bored' with it. However, it was clear that as well as being interested in quantitative information they were also interested in qualitative research keys.

In the next section we consider three broad modes of qualitative research: phenomenology, ethnography and action research. We do not intend this description to be more than a cursory introduction to these methods of conducting research. Nor do we wish to suggest that these research modes are hermetically sealed since, in practice, researchers in one primary mode will often draw on many others. (See Table 4.1.)

Phenomenology

The Hank Aaron group's research question concentrated on the life of an individual: How did Hank Aaron get to be so great at Baseball? Yet significantly they had not considered how Hank Aaron had experienced his world. After a few minutes of talking about their topic it became apparent to Brian that the students were interested in the particular experiences of Hank Aaron — their research question had a phenomenological undertone.

Phenomenologists describe and interpret the phenomena of personal lived experiences. 'Phenomenology is the study of lived or existential meanings . . . it attempts to explicate the meanings as we live them in our everyday lives' (Van Manen, 1990, p. 11). They may research their own or other people's experiences. Though phenomenologists study people in social settings they are ultimately interested in people's unique, specific, personal experiences and realities, and are thus interested in personal stories and interpretations in themselves. They ask a general interpretive question like, What are the lived experiences for particular people in particular contexts? The end-in-view is to understand and record the meanings which people make from their individual experiences in specific contexts.

Though drama experiences are imaginary, they can nevertheless be deeply felt personal lived experiences or phenomenological experiences for the students. Part of the compelling nature of drama is the potential for students' *lived through experience.* As Dorothy Heathcote (1984) notes, 'Drama is about filling the spaces between people with meaningful [emotional] experiences . . . Out of these we can build reflective processes' (p. 97). Sean and Chris stressed the importance for them of trying to appreciate people's feelings and life experiences. Sean said that drama was 'a good way to really get into it about what life was like and how it would feel.' Chris added that 'you have to feel it before you can help someone else feel it.'

Phenomenologists agree. *Talk* about experiences and problems cannot substitute for the complex situated *experiences* of people who are living through those problems. Rather than privileging any detached objective view as desirable, phenomenologists argue that the viewpoints of subjective experiences are essential if we want to record or find out how we and others experience everyday reality.

All moves in the first Hank Aaron drama session were guided by the end-in-view of enabling the students to find meaning in the imagined experiences of one individual, Hank Aaron, as he experienced contexts about which they had only read. Brian structured the work so that the students were able to experience the world of Hank Aaron from a variety of perspectives and to reflect as researchers on the meanings of his personal experiences. Aaron became the primary informant in his interactions with others: playing baseball as a child, reading hate mail, in the locker room overhearing racist remarks, out in the ball park hitting a home run, talking to the manager of the Major League club, returning to his Negro League club, talking with his family and reacting to white players. All four students had the opportunity to represent Hank Aaron, two chose to do so. Brian took on roles with the four students as they created these contexts: a player, a relative, a manager, the voice of conscience, a narrator. Knowing that the students were asking a phenomenological question gave Brian a key in which to improvise. He foregrounded Aaron's possible multiple perspectives thus placing broader issues like institutionalized racism in the background.

After the drama work the students reviewed their drama experiences and realizations. In preparing their presentations, the students scripted their own scenes which drew on and extended the drama work. In addition to their role as Hank Aaron, they imagined they were people who wrote hate mail, sportswriters, Negro League teammates, white minor league and Major League teammates, baseball fans, and his family. They revised their research questions and continued their research as they re-read material and altered their scripts. Interestingly, they began to ask themselves additional phenomenological questions: How would Hank's experience have been different if he were white? What was his experience as a black ballplayer in a profession dominated by whites? How did the hate mail they had read about affect Hank and his family?

Andy explained how his group changed their priorities and realized the importance of considering Aaron's inner experiences in order to find out 'what it was like for him'. He noted that, 'We realized that the most important things he had to put up with and get over were things like fighting through prejudice. If he couldn't do that then he could never be a great ballplayer. He did both and that's why he's great.'

Ethnography

If the students in the Hank Aaron drama had asked a question like, How did African-Americans in the 1950s cope with institutionalized racism in baseball? then Brian would have made quite different moves. If they had started from such a question Brian would have structured the work so that the students would have examined the interplay of racist structures with fans, players, school children and the game as a whole. He would not have concentrated on the experiences of one player. He would have made these moves because the students would have had an ethnographic end-in-view rather than a phenomenological end-in-view.

Ethnographers are not only participants in everyday events, they are also observers of their social worlds. Ethnographers interpret social realities as they 'participate, overtly or covertly, in people's lives for an extended period of time, watching what happens, listening to what is said, asking questions' (Hammersley and Atkinson, 1983, p. 2). As participant-observers they record what informants do and say, interpret what seems to be going on from multiple perspectives, and thereby over time construct their own understandings about social realities.

Ethnographers can research in complex cultural settings like Bali or in familiar cultural contexts like classrooms. They ask a general interpretive question like, What are the patterns of experience for these people in general? Ethnography is complementary to phenomenology. The ethnographer looks for commonalities whereas the phenomenologist looks for individual differences. Whereas the phenomenologist is interested in understanding a person's *particular* experiences, an ethnographer's end-in-view is understanding *general and shared* social and cultural realities.

Students are often just as confused about what is going on in the events described in books as any ethnographer might be in Bosnia. A 13-year-old trying to understand the behaviors of people in the world of Major League baseball as the racial barrier was broken, has tasks similar to those of an ethnographer trying to make sense of behaviors, relationships and attitudes in an unfamiliar culture.

Though students cannot *actually* do ethnographic research in societies from which they are separated by time and/or space, it is useful to use ethnography as a metaphor to explore how students can use drama to research *imaginatively* questions about other cultures or worlds which would otherwise be difficult or impossible for students to access. Like ethnographers, students in drama can explore and interpret imagined social contexts.

If the students want to explore an ethnographic question then the teacher's moves will be guided by an end-in-view which concentrates on making sense across many interactions. One perspective will be insufficient, the students will need to experience from multiple points of view as they play in an ethnographic key and try to make sense of a social context. In successive drama contexts the students can depict the actions of various informants and like ethnographers they can interview them, observe them, overhear them. When they reflect as researchers they can try to generalize and look for commonalities of meaning and patterns of experience for the people in general.

For example, the Holocaust group asked the question, What was life like in the Nazi concentration camps? The students clearly wanted to know about general patterns of experience in the camps. They drew on and extended their understandings of the camps as they created the drama world. Brian's moves were guided by an end-in-view of shared social meanings. He wanted the students to experience the camps from multiple perspectives and find meaning in their reflections on this most horrific reality. They imagined the experiences of inmates as they were examined on arrival, as they sorted through clothing and shoes, as they tried to convince a guard to let them escape. Brian took on the roles of interrogator, organizer and fellow guard. The students also looked at the camps and the inmates from other perspectives: the Germans who lived near the camps, survivors of the Holocaust, and Nazi guards. Those outside the camp were interviewed as potential witnesses at the Nuremburg trials. They were asked what they saw and what they knew by Brian in role as an incredulous allied officer. The guards contemplated the risks and pointlessness of trying to hide someone and the survivors remembered what sustained them.

Like ethnographers, the students in reflection looked and listened for patterns across different people's experiences and views of their world. For example, though at first Chris had wondered why people did not escape from the camps, through the drama work he said he began to see a pattern of helplessness in the face of the extensiveness of the Holocaust. He began to realize that the Holocaust 'was so big. I knew it was bad, but not that bad. There were so many people. It was just so big and there was no escape.' Though he had created drama with only three others, in his imagination he had begun to see,

> How many were killed in one day because they were weak, old, tired of . . . for just *no* reason . . . just how many there were and how Nazis were so in control they could make up fake little things and contests and jobs so that they could make them suffer and kill them.

He concluded that, 'It was hard how it was like a game to kill and a game to stay alive.' In attempting to make sense of the ongoing genocide and find a pattern, he used the metaphor of a game, a game which was deadly and dehumanizing in very different ways for both perpetrators and victims. Chris was making social meaning about the Holocaust which was deeply felt and with a breadth he had not previously demonstrated. However, it is important to stress that his views were not treated as definitive. They were ideas which opened up discussion and led to additional research about resistance to the Nazis.

Action Research

The first session with the Hank Aaron group was structured phenomenologic-ally to focus on Hank's individual experiences, but by the second session the group's research question had taken an action research turn. During the first session the students had invented whispered racist remarks, hate mail, and veiled threats in the locker room. By the end of the session, Aaron (repres-ented by Mike) had decided to quit and return to the Negro League, yet when Brian spoke as Aaron's conscience and asked if he wanted to be remembered as a quitter, Mike had paused unable to walk out as he had planned. At the beginning of the second session the boys wondered what else Aaron could have done in response to the racist attitudes he had experienced in the Major League. They decided that he could not have just walked out because what he did would make a difference for other African-Americans. The group's research question in effect had become: What could Hank Aaron have done in response to racism? Their end-in-view was now less concerned solely with the personal experiences of Hank Aaron and more with the choices he had in response to racism. They were now thinking like action researchers.

Action research is the third research mode we will consider metaphoric-ally to classify students' questions. Playing in an action research key provides us with a different end-in-view for the moves we make as we structure drama work. Action research is recursive and reflexive, with researchers examining and re-examining how changes in their actions change their situations. Over time, they proceed in an action research cycle — an ongoing spiral of steps: planning, taking action, observing and reflecting. They make time for all four steps. They plan what their actions will be, act, observe how these actions seem to change the context and relationships between people, and reflect in order to make sense of what is happening and how they might alter their actions.

Action researchers are, in a sense, hybrids between ethnographers and phenomenologists since they are interested, not only in the social realities of the culture of which they are a part, but also their own experiences as they take action in particular contexts. However, in addition they want to learn from their experiences in order to act more effectively in context to achieve whatever their aims may be. Action researchers' end-in-view is to consider how their actions change the context and effect the relationships between people. As they reflect they ask a general interpretive question like, What could I have done differently to achieve my goal?

When students reflect and wonder about what choices they have in a particular fictional context they are entering an action research mode. Now they are interested in the difference people can make in a situation. With this end-in-view we can structure for an action research-like cycle of action, observation, reflection and planning.

In the second Hank Aaron session there was an action research-like cycle. The students tried out several actions: explaining to his family that he could not quit; ignoring racist remarks; refusing to fight back; returning to talk to his former players in the Negro League. They also reflected in the voices of his conscience, his family and Negro League players.

The group researching the Great Depression formed an action research-type question for their drama session: Why didn't the poor just get jobs? The girls were in effect saying that if they had lived in the 1930s they would have acted to find work. Brian's moves in the drama session were all guided by this question. Christine records both the moves which Brian made and how she was thinking about the choices people had when they became impoverished,

> When we started I didn't understand how all the people were so poor.
> I just thought they were lazy or something and that they should have
> tried harder to get a job, or should have moved where the jobs were.
> So then we tried it out in the drama and I couldn't get a job. Then I
> got one and somebody accepted less pay, and then only meals, but
> I had a family so I couldn't do that. And I moved, but I couldn't find
> work there either and in the end I lived in a cardboard box and I was
> really frustrated and angry . . . asking myself 'what could I do?'

We are not suggesting that the students reached some final realization through the drama work. The students explored and raised questions but these questions also focused their classroom investigations.

Conclusion

This chapter is like a written-down score which tries to capture insights developed during and after hours of improvised teaching. It is not a definitive record of how to teach. The templates discussed were not discovered in books and then applied to teaching; the understandings were developed in action research and reflective drama practice.

We trust that readers will approach teaching and research in a similar spirit. We hope that you find the ideas we have outlined useful as you conduct your own action research and strive to become a more reflective practitioner. Mike's insights about the power of drama have relevance for us as action research and reflective drama practitioners: 'Drama takes facts and asks how they might have been different or how the facts might do something to you or someone else and how all that would feel. That's why I like drama.' If we pay attention to our feelings and our imaginations we will look beyond the facts of our teaching situations to ask how we and the students experience them and how they could be different. In doing so, we will become action researchers and reflective drama practitioners.

References

HAMMERSLEY, M. and ATKINSON, P. (1983) *Ethnography: Principles and Practice*, London, Tavistock.

HEATHCOTE, D. (1984) 'Drama and learning', in JOHNSON, L. and O'NEILL, C. (eds) *Dorothy Heathcote: Collected Writings on Education and Drama*, London, Hutchinson.

OBERG, A. and McCUTCHEON, G. (1987) 'Teachers experience doing action research', *Peabody Journal of Education*, **64**(2), pp. 116–27.

SCHÖN, D. (1987) *Educating the Reflective Practitioner*, San Francisco, Jossey Bass.

SHORT, K., HARSTE, J. and BURKE, C. (1996) *Creating Classrooms for Authors and Readers* (2nd edn), New Hampshire, Heinemann.

VAN MANEN, M. (1990) *Researching Lived Experience: Human Science for an Action Sensitive Pedagogy*, Albany, State University of New York Press.

5 History as Drama/Drama as History: The Case for Historical Reconstruction as a Research Paradigm

Lowell Swortzell

Each time we leave a performance, we are reminded that theatre and dance are the most evanescent of art forms, and that what we have just seen can never be beheld again in the exact same way. Even if we should return the next night to repeat the aesthetic process, a second viewing cannot reproduce the reaction of the first because we have been changed, by both the production and by everything else that has happened to us in the interim. A second or third inspection in turn will continue to alter our perceptions, each in its own way. And so, theatrical productions on the commercial stage evaporate from sight eight times a week; Act One is already part of the past even as Act Two is still being played. Theatre in effect has been vanishing ever since the first storyteller finished telling the first story, a truly chronic condition that underscores the need for historical investigators to salvage and preserve what they can of the 'now you see it; now you don't' transience of the performing arts.

The Challenge of Historical Reconstruction

The crumbling stones of ancient theatres in Greece and the recently unearthed foundations of several Elizabethan playhouses in London are artefacts that invite us to imagine how plays appeared in performance in those distant ages. But even today, most theatrical presentations rarely leave behind more than scattered ephemera such as prompt books, ticket stubs, programs, posters, a ragged piece of scenery here, a fading costume there. If lucky, the researcher may discover a descriptive comment in a letter from an audience member or a revealing reference in an actor's memoir that allows a sudden glimpse into what took place on a stage of the past. Through an examination of diaries and other personal memorabilia, we sometimes can observe the acting techniques of great stars of the past; if not of Greece and Shakespeare's colleagues, then, of such fascinating leading ladies of the nineteenth-century stage as, for instance, Laura Keene and Charlotte Cushman. We can see them posing in their

actual costumes (photographs taken in studios, not on stage) that may indicate their individual intelligence, demeanor and, in the case of these two, their
surprising lack of beauty. The texts of the plays in which they appeared, if
reliable, will suggest the basic dramatic and theatrical demands of their productions. Newspaper reviews may provide additional information although,
until this century, few were comprehensive enough to be of great help.

Records of more recent performances, of course, benefit from modern
technology that enables us to see and hear great performers at work. The
fabled Lunts, for example, are available alive and kicking in their film version
of Molnar's *The Guardsman* (1931). But, alas, their immortal shadows flickering
on the screen don't seem comfortable before the cameras and little of their
sophisticated interplay is conveyed here, as we are told it existed in abund-
ance on stage. Or we can hear John Barrymore reciting speeches from his
legendary *Hamlet* (1922) but we must remember they were recorded in the
intimacy of a sound studio and may not reflect how he actually came across
in the theatre. Even today, with close-up recordings on video and with high-
fidelity sound, a stage performance when viewed on a small screen looks
vastly different from its appearance alive on a real stage. An American commercial for camcorders likes to remind us that 'Time steals memories', and
indeed it does but technology does not necessarily give memories back with
any absolute accuracy.

So to document both past and present performances, we rely heavily on
historical scraps, the surviving bits and pieces of those who strut their hour
upon the stage and are heard no more. But even with these treasured posses-
sions before us, the picture mostly remains far from complete. The rest of the
restoration, to the degree that such is ever fully possible, becomes the responsibility of the historian who seeks to reconstruct the past.

Historical Reconstruction in Education

Historians of theatre education face similar challenges in documenting the lectures, classes and workshops of leaders whose skills deserve to be preserved
for subsequent analysis and appreciation. Through their books, some photographs, and descriptions by colleagues and students, we can learn about past
great teachers, pioneers like Caldwell Cook, Peter Slade and Winifred Ward,
as they went about defining and establishing drama in British and American
schools in the first half of this century. But unless we are old and lucky enough
to have met or worked with them, little evidence remains that allows us to hear
their voices, to come under the spell of their personalities or even to par-
tially experience their individual educational talents. Thanks to films and tapes
depicting more recent work of, say, Dorothy Heathcote and Gavin Bolton, we
are at a better advantage; even so, we still may find it difficult to demonstrate
to future students with any adequacy the techniques practiced by other recent
notable leaders such as Geraldine Brain Siks, Nellie McCaslin and Brian Way.

It is not surprising that we are without films that record key productions for children presented early in the century (if we could behold even a moment or two of Maude Adams' portrayal of Peter Pan, how richer the history of theatre for young audiences would be!), yet we have little more information that reveals the work of later, seminal directors such as Clare Tree Major, Charlotte Chorpenning, or even the more recent achievements of the Paper Bag Players in New York and the Unicorn Theatre in London. The stage history of children's theatre in America remains mostly in two reference works by Nellie McCaslin and in the scripts of the plays that survive. Unfortunately, at present there is no complete published record documenting the development of theatre for young audiences in Great Britain, Canada and Australia.

So historians of theatre and theatre education face the same challenge: they must reconstruct, as best they can, the subject of their study in order to determine its significance in the continuum of the stage and education. Frequently, of course, too little data survives to ascertain in adequate terms the look, the sound, or emotional depth of either a performance or a class. And not just figures of the distant past continue to disappear but also those performing and teaching as recently as last season, even last week.

The Vocabulary of Historical Reconstruction

As in every method of research, here, too, we must follow principles and speak a common language. In undertaking historical reconstructions, we are employing a critical form of inquiry that attempts to discover, order and utilize facts in a search for truth. Basically, we are documenting the causes and effects of human behavior at stipulated times in the distant or recent past in a study of a person, period, institution or movement. If we elect to be pursuers of pure research, we rely solely on the collection and verification of primary sources which normally exist in special collections, libraries, private hands or are obtained through interviews and personal observations. From these sources, we search for evidence to prove a truth or validate a statement. If we choose to employ secondary sources, we will learn how past researchers have used this information or speculated upon the significance of the subject under investigation. Once our findings are authenticated for their accuracy, we are ready to analyse the evidence and to determine its function and place in the study.

The Method of Historical Reconstruction

The vast subject of historical research has been defined in detail by scholars such as Jacques Barzun, Peter Gay, Oscar Handlin, Claude Levi-Strauss, Hilary Putnam and others whose works are listed at the end of this chapter. The purpose here is not to review their principles but to suggest a departure and outgrowth emerging from them.

The three essential stages of investigation — discovery, order and utilization — already have been designated above. First, comes the collection of data, which for many students is the most inviting period because it is the most physically active. We make trips to libraries, conduct interviews, and stalk the trail of information just as a detective does, until every clue reveals its location. But as many a sleuth has learned, clues also can misdirect, misinform and lead to dead ends. So, we must proceed with caution, exercising patience as we would in the pursuit of any good adventure. And while the sport of this hunt may not be on horseback or to the sound of horns, it can be equally as colorful: librarians and curators often are amusing people and the subjects we interview may even become lifelong friends. Certainly, the factual rewards, even if negligible, beat that of a dead fox!

The second stage is the synthesizing and ordering of the data to determine how it best can be used. From this point on, the researcher largely is working alone and usually sequestered, either at home or in the library with notes and sources close at hand for quick reference. The third phase, of course, is the carrying out of the form the presentation will take, as a written report, speech, scholarly article, contribution to the Internet or, in the present case, as a historical reconstruction.

Each of these stages includes a number of steps within it. Obviously, before we can begin to collect data we must determine the type of information we need, the places where it can be located, and the identity of experts or associates we need to consult. To guide our pursuit and to keep us from getting lost in the fascinating but non-essential materials that are bound to emerge in the course of our work, we should keep a research problem or hypothesis before us at all times. Synthesizing the data involves establishing its authenticity by validating the authority of each source. This is done through an examination of external factors which determine that a work is legitimate in its authorship and publication credentials. Internal evidence reveals the validity of the statements contained within the source itself and establishes their credibility. The researcher tests the competency of the observer, the meaning of the observation and questions the presence of any bias or prejudice it may contain.

To make a case for historical reconstruction as well as to demonstrate ways in which it can be done, this chapter will examine examples drawn from three different approaches, that of a practicing historian, Barbara Tuchman; of a former theatre critic, Walter Kerr; and a theatre historian, myself. Together, they illustrate the wide range of possibilities in reconstructing key moments, from general history, performance, and theatre education.

* * *

Barbara Tuchman in her valuable book, *Practicing History*, says that her personal goal as a writer is to 'enthrall' her readers by making the subject as 'captivating' and 'exciting' to them as it is to her (Tuchman, 1981, p. 17). And the worldwide bestseller statistics of her *The Guns of August* and *A Distant*

Mirror, among others, indicate she succeeds as few other historians do in encapsulating high principles of research and in entertaining her audiences at the same time. Since the words 'enthralling', 'captivating', and 'exciting' are not often bandied about by either writers or readers of histories of theatre, education and the arts, we may profit from a brief examination of how she achieves her aim to keep readers turning pages by providing them with what she calls 'a developing dramatic narrative' (Tuchman, 1981, p. 17).

The first chapter of *The Guns of August* (Tuchman, 1962) entitled 'A Funeral' quickly became a classic example of a historian's power to ensnare readers into a carefully devised trap, for once read, there is little chance they will not leap forward, eager for the rest of the story. She has crafted in these fourteen pages a spectacular drama which Aristotle himself would have to applaud for its adherence to his own classical requirements. It takes place in less than one revolution of the sun; it contains a cast of notable nobles, along with Arthur Conan Doyle looking on from the sidelines as a reporter. And its plot centers around an assemblage of representatives from seventy nations at a turning point in their collective lives. It offers memorable dialogue: 'He is Satan. You cannot imagine what a Satan he is' (Tuchman, 1962, p. 2). Its theme boasts the impending fall of the royal houses of Europe, as the evil Kaiser uses every opportunity to scrutinize his enemies. Its mood and atmosphere offer the pomp and pageantry of a funeral procession of 'splendidly mounted princes'; and its rhythms range from rolls of muffled drums and wails of bagpipes to the solemn 'Dead March' from *Saul* (Handel, written in 1739). Hovering above these ingredients is the suspenseful sense of irony the author creates, even in her first sentence, which she meticulously maintains throughout: 'So gorgeous was the spectacle on the May morning of 1910 when nine kings rode in the funeral of Edward VIII of England that the crowd, waiting in hushed and black-clad awe, could not keep back gasps of admiration' (Tuchman, 1962, p. 1). Of course, we want to know who and what they saw, and, as we keep reading, the drama unfolds in full color, complete with movement and sound, almost as if we are watching it on the stage or screen.

To enable readers to so directly experience a funeral that took place almost a century ago is no small accomplishment, to be sure, but when Ms Tuchman tells us she uses only primary sources to reconstruct such events, we must appreciate her achievements all the more. She invents nothing, not even the weather. In bringing the past to life she allows us to know it vicariously and to extract from that re-enactment its meaning and the purpose it serves in developing her 'dramatic narrative'.

* * *

One of the best American theatre critics of this century, Walter Kerr, writing first for the *New York Herald Tribune* and later for *The New York Times*, possessed the ability to capture a moment in the play or performance that epitomized the quality of the entire production. After just several sentences, or a few paragraphs at most, the reader knew whether or not to order tickets. Kerr, of course, having been a professor of theatre, a playwright and director himself, understood the necessity for a production to make the most of its key moments. He also knew that by bringing them to life in his reviews, he would make his columns eminently readable. Notice how the original Broadway production of *Cabaret* remains alive in this account from *The New York Times* (21 November 1966, p. 492):

> The first thing you see as you enter the Broadhurst is yourself. Designer Boris Aronson, whose scenery is so imaginative that even a gray green fruit store comes up like a warm summer dawn, has sent converging strings of frosted lamps swinging toward a vanishing point at upstage center. Occupying the vanishing point is a great geometric mirror, and in the mirror the gathering audience is reflected. We have come for the floor show, we are all at tables tonight and anything we learn of life during the evening is going to be learned through the tipsy, tinkling, angular vision of sleek rouged-up clowns, who inhabit a world that rains silver.

Into this vividly captured atmosphere bursts Joel Grey as the Master of Ceremonies who sings a song of welcome 'that has something of the old *Blue Angel* in it, something of Kurt Weill, and something of all the patent-leather night club tunes that ever seduced us into feeling friendly toward sleek entertainers who twirled canes as they worked.' According to Kerr, Grey, standing before us with 'sunburst eyes gleaming out of a cold-cream face', and sporting a pink vest, is at once 'charming, soulless, and conspiratorially wicked . . . the gleeful puppet of pretended joy, sin on a string.' Kerr lets us see him performing here even if we never saw him do so in a theatre: 'Mr Grey comes bouncing from the portals to grab a gorilla in rose tulle. The two spin into a hesitation waltz with the prim and stately delicacy of partners well-met. Let the world lose its mind, let the waltz go on' (1973, pp. 490–2). In these words, Joel Grey, the gorilla and *Cabaret* still dance, which is the goal most writers seek for their subjects, to instill life that lives long years later.

As historians, we may profit from the examples of Tuchman and Kerr by looking in our research for those reflective episodes that serve as crossroads and indices to past, present and future events. Once we determine a defining moment, one which can be documented second by second, we are ready to transform history into drama, as the following example illustrates.

* * *

In editing *Six Plays for Young People from the Federal Theatre Project (1936–1939)*, I sought such a 'defining moment' to launch my introduction which needed first to arrest readers' attention and then to lead them through the background information required before discussing the specific plays selected for the collection. Looking at a number of possible moments, ranging from the first gathering of leaders summoned to create this project to the last night of its existence, I decided that the most graphic incident I could reconstruct was to start at the end. The other choices offered little to match the high tension of the project's demise:

> When the Federal Theatre Project (FTP) came to an end on the night of June 30, 1939, the Children's Theatre unit revised the final curtain of its production of *Pinocchio*, a Broadway hit which had been play-ing to capacity houses since the preceding December. Instead of ending with the customary scene of a birthday party celebrating Pinocchio's transformation from a marionette into a human boy, the new conclu-sion, hurriedly arranged by director/author Yasha Frank, contained a surprise calculated to stun the audience. In the midst of the happy anticipation of Pinocchio's last heroic entrance there suddenly came the sound of an offstage gun explosion, followed by a booming voice solemnly announcing, 'Pinocchio is dead!' 'Shivers just went up and down everybody's spine,' an actress onstage at that moment later remembered. 'You could hear the silence, it was so dramatic.' Then voices cried out from associates Frank had planted in the audience: 'Who killed Pinocchio? Who killed Pinocchio?' The mysterious off-stage voice spoke again, 'I will tell you who killed Pinocchio,' and began to list by name each Congressman who had voted against the appropriation to continue the FTP.
>
> Summoned to record these last moments, *Life* photographed the cast assembled in mourning, with old Gepetto and his cat kneeling in prayer in front of Pinocchio's bier, all weeping over the dead figure who only minutes before had been cheered by children and adults alike. Lifting the coffin, the cast and audience together marched out of the theatre and proceeded to Times Square chanting, 'Save the Federal Theatre!' The next day, newspaper headlines repeated: 'PINOCCHIO IS DEAD. WHO KILLED PINOCCHIO?' *Life* printed a second photo-graph showing the abandoned puppet stretched out lifeless on the floor of the empty stage, accompanied by the caption: 'Left behind was the image of Pinocchio, limp and alone beside the stagehand's working light.' So a dead Pinocchio became the public symbol for the demise of the FTP and its nearly 8,000 actors and employees across the country who that same night lost their jobs. The next day they found themselves locked out of offices and barred from playhouses in cities that for the last three and a half years had been part of a national theatre movement never before experienced by American audiences. (Swortzell, 1986, pp. 2–3)

If the reconstruction of this defining moment has made us want to know the rest of the story, we are ready to receive the background information regard-ing the creation, function and cancellation of a theatre killed by Congress nearly sixty years earlier.

Conclusion

Gripping as they may be, reconstructions alone cannot tell the entire story, of course. Historians also must provide the facts and figures that fully document the person or event under consideration, presented in traditional narrative forms, as well as in diagrams, charts and graphs. Such descriptive accounts can be both illuminating and entertaining in their own way, to be certain. But, as I trust Tuchman, Kerr and I have demonstrated, history can gain the added pulse, the intimacy and immediacy of another time if the investigator also employs the tools of the dramatist. Then the meaning of those defining moments will be preserved because they have been recreated, experienced and understood anew. The voices of artists and teachers, past and present, instead of being lost to silence, will be heard once more. And those historians who resurrect their subjects will come to know, however fleetingly, powers once thought to be possessed only by a divinity.

Can a researcher ask for anything more?

References

BARZUN, J. (1974) *Clio and the Doctors: Psycho-History, Quanto-History and History*, Chicago and London, University of Chicago Press.

GAY, P. (1974) *Style in History*, New York, Basic Books.

HANDLIN, O. (1979) *Truth in History*, Cambridge, Mass., Belknap Press.

KERR, W. (1973) 'Cabaret' review *New York Times* 21 November 1966, reprinted in BECKERMAN, B. and SIEGMAN, H. (eds) *On Stage: Selected Theater Reviews from the New York Times 1920–1970*, New York, Arno Press.

LEVI-STRAUSS, C. (1966) *The Savage Mind*, London, George Weidenfeld and Nicholson Ltd.

POSTLEWAIT, T. and McCONACHIE, B. (eds) (1989) *Interpreting the Theatrical Past: Essays in the Historiography of Performance*, Iowa City, University of Iowa Press.

PUTMAN, H. (1981) *Reason, Truth and History*, Cambridge, Cambridge University Press.

SWORTZELL, L. (ed.) (1986) *Six Plays for Young People from the Federal Theatre Project (1936–1939): An Introductory Analysis and Six Representative Plays*, New York, Greenwood Press.

TUCHMAN, B. (1962) *The Guns of August*, New York, Macmillan.

TUCHMAN, B. (1981) *Practicing History: Selected Essays*, New York, Alfred A. Knopf.

6   Restoring our Dramatic Past

Angela O'Brien

For many younger scholars and practitioners, historical research may seem dull and outmoded. Apart from changes of fashion in research and criticism, there are two reasons for this. First, students who have undertaken traditional history of theatre subjects at universities in the western world will have been subjected to lectures which rely on secondary source materials that suggest there is a body of factual information which can be learnt. These historical texts tend to be received by students as a kind of scripture and verse of theatre history, without question, and often without reference to their political and social context.

Secondly, for generations of students, a study of theatre history was based on a detailed study of text, often elaborated by the scant factual approach to performance history. While this method of critical appreciation might be appropriate for plays that were intended to be viewed primarily as literary texts, such as Shelley's *Prometheus Unbound*, it provides minimal insight into texts written either for theatrical performance, or developed and modified during the process of performance.

Theatre is a collaborative and a community art form. It draws on all the senses, and appeals to intellect as well as emotion. When it comes to history, the task of talking about something that is best enacted seems peripheral to the seductive and engaging process of making theatre. Even reflective processes, so often used in contemporary theatre research, place the emphasis on analysis of experience rather than the recording of experience.

It is worth recalling the aphorism that those who ignore the lessons of history do so at the risk of repeating its mistakes. Histories are stories about the past, and reconstructing that past will involve elements of mythologizing, from the political and theoretical stance of the historian. Reconstructions of any historical event become more complex when we import our own contemporary geographical, national or ethnic views of things into our interpretations of the past. In late twentieth-century literature, there is a recognized blurring of the boundaries between fact and fiction, and an increasingly common 'new' journalistic stance that even the news of today is subject to interpretation. This approach to recording is ideal for the theatre historian, who must find a way to offer a single interpretation of the theatrical experience constructed from multiple sources.

How Do We Deal with Theatre History?

A useful approach to the recording of theatre history is to see it as a jigsaw puzzle, where each piece must be fitted in place when building up the whole picture. The script alone tells us very little about the setting, the performance style, the directorial intention, the visual effects, the interpretation of characters by the performers, and the response of the audience. Critical commentary provides only scraps of information. But if we have not seen a particular performance, then a combination of script and critical commentary will provide us with more understanding of the experience, as will photographs, pictures of stage settings, recordings, the memories of audience members, and the many other pieces of evidence available to the historian. This time-consuming process of verification is crucial for the theatre historian.

Sometimes, of course, the jigsaw pieces may not be readily available. The historian must become a detective, hunting out bits and pieces of information, recognizing those which are real treasures, and discarding others that may not fit the particular style of history being compiled. Historical research in drama is as wide as the imagination. Research topics, particularly those in the theatre, grow like topsy. Because little work has been done on recording theatre history, what we imagine to be a relatively confined exercise may turn out to be an extensive one. Many years ago I engaged on a project to consider the development of a left-wing movement in Australia. My starting point was little more than a few short journal articles, and a box of old programs and photos. As I extended the research and began to uncover scripts, programs, and newspaper reviews, the project grew beyond my control. When I discovered that there were over 1,000 productions of left-wing theatre throughout Australia I knew that herein lay a lifetime's research!

Research Resources

There are two kinds of information available to the historical researcher: secondary source material and primary source material. Secondary source material includes books written about the event, including critical commentaries, biographies, histories, literary analyses of texts, stories about performances told by those who were or weren't there. There is also a body of evidence we might describe as primary. Primary sources are archival evidence which provide firsthand insight into the event or period we are researching. It is important for the historian to explore both secondary and primary sources. Sometimes it can be difficult to differentiate between them. A good deal of secondary source material becomes primary source material in another context. Robert Lewis's (1960) text, *Method or Madness?*, is both an interpretation of the writing and teaching of Stanislavski, as well as a firsthand account of method acting as developed by Lee Strasburg in the Group Theatre.

Secondary Source Material

Researchers have a responsibility to undertake a survey of the studies that have been done in a specific field. There is not much point in starting from the beginning when another researcher has already done considerable work in the area. As relatively little investigative work is being done in theatre, researchers cannot afford to duplicate efforts. Bibliographic research can help us survey the field. Such searches are best undertaken using the latest electronic search methods, and by employing the many data bases now available on CD-ROM. Also, there is still value in undertaking a manual search in the library as electronic searches will only yield selective information based on how they have been programmed.

Sometimes, it is not the obvious secondary sources which are the most useful. For example, when researching the history of a theatre in education project or youth theatre, information about educational practice will be just as illuminating as information about contemporary theatre theory. Similarly, when researching political theatre, investigators might need to move into a study of conventional political history. Professional and educational drama is volatile in its response to general social and political issues. The plays of Aristophanes, which include so many specific local and historical references, provide a useful illustration. These comedies have become quite difficult to appreciate, without translation into contemporary form, and this is despite the fact that late twentieth-century theatre shares an interest in political and social satire. How might contemporary topical self-referencing in Berkoff's *Sink the Belgrano*, Sondheim's *Assassins*, Williamson's *Dead White Males*, or the popular culture exemplified by *The Simpsons*, survive sensible interpretation in the twenty-fifth century?

Another challenge with selecting secondary source material is the question, How much should be read? Areas where there have been considerable commentary, for example, the plays of William Shakespeare or Samuel Beckett, require that researchers define their questions, and limit their studies to those secondary texts which are clearly apposite. If a topic is chronologically recent, or has received little attention, then investigators may need to read widely before they have enough material to define their topic's parameters. As work on the left-wing theatre of the thirties in America, Australia and Britain received scant attention until recently, it is still manageable to compile a short bibliography of definitive texts.

Primary Source Material

Primary resource material may be readily available in collected archives. However, there may be no central location for the body of primary archival material sought. In Australia, there has been minimal systematic collection of theatre material up until the last decade. Very often collections will be split up all over the country, or held by hundreds of individuals in their personal papers.

The following kinds of archival material will be useful but the list should not be seen as exhaustive.

The script

There is a tendency to take the script for granted as 'fact', perhaps because scripts have been the only surviving documents readily available to researchers in the theatre. We have begun recently to differentiate between the literary text which provides the source material, and performance text which translates that source material into living performance.

The script is not always reliable evidence. The controversy over whether or not Shakespeare wrote a number of his plays gives some indication as to the difficulties faced because records have either been destroyed or lost. Today, with so many companies and educational institutions engaged in group devised shows, or performances where writers work with actors to develop performance text, the published text is not necessarily a literary record of the performance text. Furthermore, if a text becomes internationally known, it may go through many incarnations before being published, or the published literary text used in the first production may not necessarily be a record of subsequent performance texts.

In recent years, many theatre arts publishers have begun systematic publication of play texts, with program notes available for premier productions of new plays. These can include cast lists, and sometimes still photographs of the performance. Published texts should be seen as blueprints for theatrical production, or texts for literary analysis, rather than records. The issue of translated scripts poses further problems with relation to the translation used, and contribution of the translator to the work. In some instances, translation goes well beyond moving a script from page to stage. Tadashi Suzuki's 'translation' of *Macbeth* sees a script so modified to accommodate Japanese performance styles, that it would be misleading for researchers to assume that much could be discovered from reading only the Shakespeare text.

Also, plays in manuscript form can be misleading. In the left-wing theatre movement of the 1930s, plays were syndicated between New Theatres in America and Australia, and Unity Theatres in Britain and Australia, as well as between the various New Theatres or Unity Theatres within each country. Because these plays were performed in the context of art as a political weapon, they were often manipulated to suit the local situation.

Programs and critics

As I write this chapter, theatre programs are laid out in front of me. First, there is the program from the Old Vic tour of Australia in 1948 which starred Laurence Olivier and Vivien Leigh. This program is an expensive publication, and was produced with other material of archival interest, including a pamphlet entitled

The Oliviers: A Brief Chronicle, which gives biographical information, photos and cast lists, a brief history of the Australian and New Zealand tour, designs for program covers, as well as contemporary critical commentaries on the plays. There is also information about the theatres in Australia where the company played, and photographs and biographies of other performing and technical staff of the period.

The second program is the Australian production of *Hair, the Rock Musical*, which toured in 1970. This program is a glossy journal, and includes a wealth of information about the director and cast, and background material. It also includes photographs of the production. But perhaps most useful to the historian are the many advertisements which give real insight into the clothing, the hairstyles and the spirit of the Age of Aquarius.

The third program is more modest as a publication, and records the Royal Court production of an Australian play, *Don's Party* by David Williamson. There are no photographs of the play, brief biographies of the performers, most of whom are Australian. A most interesting aspect of this program are the political notes and glossary of Australian terms. One might interpret this program as exemplifying the curiosity value of a 'down-under' show playing in a West End Theatre.

As well as programs, critical response can have an enormous impact on the way in which a play is received, and whether or not it has a successful run. The Australian play *Summer of the Seventeenth Doll* was well served by excellent critical acclaim which meant it was successfully exported to England, and became the basis for an American feature film. Critical response is seldom reliable in its own right, but it can assist with a narrative of the story of the play and provide a description of the visual effects, or a comment about performance style and quality.

Criticism provides a firsthand account of a performance, presumably written while the performance is still fresh in the writer's mind. Not all useful 'criticism' flows from the pen of professional critics. Useful criticism can be found in autobiographies, letters and journals. This record of the first production of Clifford Odet's *Waiting for Lefty* on 5 January 1935, brings the performance to light with a real immediacy:

> The first scene of Lefty had not played two minutes when a shock of delighted recognition struck the audience like a tidal wave. Deep laughter, hot assent, a kind of joyous fervour seemed to sweep the audience towards the stage. The actors no longer performed; they were being carried along as if by an exultancy of communication such as I have never witnessed in the theatre before. Audience and actors had become one. Line after line brought applause, whistles, bravos and heartfelt shouts of kinship. The taxi strike of 1934 had been a minor incident in the labour crisis of the period. There were very few taxi-drivers in that first audience I am sure; very few indeed who had ever been directly connected with such an event as the union meeting that

provides the play with its pivotal meeting. When the audiences at the end of the play responded to the militant question from the stage: 'Well, what's the answer?' with a spontaneous roar of 'Strike! Strike!' it was something more than a tribute to the play's effectiveness, more even than a testimony of the audience's hunger for constructive social action. It was the birth cry of the thirties. Our youth had found its voice. (Clurman, 1946/1960, p. 148)

If possible it is useful to have some understanding of the role of the critic within the drama community under consideration, and the critic's relationship with the company, and to recognize the power of the critic, particularly within the commercial theatre.

Newspapers and journals

Newspapers and local magazines are useful sources of archival material. In research on left-wing theatre or off-off-Broadway, where virtually no documentation exists, newspapers are a vital source in allowing the researcher to piece together a chronological skeleton which can then be fleshed out. When little information exists about a play or company or performance event, the newspapers can offer the following: advertisements which date the first performance; pre-publicity 'puff' which may give information about the company, the writer, the narrative or the performers; a critical review, which will provide additional information about the performers and details about the play's content.

Newspapers can also provide a social and political context for performances. Just as the *Hair* program gives the researcher some indication of the commercial impact of the play, which spoke for the 1970s in much the same way as *Lefty* had spoken for the 1930s, the news items, articles, and advertisements provide insight into the event's milieu. Luck can come into play here as was the case with a recent project involving the reconstruction of a play, *Thirteen Dead*, initially performed in Melbourne, Australia in 1936. After I located the script and one or two limited reviews, a newspaper article came to light in which the director of the play discussed both the group writing of the play, and the way in which the company intended to stage the piece.[1]

Newspapers, however, like critics, must be considered in relation to editorial policy. Writing on left-wing theatre in Australia was found in the Communist Party weeklies, *The Guardian* and *The Workers' Voice*, or, in syndicated articles coming out of American journals such as *New Masses*. Reviews in these papers and magazines can be deceptively celebratory, and can be at odds with the mainstream papers of the day. Remember that just as left-wing papers tended to be uncritical, right-wing papers, if they reviewed at all, were often loathe to praise works which were considered subversive.

The artistic, cultural and commercial milieu

Theatrical companies, academic institutions, schools, community groups and other production organizations are seldom apolitical. Similarly, writers, directors, designers and actors are influenced by the milieu in which they operate. Writers, directors and actors may find their artistic activity directed by company policy or even political policy. In the Soviet Union in the mid-1930s, a change in cultural policy saw a major shift from the agitprop style to socialist realism, styles which are diametrically opposed. The Chinese cultural revolution saw a similar about-face. Shifts in company policy in America, Europe and Australia, whether pressured by box office, funding policy or politics, can be as significant to the historian, if sometimes more difficult to pinpoint.

Theatre company records, including statements of policy, board meetings and publications are all useful evidence. Government policy and funding records are invaluable for some periods in countries with developed theatre subsidy.

Visual and aural representations

An excessive emphasis on verbal text has overshadowed the visual impact of the theatre. In recent years, the development of physical or kinaesthetic theatre, and the interrelationship of dance and music diminishes the value of script as primary document. The availability of set designs, costume designs, sketches of settings and photographs of productions provides valuable evidence in reconstructing the theatrical past.

Much of what we know about Greek theatre forms and costumes have been gleaned from frieze or other decorative art featuring representations of performance work. The famous de Witt drawing continues to be influential as a depiction of what an Elizabethan theatre looked like, just as paintings of eighteenth-century plays throughout Europe provide a sense of the actor within the setting. The still painting or the photograph provides us with no more than a static representation of any one moment in a performance. On the other hand, recording of contemporary theatre performance has moved to multi-directional video-taping and serial photography, in an effort to capture its kinaesthetic effect.

Sound can be just as elusive as the visual effect. Prior to the development of electronic recording devices, it has been difficult to reconstruct the way in which a performance was heard. Where theatre records are available — for example, records of lighting or sound designs — there will be an indication of what kinds of incidental music were used, but no indication of how. In the case of *Hair*, a combination of the recording of the musical, the program, and newspaper reviews can provide the basis for a short, interesting piece of research, particularly when considered in the context of the social upheavals of the late 1960s.

Memories and oral history

The theoretical and autobiographical writings of performers, directors, and theatre managers are useful evidentiary material. These can form the basis for later detailed study of companies, genre and the development of directorial or acting styles. It is through this kind of writing that we are able to reconstruct some of the more difficult aspects of theatrical history, including, for example, acting styles or vocal use. Anthony Sher's (1985) *Year of the King* is a useful text for those interested in researching acting styles. Sher's diary is full of sketches which illustrate the process by which he developed his characterization. He records his observations of source material:

> Driving . . . in Chiswick, a strange coincidence: I round the corner to see a badly disabled man struggling along the pavement, his walk a weaving dance. I screech to a halt, whip out my sketch pad and, from my rear view mirror, began drawing furiously . . . I sketch him from behind as he struggles on. Looks rather like the crippled man in Satyricon. The effort of walking is so extreme it's as if the body is all disconnected. He has to sit on a low wall to rest. An attractive blonde woman passes him. He says something and reaches for her. She breaks into a little run. Lady Anne? (Sher, 1985, pp. 108–9)

Such descriptions provide useful source material for a variety of research questions relating to acting styles, interpretations of Shakespeare, or the theatre at work in Britain during the 1980s.

When researching a specific local company, in-house publications can be valuable. Herbert Kline's brief comments in *New Theatre and Film*, a left-wing magazine published out of the New Theatre Movement, are particularly inspiring:

> From now, 1984, try to imagine that you were like us then, impassioned participants in the theatre arts renaissance that New Theatre helped generate from 1934 through 1936. Three rebellious, creative, challenging years of dramatising the harsh realities of American life and the imminent dangers of fascist triggered wars. Also three years of growing faith in America's future, in Franklin Delano Roosevelt's 'New Deal' presidency after suffering deprivations in the most terrible depression in our country's history . . . Our beliefs were a kind of all embracing humanism stemming from America Revolutionary ideas of Democracy, but strongly and openly leftist. (Kline, 1985, p. 7)

Because of the nature of theatre, so little has been written down. Memories of theatre workers and audience members have become increasingly important in the past few decades. The transcribed interview has become a staple in academic texts. The spoken memory can often be more immediate and powerful as a way of capturing the spirit of the past, as is the following memory of Australian playwright, Jim Crawford, about the *Roving Red Revue*, a robust proletarian company which developed out of the unemployed workers' movement in the early days of the depression:

> ... it operated on what could be called an arbitrary basis without any refinements whatsoever in such things as play writing, casting, production and so on. It worked on a strictly utilitarian basis ... it was organised to raise funds for the Unemployed Workers' Movement and other militant bodies. When some sort of program had been decided on the committee cast the sketches by the simple expedient of going along to the bagman's tent, humpy, semi-cave or sleeper shelter and telling the particular inmate, 'Hey Boofhead, you're playing this' ... They turned out purely and simply in the interests of solidarity. There evolved a technique of assessing their parts in terms of rum, to give both verve and nerve ... A walk-on was rated as a two-rummer, while a lead part rated anything up to eight or ten rums, according to a player's purse. (O'Brien, 1989, p. 46)

There are pitfalls in the process of taping oral history. Ensure the recorder is working; innumerable researchers have left an interview excited by a fruitful interview only to find that they do not have a recording. Notes should also be taken as well as consideration of the questions to be asked. Researchers should transcribe tapes immediately as it can be disconcerting to be surrounded months later by a box of tapes and no transcriptions.

The Researcher's Responsibility

The telling of others' stories imposes a responsibility on the researcher to deal sensitively and ethically with the material. Many universities now have a Research Ethics Policy which establish a study's parameters. While celebratory tones might motivate a researcher's written report, such accolades should be balanced against a public responsibility to give a fair and honest account. Sometimes it is more appropriate to allow the material to speak for itself, with minimal authorial commentary.

The qualifications for researchers using this paradigm are not only a love of theatre; as well, they need the curiosity of a cat, the determination and skill of a detective, and an open-minded fascination with the complexity of human creative behaviour.

Note

1   Catherine Duncan, 'Building a play on the Wonthaggi disaster', *The Herald*, 1 July 1937. The text of 'Thirteen Dead', and a discussion about the play is published in O'Brien, A. (ed.) (1993) *Thirteen Dead*, Melbourne, New Theatre Publications.

Angela O'Brien

References

CLURMAN, H. (1946/1960) *The Fervent Years*, London, Dennis Dobson.

KLINE, H. (1985) *New Theatre and Film 1934 to 1937*, Florida, Harcourt Brace Jovanovich.

LEWIS, R. (1960) *Method or Madness?* London, Heinemann.

O'BRIEN, A. (1989) 'The road not taken: Political and performance ideologies at Melbourne New Theatre 1935–1960.' Unpublished PhD thesis, Monash University.

SHER, A. (1985) *Year of the King*, London, Methuen.

7 An Overview of Experimental Research Principles for Studies in Drama and Theatre for Youth

Johnny Saldaña with Lin Wright

We are neither statisticians nor experts in experimental research design. We are artist-educators with an interest in research who conduct it to the best of our abilities while acknowledging the limitations of our training and experiences. Discussed below is a very general outline of experimental design principles, given the restrictions of chapter length. Readers are encouraged to refer to more comprehensive works on the topic (e.g., Babbie, 1995; Creswell, 1994; Fraenkel and Wallen, 1993; Isaac and Michael, 1981; Menard, 1991; Miller, 1991; Smith and Glass, 1987), and to conduct their studies under the supervision of knowledgeable mentors in their fields.

When is Experimental Research Appropriate?

Theatre critic Sylvia Drake once proposed that the true test of a play script's suitability for presentation through live theatre is when the material loses its impact if it is adapted for electronic media. Hence, she encouraged playwrights to ask themselves, Will my story be best told through television, film, or live theatre? The impact of a research effort can be assessed similarly if you ask yourself: Will the answers to my particular research questions be best revealed through quantitative methods, qualitative methods, or a particular combination of both? This chapter focuses primarily on the former.

The *purpose* of your research effort and the most suitable form of *answers for your central research questions* guide your decisions for selecting the most appropriate methodology and methods. It is unwise to assume automatically that some form of experimentation should be conducted as part of your study. Neither should a fascination for naturalistic inquiry dictate that particular approach to your work. An empirical researcher should have a working knowledge of both quantitative *and* qualitative methods to enable him or her to make the most appropriate choice(s) for a study.

Experimental research may be an appropriate choice when there is a need to assess the *effects* or *outcomes* of a particular *treatment* or process on a group of young people. For example, will a playwriting unit with a randomly selected group of junior high school students improve their grades in English composition assignments? Experimental research may also be an appropriate choice when the research question is tightly focused and measurable variables of interest are stated: Does a series of ten, half-hour improvisational drama sessions conducted in Spanish assist with retention of Spanish-language vocabulary with fifth grade English speaking students? Experimental research is also appropriate when you explore pre-existing instrumentation not yet applied to theatre for youth research. For example, the semantic differential study (Saldaña and Otero, 1990) experimented with the instrument's use as *one* possible measure of theatre response from young people.

Experimental research may also be appropriate when the audience is composed of policy-makers. Saldaña receives phone calls from various theatre companies and programs, desperately in need of research studies that 'prove theatre for youth "works"'. Time is taken to explain that research does not 'prove' anything — it merely suggests and presents the interpretations of a researcher's observations. But studies that illustrate and suggest a program's merit or 'payoff' for children may be a convincing political tool for retaining or supporting a particular program. Depending on the research orientation of decision-makers, there may be a preference for quantitative rather than qualitative studies. Hence, research will have to be designed that defers to their needs. In a related vein, experimental research can be used to illustrate not only the effects of a treatment on a particular group, but also the consequences for another group when the treatment has been withheld from them. This comparison may build a stronger argument (if results are significant) for the inclusion or revision of particular programs.

Qualitative studies most often explore social action in naturalistic environments where a 'treatment' is not purposely administered. If the research purpose does not lend itself to naturalistic inquiry, an experimental design may be appropriate. But statistical data still can be used as an additional data record for selected qualitative studies (Erickson, 1986; Glesne and Peshkin, 1992; Marín and Marín, 1991; Miles and Huberman, 1994). Demographic data, such as the percentages of different ethnic groups represented at a school; the mean (average) standardized test score of a particular classroom; or category percentages of a phenomenon (e.g., teacher talk during a drama session: 55 per cent classroom management; 20 per cent teacher-in-role; 5 per cent directions; 15 per cent reflection; 5 per cent other), can inform and enhance the analysis.

Strengths and Weaknesses

There are several strengths to experimental designs. First, experimental studies are tightly focused on specific variables of interest. The parameters of the study will be well defined from the beginning when a precisely written research question is developed. Second, a researcher in need of structure and organized frameworks can rely on the standardized procedures established for experimental research. There are a number of 'how to' texts that describe the procedures to follow. Creswell (1994) and Fraenkel and Wallen (1993) are highly recommended for initial guidance. Finally, the availability of computer software programs for statistical analysis, such as SPSS (Statistical Package for the Social Sciences), make storing and analysing quantitative data remarkably easy for the researcher. However, a working knowledge of statistical reasoning is essential before using any computer program designed to 'number crunch'. The user must still make decisions about the most appropriate statistical tests to employ, and then interpret the statistical results.

There are also weaknesses and limitations to experimental research. First, since an experimental study is strongly focused, results and thus knowledge gained tend to be narrow. Depending on the scope of the project, a tremendous amount of time and energy may be expended for a small piece of generalizable information. Second, experimental research is subject to more rigorous review and critique by supervisors and peers. Strict adherence to the 'rules' of the paradigm may be demanded, and the *validity* and *reliability* of your work (discussed below) may be in jeopardy if the research is not carefully designed and conducted. Finally, for some, the quantitative orientation of experimental research negates the 'heart and soul' of the aesthetic experience in theatre. Supplementing your statistical data with respondent quotes or other descriptive examples may provide more meaning to the numbers generated from quantitative analysis (see Klein, 1995).

The 'Politics' of the Paradigm

If you agree to play a particular game, it is expected that you adhere to its particular rules. Classic experimental research designs embody a set of prescribed, standardized procedures and rules to follow from the study's preparation to the reporting of results. The methodology is *positivist*, a paradigm rooted in natural science research and later adopted by the social sciences (e.g., psychology, sociology, and education). Although qualitative or naturalistic inquiry is another method of research in current use, the traditional quantitative paradigm still maintains a strong presence in selected fields, including education.

Yet, despite its efforts to be 'objective' and 'rigorous' in its search for 'truth', quantitative research is actually a value-laden enterprise. Smith (1995) promotes that *any* study and its consequent analysis are 'constructions of the researcher'. Statistics are not neutral; there are assumptions behind every number. Researcher decisions on what constitutes the phenomenon of interest and its measurement are choices based on what he or she may interpret as important or more salient than the alternatives.

Within the academic community there are some who question the utility of quantitative research in theatre (Grady, 1995), those who question the validity of qualitative approaches altogether (Cizek, 1995), and those who strive to reconcile and combine the two methodologies (Creswell, 1994; Howe, 1992). Mary Lee Smith, an educational researcher experienced in both approaches, advocates that the research question leads to the methodology, and the ultimate choice and appropriateness of a paradigm is subject to 'political negotiation' between the researcher and reader. Thomas Barone (1995), an eminent qualitative researcher in the US, promotes the need for a spectrum of research 'genres' and acknowledges that there is still a place today for good quantitative research in education.

What is Experimental Research?

In this chapter, the term *experimental research* is used quite broadly, and the discussion will be limited to a selected number of study designs.

True and Quasi-experimental Research

True experimental research investigates whether a cause-and-effect relationship may exist between a treatment condition (i.e., *independent variable*) conducted with a *randomly* selected group of participants, and the outcome or consequences (i.e., *dependent variable*) of that treatment on the participants. The possible relationship between the independent and dependent variables is determined through quantitative measurement of the treatment outcomes and statistical testing of the data. To use an example from above: Will a playwriting unit (the treatment condition or independent variable) with a randomly selected group of junior high school students (the participants) improve their grades in English composition assignments (the outcome or dependent variable)?

Most researchers, particularly those working at one school site, are not always able to secure a truly random group of participants. True experimental research becomes *quasi-experimental* when the random assignment of participants to the treatment or control conditions is not possible, or when the researcher has only partial control over the treatment condition (the independent variable). For example, one particular school classroom of thirty children is not necessarily composed of a sample of young people that can adequately represent the population characteristics of *all* classrooms of a similar grade level. Concessions are made for the sake of convenience and management of the research effort when we elect to work with one particular classroom at one particular school site with particular demographics, socio-economics and curriculum.

One experimental research approach is a *pre-test/post-test design*. Suppose a researcher would like to explore if a series of ten drama sessions focusing on multi-ethnic themes conducted with an ethnically diverse class of eighth-grade students contributes to prejudice reduction among the group. A written survey that assesses their beliefs and attitudes toward various ethnic groups is administered to the group before the drama series (this is the pre-test before the treatment). The ten sessions are conducted, and the post-test surveying their beliefs and attitudes is then administered. Statistical results from the pre-test and post-test are compared to assess any change in the group which might have occurred as a consequence of the drama treatment. Keep in mind that this is a very simple example. A host of complexities and validity problems are involved with the design and execution of this type of study.

Another approach is a *control group design*. To enhance the *internal validity* of a study (discussed below) the outcome, or dependent variable, of the *treatment group* is compared to a second group that does *not* receive the treatment. This group is called the *control group* because the researcher is trying to control possible error effects or other possible influences on the outcome of the study. Suppose that a researcher is bringing two groups of high schoolers to see a production of an absurdist play. The first group receives a pre-performance workshop by one of the actors in the production who discusses the absurdist genre and the background of the specific play they will attend, and then conducts a drama session with the students that explores the challenges facing the actors and audience members in the production. They might also become acquainted with the scenography created for the production through renderings and discuss their symbolic meaning. The second high school group (the control group) attending the absurdist production receives no pre-performance workshop. Both groups attend the production; immediately afterwards, a questionnaire is administered to both groups of teenagers. This data gathering *instrument* (the questionnaire) might ask them such short-answer questions as recall of the character's names or specific moments of action, interpretations of non-realistic dialogue, acting challenges faced by the performers, and the relationship between scenic elements and the meaning of the play. Questionnaire results from both groups are then coded or rated by a panel of adults trained by the researcher. Then the results are compared to assess the effects of the pre-performance workshop on the treatment group's interpretations of the production and the consequences of no pre-performance workshop on the control group's interpretations. Again, this is a very simple example and does not illustrate the problematic interplay between the treatment, the students, the production, and the instrumentation.

Causal-comparative Research

Cause-and-effect studies become *causal-comparative* when the researcher has no control over the independent variable. In other words, the investigator is looking at differences that already exist between or among groups, and explores possible effects, causes, or consequences of an intervention. For example, which kind of drama teacher exhibits better classroom management skills — those trained in linear or holistic approaches? The independent variable, the drama teacher's training, is something the researcher cannot manipulate or control; the teacher's training has already occurred. But investigating the dependent variable, their classroom management skills, is still possible and observable (and theoretically measurable).

Some research methdologists may call this type of study a *between-groups design*, which classifies participants into subgroups according to some shared characteristic such as gender, ethnicity and grade level. Statistical comparison is made between two or more subgroups to determine if there is a relationship between the outcome (dependent variable) and the subgroup characteristic (independent variable). For example, is there a relationship between an adolescent's gender and his or her capacity for empathizing with a male character's actions in a play? Is there a relationship between a child's ethnicity and the attentiveness she or he sustains while watching a Spanish-English bilingual play production with an all-Hispanic cast?

Limitations of space do not permit us to explain fully the particular components or subtleties of each methodology outlined above. In fact, there are many other research designs which have not been discussed in this section. Refer to other sources in research design for more detail.

What is a Statistic?

Experimental studies gather data in various forms (e.g., words, scales, actions) that are generally transformed into meaningful numbers — statistics — for analysis. Permit us to define *statistic* in an inescapably dense manner; an example will follow: A statistic is an approximate, numeric symbol for a socially constructed measurement of a phenomenon or action (i.e., a variable), or a group of data.

Imagine that we have designed a written survey to be administered to a group of fourth-grade children after they have seen a theatre for youth production. One of the statements on this survey is: 'The acting was good in the play.' The child has been instructed to select and circle one of four possible agreement ratings:

4 = 'I agree a lot'
3 = 'I agree a little'
2 = 'I don't agree a little'
1 = 'I don't agree at all'

When Luis reads the survey statement, 'The acting was good in the play,' and circles the number '3' (which equates to 'I agree a little' on this particular survey), what is happening? Luis is examining the finite number of possible responses we as the researchers have chosen to include on this survey. He reviews the numbers and their accompanying descriptors (the numbers' symbolic associations) and negotiates within himself which number most accurately

reflects his own point of view. He has transposed his experiences and interpretation of the acting effectiveness into a number we have negotiated (or
socially constructed) to represent and approximate his response. Luis is also
interpreting the acting quality not according to our criteria of what constitutes
good acting, but according to his own meaning perspective (Erickson, 1986)
of what he experienced. He is representing, through his particular rating choice,
his *personal* interpretation of the acting, not the acting as perceived by others.
In this example, '3' is the numeric symbol — a descriptive statistic — that
approximates Luis' personal opinion about the acting through his interpretation of our scale. If we survey twenty-nine more children for their responses
to the same statement, and calculate the mean rating to be 3.65, we will have
another numeric symbol — another descriptive statistic — that approximates
the group's overall response to the acting.

Types of Statistics

Descriptive statistics generally summarize the collection of individual pieces
of data and 'describe' a phenomenon or action. For example, the N (number)
of students in your sample may be 30. Their $\bar{X}$ (mean) age is 10.4 years. The
group is composed of 55 per cent girls and 45 per cent boys, and the class they
are in scored at the 75th centile nationwide of the most recent standardized
test of basic skills. District researchers have suggested that a strong correlation
(relationship) of r = .65 exists between these children's standardized test scores
and their families' annual income. Basic statistics such as these profile the group
along several variables of interest and provide general information which may
be needed for your study. They can also be used for certain tests of significic-
ance which generate *inferential* statistics.

Inferences can be made about the data you've collected when they are
taken through selected, standardized mathematical formulas that suggest the
probability of outcome error. Seen loosely in another way: the probability that
the results you achieved are due to a treatment effect can be calculated statistically, suggesting the amount of *significant difference* between the groups
you examined. Some of these procedures are the *t* test, which examines any
significant difference between a variable's means from two groups; or the *F*
test (analysis of variance, or ANOVA) which examines any significant difference between the means of three or more groups on a variable. This chapter
cannot go into great detail about these or other tests, but note that the results
are used to accept or reject any predetermined *hypotheses* you have developed
for the research study (discussed below).

This chapter also cannot fully explain the criteria for selecting the most
appropriate statistical test of significance for the kind of data you collect. But
do be aware that there are two types of statistical analytic procedures with
corresponding tests: *parametric* and *nonparametric*. Briefly, the most appropriate procedure to use depends on the type of measurement scale(s) used in

your instrumentation, the size of your sample, the precision of your measurements, and other factors. For example, analysis of data gathered through Likert scales, a common form of survey measurement (such as the 4 point scale used above with 'The acting was good in the play'), should employ nonparametric procedures because the scale measures an artificial, not an actual, magnitude. For more details and an excellent overview of criteria for nonparametric tests of significance, see Gibbons (1993, pp. 63–4). Standard textbooks on statistical reasoning will explain parametric procedures in detail.

The language of 'number crunching' can be confusing and intimidating at first. Vogt's *Dictionary of Statistics and Methodology* (1993) is an excellent reference book of terms for practitioners. Huff's *How to Lie with Statistics* (1982) is a layperson's guide to bias, reliability, and validity in everyday applications of statistics, and a 'user-friendly' orientation to descriptive statistical meaning. References aside, college level coursework in data analysis and measurement are essential prerequisites for experimental researchers.

What are the Major Steps for Preparing and Conducting Experimental Research?

After you have determined that the purpose of your research and the answer to your research questions are best suited to experimental, quantitative approaches, write your preliminary research question on paper, keeping in mind that it should be as clear as possible and manageable given the limitations of time and available resources. Also realize that the question will become fine-tuned as further steps are taken with the design preparation.

Though textbooks in experimental research are good references for step-by-step procedures, individuals who have successfully conducted this kind of research may be more valuable as mentors and advisors for your own work. Discussed below are just a few of the major steps in preparing and conducting experimental research. They are not necessarily discrete procedures — there will be some overlap as you negotiate with a school for permission to conduct your study; find previous research that reshapes your conception of the topic; and, rewrite a possible interview question after a teacher shares that it's too vague for children.

Conduct a Literature Review

A review of literature in your field of study is essential to determine whether research in the area has already been conducted; whether a lack of research exists; whether relevant instruments have already been developed; what previous research has observed; and how previous research may inform your own study. Make no mistake: a literature review is essential because it reshapes your thinking about the topic and contributes greatly to the design of your work.

Your own project builds on previous theory to develop new theory, and fills a gap in the extant knowledge base. Experimental research is in its infancy with theatre for young audiences; it has been more widely applied to studies in classroom drama. Dissertation literature reviews and articles that survey numerous studies in the field of drama and theatre are good starting points for a more indepth review (see Kardash and Wright, 1987; Morrison Institute, 1995; O'Farrell, 1993; Saldaña, 1988; Vitz, 1983; Wagner, 1988; and Wilkinson, 1988).

Define Relevant Terms and Variables

As your literature review progresses, rewrite your central research question, keeping in mind that terms and variables will become more defined. For example, 'story drama', 'improvisation', and 'holistic' may be interpreted differently by several drama practitioners. Specify what the relevant terms mean to you as the researcher and how they will be realized in your study. Likewise, other variables of interest such as 'prejudice reduction', 'classroom management skills', or 'oral fluency' also need precise definitions and an explanation of how these will be measured.

Locate a Participant Sample

A *sample* is a small portion of the population at large. The participants in the sample, if randomly selected to form a large enough group, theoretically represent the 'universe' of people who share similar traits. For example, a randomly selected group of thirty 9-year-olds serves as a sample intended to represent all 9-year-olds. Hence, the results obtained from an experimental study with these thirty children, if internally and externally valid, should *generally* apply to other groups or individuals sharing similar traits. Naturalistic inquiry rejects this assumption and operates under local and context-specific conditions. Transferability of findings to other groups is a consideration by the researcher and reader of the report.

Most researchers in theatre and drama do not have the luxury of random sampling. Depending on the design, most often our participants are drawn from one or a few school settings, or even limited to the children available in one classroom. Nevertheless, determining the most appropriate number of participants in your study is one of the first formal operational construct decisions. Perhaps it may be a classroom of twenty-five children for a pre-test/post-test design, or two classrooms of twenty-seven children each for a control group design. Depending on the reliability and validity needs of your study, plus the statistical tests of significance you choose, a minimum number of participants may be required, such as thirty or forty. Smaller groups such as ten children can still be used in experimental research, but any statistical tests of significance employed should be nonparametric. Needless to say, the larger the number of participants, the greater your data base for analysis and the greater your confidence when interpreting the results.

If your study is conducted in a school setting, permission for research with minors usually will be required by the school's administration. You will be expected to submit your research agenda in writing, sign any necessary forms, and follow a code of ethics when you work with children, e.g., securing parental consent, no coercion of young people to participate, maintaining the confidentiality of participants. Other legal requirements and protocols may be stated by funding agencies or instititutions for whom you work.

Select the Instrumentation

Depending on the children's age or reading and writing skills, data can be gathered from young people in such *written forms* as questionnaires, tests, attitude scales, or journals. The written data might be provided by a child participant, or scored by an adult observer using a rating scale or checklist from a survey. Tape recorded *interviews* with young children can be transcribed and coded. Predetermined or emergent categories of response in the data such as 'recall', 'empathy', 'scenography-lighting', and, 'evaluation of acting', can be discerned, coded, rated, or counted. *Other forms* of data gathering can be content analyses of art work response or video tapes of drama sessions, among others. How and why these general forms of data gathering are chosen, constructed, and designed to help answer your central research question is your *instrumentation.*

Selected studies in drama and theatre for youth have adapted or developed original instrumentation for measurement and assessment of children's work or responses. These methods or instruments can be replicated for your particular study if the original developer has found them to be both acceptably reliable and valid. Since many studies are specialized and context-specific, it may be best to generate your own instrumentation or adapt others for the needs of your particular study. For a spectrum of instrument and research method examples in drama and theatre, see Brown, 1992; Cooper, 1983; Furman, 1981; Gourgey, Bosseau, and Delgado, 1985; Kaaland-Wells, 1994; Klein and Fitch, 1990; Moore and Caldwell, 1990; Rosen and Koziol, 1990; Rosenberg, Pinciotti, and Smith, 1983; Saldaña and Otero, 1990; and Vitz, 1984. Carter (1982), commenting on the credibility and utility of experimental research, is essential reading.

Assess the Study's Validity and Reliability

In an experimental study you should be accountable for its *validity* and *reliability.* *Validity* insures that the instrument you use for gathering data in your study measures what it is designed to measure and leads to appropriate inferences by the researcher. To use a rather obvious example, you cannot validly assess a child's verbal improvisation skills through a written test. A more appropriate, or more valid, measuring instrument is an audio or video-tape recording of the child's improvisational work during a drama session. The *internal validity* of a study refers to what extent you can justify that the results obtained are a consequence of the treatment and not from errors or other factors in your research design. *External validity* refers to the generalizability of your results to other groups of young people aside from those who participated in your study.

Reliability also refers to the extent that a measurement is free of error, but in this case, reliability refers to the *consistency* of a measure after several repeated uses. For example, a rating system you develop for classifying children's responses to a probing question includes four possible ratings by an adult: 'high', 'average', 'low', or 'no response'. Raters working independently on coding the responses should have some consistency between them. All or most of them should agree that a particular response merits the same rating for the instrument to be reliable. Justifying your study's validity is most often a case of your ability to demonstrate the internal logic of your study or instrumentation; reliability coefficients can be calculated statistically.

Write and Test the Study's Null and Research Hypotheses

Once there is specificity to your research question, and logistical decisions have been made about the size of your sample, the amount and type of treatment, and the most appropriate instrumentation, it is time to put your theory to the test.

A *hypothesis* is a statement, rooted in the central research question, that can be subjected to empirical evidence to confirm or disconfirm its accuracy. For example, a researcher's central question might be: Is improvisational drama a more effective method than lecture/discussion for adolescents to learn anger management skills? From this question, a *null hypothesis* is developed. Read the following example:

> *Null Hypothesis*: Tenth grade students who learn anger management skills through improvisational drama will not be more proficient at them than students who learn these skills through the lecture/discussion method.

A null hypothesis is used as a theory-testing method and phrased in the negative form since it is more accurate to confirm that a statement is definitely false than it is to confirm that a statement is probably true. Remember — you are trying to reduce the possibility of error in your research efforts.

Each group receives its training through drama or lecture/discussion. Then the researcher assesses each group's proficiency at anger management through behavior checklists and anecdotal records about the students submitted by the school faculty and counselors, along with the researcher's own checklists and records. The data collection period might extend over a month's period of time after the anger management instruction. These data (e.g., the number of positive and negative incidents/observations about each participant's anger management) could then be transformed into frequencies or scores, and the two groups' means would be compared. The evidence obtained from data collection and statistical analysis is then applied to the null hypothesis for *acceptance* or *rejection*. If the results show a statistically significant difference in means between the two groups, and the results disconfirm the null hypothesis, then the null hypothesis is *rejected* and the *research hypothesis* is *accepted*:

> *Research Hypothesis:* Tenth grade students who learn anger management skills through improvisational drama will be more proficient at them than students who learn these skills through the lecture/discussion method.

Research methods and statistics texts can more fully explain the logic behind null and research hypothesis development and how the statistical results are applied to them. (Fraenkel and Wallen, 1993, pp. 194–9, challenge some of the traditions of this procedure and present a more 'common sense' approach to hypothesis testing.)

'Friendly Advice' on Conducting Experimental Research with Children

A tremendous investment of time and energy goes into experimental research, and there are risks along every step of the way, especially if you are administering an original instrument, or researching a topic that has had little or no previous research. As time allows, it is worth conducting a *pilot study* or a 'trial run' of your research design on a different group of participants before the actual study is undertaken. Unforeseen problems or 'glitches' may become apparent, and you can modify or redesign the study and instrumentation as needed.

The following section presents recommendations for data collection from children, based on our experiences with the Arizona State University (ASU) longitudinal study.

Surveying Children

Asking adults to review your written questionnaires or surveys before you administer them to young people is strongly advised. Elementary classroom or secondary school language arts teachers can provide valuable feedback on the readability level of your instruments. Those with expertise in surveying children can share their advice and observations about children's response trends to specific instrument formats (e.g., deleting neutral responses such as 'no opinion' from Likert scales; avoiding adjective pairs that can be misinterpreted in semantic differential scales).

Observing Children

Some instruments developed for adult observers of classroom drama sessions are inventories or rating scales of selected behaviors such as movement, pantomime, concentration, and oral fluency (see Rosenberg *et al.*, 1983). Interjudge reliability (consistency between observers) with some of these instruments has been problematic, due primarily to the lack of specificity with their terms and the complex nature of the improvisational process itself. It is recommended that rubrics developed for observation in these settings be taken through multiple pilot tests for fine-tuning, and that adult observers be well trained in their use and confident about 'what behavior goes with what term'.

Interviewing Children

Record the child's responses with a hand-held microphone rather than a condensor microphone built in the tape recorder. The microphone — always held by the adult — can be placed closer to the child to record what may sometimes be spoken in a soft voice. Another technique to guarantee easier and more accurate transcription is for the adult to repeat what the child has just said — only when needed and word for word. Younger children's sentence construction and speech may sometimes be erratic or inarticulate to adult ears:

> *Child*: And then in the play they was going to [inaudible] him.
> *Interviewer*: 'Going to "heart" him'?
> *Child*: No, *hurt* him.
> *Interviewer*: Oh, '*hurt* him'.

Transcribing the child's original grammar and vocal patterns including 'ums', broken phrases, repeated words, word emphases, pauses, and responses spoken as questions rather than statements, are strongly recommended in case these aspects become important in later analysis. For example, a kindergartener might say:

> *Child*: And then Timmy's sister, she, she, she said they was gonna, um, gonna go get ice cream [giggles], but the puppet, the, Timmy said, 'No, wait for for me!' Uh, but she *didn't*.
> *Interviewer*: What happened next in the play?
> *Child*: Uh. [5 second pause] Timmy got mad?

If you feel the child's response is minimal or unclear to you as an adult, ask the child to elaborate on the response with such prompts as, 'Tell me some more about that,' 'I'm not sure I understand; please give me an example,' or 'How do you know that?' Depending on the design of your instrumentation, such prompts may not be permitted as part of the interview schedule.

Children can be interviewed individually or in small groups of three to five — generally referred to as *focus groups*. But the grade level of the children should be considered when designing the protocol. In the ASU longitudinal study we observed that children in small groups in grades K–3 tend to reach consensus, and peer influence on some individual responses is evident. Also, younger children in the interview setting tend to be fascinated by the tape recording devices. The novelty of the interview itself may lead to distracting behaviors within the group. Hence, one-to-one interviews are recommended with the lower grade levels. The group consensus pattern dissipated at grade four in small group interviews, and by grade six treatment participants even openly disagreed with others' responses to reveal 'critical' exchanges on the effectiveness or ineffectiveness of the production.

Selected researchers in multicultural education have observed that some groups, such as Hispanic adolescents, may prefer and participate more in small groups than in one-to-one interviews. There is also research available that describes unique interaction patterns within small groups composed of same-gender membership.

Goldberg's (1977) interviewing protocol and coding and category system of young people's responses to theatre was used as one of the primary data collection instruments for the ASU longitudinal study (Saldaña, 1996). Over seven years, transcripts of verbal responses were coded and transformed into quantitative measures for statistical analysis. But peer reviewers questioned both the validity and reliability of the system presented in preliminary reports. One critic felt that the statistical results did nothing more than count 'numbers of utterances' from children. Another questioned the reliability of the coding system when examples presented in the report did not accurately reflect the category definitions, according to her interpretation. Cahill (1991) also found Goldberg's coding and category systems questionable in her own study. The transformation and reduction of rich qualitative data into quantitative form, *in this case*, did not provide the best answers to the central research questions of the longitudinal study. The interview data were reanalyzed qualitatively with a new emergent category system, but percentages of children's responses in these new categories were still tallied to help inform the analysis.

Data Collection, Documentation, and Quality

In theatre for youth studies, most data have been collected during and after the performance event in the form of observations, interviews, and written instruments. But very little *pre*-testing has been conducted for comparison with data collected afterwards. We encourage researchers to consider *pre-event* interviews or other forms of data gathering from children. Assessing their current attitudes toward theatre; their knowledge and expectations of the specific event; and their background experiences with drama, theatre, and the specific play's content or themes, may yield valuable insights.

We would also like to encourage researchers to document a study's treatment, data gathering procedures, and related statistical results in greater detail for future meta-analytic work. Kardash and Wright (1987, pp. 36–7) recommend that sample sizes in drama studies should be much larger than sixteen, and any observed effects on gender, ethnic, and specific grade level subgroups should be reported. Future studies in drama might also explore sample characteristics between and among boys and girls and children from various ethnic groups, and the effects of drama on children's writing and reading skills.

Finally, the quantity *and* quality of data you collect from participants in your study does, to some degree, depend on the quality of the *treatment* itself. Superficial, unchallenging classroom drama experiences and mediocre theatre events are unlikely to yield any substantial response (i.e., data) from children. Just as there are standards for excellence in experimental research, so too should the artistic experiences we provide for young people be rigorous and 'tight' if our research is to have any value.

Final Comments

Why conduct research in drama and theatre for youth? Because the generally skeptical social climate of today, and those with power to distribute funds and mandate programs, demand justification and accountability. Research has the potential in this field not only to reveal new insights and to improve our practice, but to serve as an agent for advocacy — to show decision makers that drama and theatre for youth 'works'.

Experimental is not just a label applied traditionally to particular methods of research. It is a word that evokes a sense of trial and error, investigation, exploration, 'let's try this and see what happens'. We once consulted a child psychologist to help us think through how emotion may play a role in the child's interpretations of stage action. He jokingly but honestly replied, 'As soon as *our* field figures it out, we'll let you know,' and suggested that we, like any researcher, make an informed deduction from our observations. As non-experts who depend on the expertise and professional literature from other fields for guidance with our own research endeavors, we try to keep abreast of current trends and practices in the fields of quantitative *and* qualitative research in education, child development, psychology, and sociology. The qualitative paradigm has been evolving distinctively over the past fifteen to twenty years, and its methodology and methods are having subtle effects on the quantitative paradigm. The field of educational research is currently in flux

(Barone, 1995); hopefully, as soon as *their* field 'figures it out', they'll 'let us know'. Unfortunately, that means that, in the interim, researchers in our own field may disagree over the quality of a quantitative study (pun intended). The best we can do in the meantime is to simply make informed deductions of, and inductions from, our observations and interpretations of data. We should evaluate our colleagues' research using strong standards of excellence, but be cautious of arrogance, superiority, Eurocentrism, and narrow vision when it comes to criticism of each others' work.

References

BABBIE, E. (1995) *The Practice of Social Research* (7th edn), Belmont, Wadsworth.

BARONE, T. (1995) *Qualitative Research*, Lecture, Arizona State University (ASU), Tempe, Arizona, 17 January.

BROWN, V. (1992) 'Drama and sign language: A multisensory approach to the language acquisition of disadvantaged preschool children', *Youth Theatre Journal*, **6**(3), pp. 3–7.

CAHILL, C. (1991) 'An empirical study of proposed systems for measuring responses of children to theatre for young audiences.' Unpublished Dissertation, Southern Illinois University at Carbondale.

CARTER, H. (1982) 'What is it — Research or research?', *Children's Theatre Review*, **31**(2), pp. 26–31.

CIZEK, G. (1995) 'Crunchy Granola and the hegemony of the narrative', *Educational Researcher*, **24**(2), pp. 26–8.

COOPER, J. (1983) 'A study of the effects of pre-performance materials on the child's ability to respond to theatrical performance.' Unpublished Dissertation, University of Georgia.

CRESWELL, J. (1994) *Research Design: Qualitative and Quantitative Approaches*, Thousand Oaks, Sage.

ERICKSON, F. (1986) 'Qualitative methods in research on teaching', in WITTROCK, M. (ed.) *Handbook of Research on Teaching* (3rd edn), New York, Macmillan, pp. 119–61.

FRAENKEL, J. and WALLEN, N. (1993) *How to Design and Evaluate Research in Education* (2nd edn), New York, McGraw-Hill.

FURMAN, L. (1981) 'Creative drama as a vehicle for assessing comprehension', *Children's Theatre Review*, **30**(2), pp. 33–8.

GIBBONS, J. (1993) *Nonparametric Statistics: An Introduction*, Newbury Park, Sage.

GLESNE, C. and PESHKIN, A. (1992) *Becoming Qualitative Researchers*, New York, Longman.

GOLDBERG, P. (1977) 'Development of a category system for the analysis of the response of the young theatre audience.' Unpublished Dissertation, Florida State University.

GOURGEY, A., BOSSEAU, J. and DELAGO, J. (1985) 'The impact of an improvisational dramatics program on student attitudes and achievement', *Children's Theatre Review*, **34**(3), pp. 9–14.

GRADY, S. (1995) '"Misplaced concreteness": [Re]Searching for meaning-making', *Youth Theatre Journal*, **9**, pp. 1–13.

HOWE, K. (1992) 'Getting over the quantitative–qualitative debate', *American Journal of Education*, **100**(2), pp. 236–56.

HUFF, D. (1982) *How to Lie with Statistics*, New York, W.W. Norton.

ISAAC, S. and MICHAEL, W. (1981) *Handbook in Research and Evaluation* (2nd edn), San Diego, Edits.

KAALAND-WELLS, C. (1994) 'Classroom teachers' perceptions and uses of creative drama', *Youth Theatre Journal*, **8**(4), pp. 21–6.

KARDASH, C. and WRIGHT, L. (1987) 'Does creative drama benefit elementary school students: A meta-analysis', *Youth Theatre Journal*, **1**(3), pp. 11–18.

KLEIN, J. (1995) 'Performance factors that inhibit empathy and trigger distancing: "Crying to laugh"', *Youth Theatre Journal*, **9**, pp. 53–67.

KLEIN, J. and FITCH, M. (1990) 'First grade children's comprehension of "Noodle Doodle Box"', *Youth Theatre Journal*, **5**(2), pp. 7–13.

MARÍN, G. and MARÍN, B. (1991) *Research with Hispanic Populations*, Newbury Park, Sage.

MENARD, S. (1991) *Longitudinal Research*, Newbury Park, Sage.

MILES, M. and HUBERMAN, A. (1994) *Qualitative Data Analysis* (2nd edn), Thousand Oaks, Sage.

MILLER, D. (1991) *Handbook of Research Design and Social Measurement* (5th edn), Newbury Park, Sage.

MOORE, B. and CALDWELL, C. (1990) 'The art of planning: Drama as rehearsal for writing in the primary grades', *Youth Theatre Journal*, **4**(3), pp. 13–20.

MORRISON INSTITUTE FOR PUBLIC POLICY (1995) *Schools, Communities, and the Arts: A Research Compendium*, Washington DC, National Endowment for the Arts.

O'FARRELL, L. (1993) 'Enhancing the practice of drama in education through research', *Youth Theatre Journal*, **7**(4), pp. 25–30.

ROSEN, R. and KOZIOL, S. (1990) 'The relationship of oral reading, dramatic activities, and theatrical production to student communication skills, knowledge, comprehension, and attitudes', *Youth Theatre Journal*, **4**(3), pp. 7–10.

ROSENBERG, H., PINCIOTTI, P. and SMITH, J. (1983) 'On quantifying dramatic behavior', *Children's Theatre Review*, **32**(2), pp. 3–8.

SALDAÑA, J. (1988) 'Jed H. Davis' "Prospectus for Research in Children's Theatre": Twenty-five years later', in KLEIN, J. (ed.) *Theatre for Young Audiences: Principles and Strategies for the Future*, Lawrence, University Theatre, University of Kansas, pp. 55–86.

SALDAÑA, J. (1996) ' "Significant Differences" in child audience response: Assertions from the ASU longitudinal study', *Youth Theatre Journal*, **10**.

SALDAÑA, J. and OTERO, H. (1990) 'Experiments in assessing children's responses to theatre with the semantic differential', *Youth Theatre Journal*, **5**(1), pp. 11–19.

SMITH, M. (1995) *Research Design*, Lecture, ASU, Tempe, Arizona, 8 March.

SMITH, M. and GLASS, G. (1987) *Research and Evaluation in Education and the Social Sciences*, Englewood Cliffs, Prentice-Hall.

VITZ, K. (1983) 'A review of empirical research in drama and language', *Children's Theatre Review*, **32**(4), pp. 17–25.

VITZ, K. (1984) 'The effects of creative drama in English as a second language', *Children's Theatre Review*, **33**(2), pp. 23–6.

VOGT, P. (1993) *Dictionary of Statistics and Methodology*, Newbury Park, Sage.

WAGNER, B. (1988) 'Research currents: Does classroom drama affect the arts of language?', *Language Arts*, **65**(1), pp. 46–55.

WILKINSON, J. (1988) 'On the integration of drama in language arts', *Youth Theatre Journal*, **3**(1), pp. 10–14.

Part Two

Possibilities

8 Into the Labyrinth: Theory and Research in Drama

Cecily O'Neill

We have been working for several decades in drama in education to establish a sound theoretical base and a productive conceptual framework for our research and practice. In every discipline, the development of theory is critical for both understanding and practical dissemination. Research is generated, guided and enlarged by theory, the lens that focuses and illuminates our complex and multi-layered practice.

Theory provides the instruments through which we discover underlying similarities, patterns and relationships in our work and articulate these patterns for others. It furnishes lucid images of the characteristics and processes of drama and is fundamental in guiding and shaping our research as it is organized and displayed through the numerous alternative research paradigms now available.

The Relationship of Theory to Practice

It is certainly possible to engage in effective practice without a basis in theory and to undertake theoretical studies without any understanding of practice. We are probably all familiar with examples of this imbalance, perhaps even in our own work. Theatrical performance proliferated in the Middle Ages, but until the rediscovery of Aristotle there was no theoretical net to throw over it. The absence of theory did not reduce the number or effectiveness of the plays of that period. In *The Quest of Averroes*, Borges describes an Arab philosopher who is familiar with Aristotle's *Poetics* but lacks any conception of the meaning of 'tragedy' and 'comedy' because of the Muslim taboo on representation. Even when he encounters theatre, he cannot grasp its meaning or its relationship to his knowledge of Aristotle's text. He possesses the 'net', but can catch nothing in it (Eco, 1994, p. 102).

I worked in drama for a long time before I began to weave a net of theory to throw over my work, or even to recognize the value of doing so. The significance of theory to the growth and clarification of my own practice became apparent when I encountered Gavin Bolton's work, and watched him prepare the ground for so much subsequent theorizing in the field. As he began to classify the modes of dramatic activity in the classroom, my own practice began to come into focus (Bolton, 1979). I continue to weave my net, inevitably full of holes, from the ideas of everyone whose work I have encountered in practice or on the page. Woven into this net are all the insights and responses of the teachers and students who have guided or followed me into a myriad of drama worlds. The most exciting moments occur when some theoretical insight clarifies a knotty problem in practice, or when the obscurity of theory is illuminated by the memory of a significant dramatic event in the classroom or on stage. The loneliest times are when practice inexplicably breaks down, and when the words of thinkers who have spoken clearly to others remain opaque. Still one struggles, accumulating notes and piling up academic papers, and suffering, as Theodore Roethke (1977) puts it in his poem *Dolor*, the 'inexorable sadness of pencils', and all the 'misery of manila folders' (p. 376). It is easy to lose one's sense of direction and purpose in the struggle.

Finding Problems and Questions

The most daunting task for any researcher, however experienced, is to settle on the question, problem or hypothesis that will generate the most fruitful research and bring about the greatest enlargement of the field. These questions and problems are embedded in the context of previous theory and investigation. In my own case, they occur as a result of reflections on what I have read, particularly in dramatic theory, criticism, and aesthetics; on the work of others that I have observed and analyzed; on emerging patterns in my own work and on the relationships between all of these. Sometimes a word or phrase in the works of some commanding intellect will seize my attention and direct my thought. For example, Langer's assertion that drama is 'the mode of destiny' was the beginning of a fascination with the operation of dramatic time in both process drama and theatre (Langer, 1953). Robert Witkin's understanding that a teacher of the arts need not operate outside the creative event drew me to reflect on the functions of the teacher in role (Witkin, 1974). Hornby's insights about role-playing within the role confirmed my certainty that drama not only happens through role-play but is essentially *about* role-play (Hornby, 1986).

Whatever the focus of our research, we are never working in a vacuum, and our efforts must rest firmly on those of our predecessors if we are not to find ourselves ceaselessly reinventing the wheel. Knowledge and understanding in either science or art do not appear in a vacuum. They spring from an immersion in existing practice and theory, and an appreciation of the central traditions, rules, demands and possibilities in the field. Problem finding is as important as problem solving. We seek, formulate and explicate significant questions that are at the heart of our subject but have not yet made an impact on practice.

Surveying the Field

The first task for every researcher or theorist is to survey the field as thoroughly as possible. This is a daunting task in drama, where our concerns connect with so many other domains. An inductive survey may require us to develop at least a passing familiarity with the language and method of several other disciplines. Philosophy, psychology, anthropology and sociology have all been usefully pressed into service to illuminate our practice in drama and to guide us towards appropriate research paradigms. Although these and other disciplines have served us well, we have not always recognized that the most useful sources of illumination and enrichment may lie closest at hand — for example, in theatre and performance studies. When we attempt to draw on disciplines remote from our own in their focus, origin, period and discourse, we may betray our lack of understanding and bring confusion to ourselves and our readers. These forays may actually lead us away from the heart of our own work. The more unfamiliar the ground on which we try to build our theories, the more unstable and ephemeral the results are likely to be. This may be the price we pay for importing into our work ideas from distant disciplines and exotic fields of thought. Rigorous reflection is needed to ensure that we are not misunderstanding or misrepresenting the original significance of these studies and distorting them to suit our purposes.

Where a thorough grasp of other disciplines is achieved, fresh understandings and perspectives will clarify, articulate and enlarge our thinking about drama. We will attain an intellectually precise method of writing and talking about our work without having to resort to the creation of restrictive and separatist jargon, or to hijacking inappropriate modes of discourse from more fashionable or 'respectable' disciplines.

As theoretical principles and research frameworks gradually begin to arise from the growth of knowledge and experience in the field, the next effort is to maintain as clear and precise a focus as possible. It is important to remember that research and scholarship cannot be about *everything*. Great intellectual enterprises will fail unless they are accompanied by a sense of perspective and a capacity for prioritizing, selecting, and organizing one's efforts. One must also try to maintain one's interest in and delight in the work, so that, in George Eliot's words, our consciousness may be 'rapturously transformed into the vividness of a thought'. Otherwise our undertakings may come to resemble the sterile labours of Eliot's Mr Casaubon in *Middlemarch*, the prototype of the dry, life-denying academic, uselessly accumulating detail for his unwritten masterpiece, 'The Key to all Mythologies', and losing both his direction and his joy in the work. Aesthetic endeavor may be as demanding, and at times as apparently barren and futile as this arid scholarship, but its aim, at least, is generative. Yeats (1923) writes of the work of the artist, but it might also be of the scholar, in this striking image:

How many centuries spent the sedentary soul
In toils of measurement, beyond eagle or mole,

Beyond hearing or seeing or Archimedes' guess
To raise into being this loveliness? (p. 357)

Time, observation, intuition, measurement and the 'guess' are all part of the labour of the sedentary soul, as are the multiple perspectives gained by soaring like the eagle and digging like the mole.

Every scholar, researcher or artist must maintain a sense of perspective. A keen survey of the landscape is essential before one aspect or feature of the vista captures the gaze. To develop the metaphor, at first the flora may seem to yield most interest, but in the process of surveying the field the fauna may force itself more strongly on one's attention. In other words, with a deeper knowledge of the domain, the research topic is almost bound to alter. It is futile and unscholarly to attempt to determine a question or problem before knowing the field. Matthew Arnold's precept was to let the mind play freely around the subject until a focus emerged.

The selection of research problems and topics and the questions we raise will inevitably expose our training and our influences and reveal our deepest personal and cultural beliefs and values. Choice always has a moral and an aesthetic as well as a cognitive dimension. Theory and research can never be neutral. All knowledge is a social construction, contextual, transient and open to reconstruction. Our theory and practice will inevitably reflect contemporary taste, practice and discourse, with all their associated limitations and prejudices. The shreds and patches of these influences, ideas and values are gradually woven into our individual theoretical net. If they wished to make the effort, it would not be difficult for readers to identify my influences, interests, values, intellectual training and habits of mind from this chapter alone.

The Scientific and the Aesthetic

Values are not necessarily disconnected from and opposed to facts and knowledge. Although a destructive separation of the rational and the affective has persisted for centuries, values and commitments are no longer regarded as essentially irrational and anti-cognitive. This is good news for us in drama, since we are concerned with a medium that cannot depend for its life on facts alone. In the light of changing patterns of research in education and the humanities, we need no longer apologize for drama's subjective character, the complexity of the activity and the multi-layered experience to which it gives rise.

Like scientific research, our research in drama demands careful observation, generalization and the expression of results in a community of scholars and educators. Like science, the study of drama requires detail and precision and will emphasize certain fundamental processes. Thinking creatively and critically, solving problems, constructing knowledge, 'reading' results and developing productive theories are as essential for development in the arts as in the sciences.

The myth persists in some quarters that scientific research is value-free, although Polanyi (1962) has effectively demonstrated that scientific thinking is as personal as it is objective. Scientific knowledge, like knowledge about drama, is symbolic in nature, socially negotiated and to a significant degree dependent on imagination and intuition — 'Archimedes' guess'. Scientists need to have some imaginative sense of their theories as a whole before they can set about proving their truth, and the most prized quality for those working in the most rigorous reaches of pure mathematics and theoretical physics is intuition, the feeling for the answer in advance of the proof. Scientific thinking has a strongly heuristic side and the process of theorizing can be both creative and aesthetic. The scientific method itself, like any other explanatory process, is a dialogue between fact and fancy, the actual and the possible, between what could be true and what is in fact the case. It is the story of justifiable beliefs about possible worlds (Medawar, 1982, p. 111). There is no reason why the mental processes involved in the study of drama should be any less coherent and progressive than those required by the study of science. A precisely similar training of the mind should take place and a similar sense of the essential coherence and parameters of the subject should emerge. The enterprise of drama, as of the other arts, involves, in Shelley's phrase, 'imagining what we know', and recasting our perceptions of the world into aesthetic experience.

Rich and exact description, logical argument and clarity of thought are significant in the pursuit of every kind of research. Questioning, decoding, deducing, comparing, synthesizing, interpreting, and reasoning are all involved. Theory is never merely a matter of cataloguing processes, patterns and relationships, nor is it generated solely out of observation and experience. Theorists have the freedom to reflect, speculate, imagine, simplify, categorize, infer, exemplify, and invent, and the result of their efforts is likely to be successful in so far as these freedoms are entertained. Many influential thinkers, from Nietzsche to Barthes, have been distinguished by their playfulness and irony, and in our efforts to gain respect in the wider academic community we should not allow ourselves to lose this aspect of our work and become trapped in the 'toils of measurement'. We should not assume that scientific inquiry is the only legitimate form for our research, and neglect or abandon those qualities which I believe are inherent in our subject.

Research Characteristics

The most effective research in drama will share a number of the characteristics of scientific research. General principles are generated and refined by focusing on the central concerns of our subject. Effective and fruitful research will develop emerging representations of the ways in which drama operates in a variety of contexts. These 'principles' and the research to which they give rise are not final truths but approximations. Theorists in science also construct generalizations and approximations. Niels Bohr (Pippard, 1986) reminds us that the task of physics is not to find out how nature is. Instead, 'Physics concerns what we can say about nature' (p. 46). The scientific community develops constructs and these are formulated and imposed on natural phenomena in an effort to interpret and explain these phenomena. The rapid changes in scientific thinking demonstrate that these constructs are not final truths about the physical world and its attributes. In drama we are dealing with imagined worlds, and the constructs we impose upon these worlds will always remain approximate.

Some subjects, for example the study of history, can be both a science and an art. Scientific principles are involved in the historian's treatment of evidence, and the presence of these elements is what helps to distinguish history from myth, legend and propaganda. Scientific implies systematic, logical and progressive. A scientific approach to any subject changes its character from the casual to the causal, from the random to the systematic. But this kind of approach also implies a sense of consolidating progress. Theory and research may begin in the 'background' of the work and, as they proceed, start organizing the 'foreground' as well. There is nothing in these notions of logic and progression that makes them inherently antagonistic to inquiry in drama. Sterile and inappropriate number-crunching is not necessarily implied.

If scientific concepts have significance for an art process, aesthetic concerns may also have relevance for science. Many scientists take a strongly aesthetic view of their enterprises. They point out that there are awkward problems, ugly theories and messy results, and see a definite correlation between the ugly and the wrong. Philip Anderson (1994), the Nobel prize-winning physicist, believes the aesthetic principle operates powerfully in science. The breadth and significance of the work, the subtle and unexpected connections it makes to other fields and the depth to which it delves into nature are among the essentially aesthetic considerations Anderson uses to establish the significance of an inquiry. He sees the idea of broken symmetry in physics as having much in common with the literary meaning of the term 'ambiguity', that is, the number of layers of meaning that can be crammed into one idea. It is not easy to associate ambiguity with what we may be accustomed to admiring as the clarity and logic of the scientific approach.

Questions and Hypotheses

Finding the central questions that will guide their studies is the toughest part of the endeavor for most researchers. Drama offers almost too rich an array of topics and potential lines of inquiry. What's happening in drama? How does it happen? Where does it come from? Who is in charge? What ideas are in play? What kinds of communication arise? Who talks? How much? What about? Who listens? How does drama relate to other kinds of performance? To educational theories? To narrative? To text? To other art forms? Even these few apparently basic and simple questions may be far too wide for a single study and will inevitably generate many further questions. The guiding problem or question must be refined and clarified before it can be serviceable in research.

We must guard against the temptation to consider only problems to which we already know the answers. These questions are inauthentic. Although they may confirm our beliefs, no surprises will occur along the way, and no real discoveries will be made. It may be more genuinely authentic and aesthetic, if rather terrifying, to pose a problem for which there may be no final answers. That will be a true quest, although it may not endear us to our supervisors or colleagues.

Having developed an hypothesis, which is after all only an instrument, a guide, we must also guard against allowing ourselves to become possessed by it. As Sterne (1983) reminds us in his ironical masterpiece, *Tristram Shandy*,

> It is in the nature of a hypothesis . . . that it assimilates everything to itself as proper nourishment; and, from the first moment of your begetting it, it generally grows the stronger by everything you see, read, or understand. That is of great use. (p. 110)

Once we have developed a hypothesis, a set of criteria, a model or a pattern, the temptation is to locate at all costs more and more instances that seem to fit our pattern. Every occasion or event is seized upon as yet another example of the truth of our theory or model or hypothesis. We crush them into our hypothesis or model like the Ugly Sisters' toes into the glass slipper. We distort examples that do not quite fit the model or overlook those that form a different pattern entirely. When we find ourselves declaring that apples are in fact oranges, or dismissing them as faulty oranges, we know we are in danger. The trick is to develop as great a skepticism about our own hypothesis as about those of others, and remain flexible in testing alternatives. When these mental habits are not cultivated, even sensitive and knowledgeable researchers descend into fiction, advocacy, gainsaying and delusion.

The Labyrinth

The research question or topic crouches like the Minotaur at the centre of the labyrinth of scholarship, with a maze of pathways and blind alleys leading off in all directions. The words of the great scholars who have gone before us echo distractingly in the gloom. Where is the Ariadne's thread that will guide us? It is unlikely that we will be able to approach our goal by a direct route. Instead, it may be best to seek it indirectly, uncovering assumptions, raising questions, looking up quotations, following footnotes and pursuing intuitions. The metaphor of the researcher as hero struggling to find a way through the labyrinth seems an illuminating one.

This chapter has already employed at least two other metaphors, the net of theory and the field of study. Metaphor is a device for seeing something in terms of something else. It can supply us with a range of new perspectives on our topic. The nature of even the simplest object will be clarified by considering it from as many viewpoints as possible. Metaphor suggests diverse modes and approaches to inquiry. It calls imagination into play, the cognitive capacity that allows us to construct alternative worlds. It is the very enterprise of drama.

Increasingly, researchers are being encouraged to turn to metaphor and imagination in order to resolve or bypass long-standing conflicts between the quantitative and the qualitative, the subjective and the objective. These approaches reconcile old oppositions by linking theory and experience together in new and dynamic ways, helping us to attend to a multiplicity of voices and to interpret what we encounter from a plurality of points of view. Open structures of thought and practice that are always in the process of reconstruction and never promise final resolution are advocated. As Merleau-Ponty (1967) puts it, rationality implies that 'Perspectives blend, perceptions confirm each other, a meaning emerges' (pp. xix–xx). When various experiences intersect, we weave our past experiences into those of the present and other people's lives into our own.

It is frustrating that so many researchers, including those on university PhD committees, still seem to believe that quantitative methods carry more weight, more 'truth', and are more persuasive than other methods. In *The Journal of Creative Behavior*, for instance, surely an obvious arena for potentially creative and adventurous research paradigms, the quantitative seems by far the most acceptable method of inquiry. What is this urge to pin down creativity with numbers? Is there a strict ratio between the elusiveness of a subject and the stringency (and inappropriateness) of the kinds of measurements applied to it?

The Laboratory of Drama

We should be encouraged in our pursuit of the aesthetic and metaphoric, not just by the scientists and researchers who operate in this way but by the fact that many theorists in a variety of subject areas use drama as a model or metaphor for their own thinking. Burke, Goffman and Burns, among others, have viewed their subject through the lens of drama. Drama provides a tight structure or paradigm for human behavior, an experimentally controlled example of human interaction. Our research site, the field of drama, is itself a laboratory. People are segregated in a space, sometimes the theatre, sometimes a studio or classroom, where human behavior can be displayed and manipulated through metaphor, repetition and exaggeration. Drama is not a model of every kind of human action but always of the most perplexing, problematic and forbidden activities. It is not surprising if our research is also perplexing and problematic.

We can use graphic means, perhaps even another model, to explicate the drama model. The advantage of constructing models and diagrams is that they are simple graphic representations of the structure of an idea or process. A model provides the outline of an action or event and has the advantage of brevity and precision. It should be as broadly applicable as possible if it is to be useful in focusing subsequent attempts at investigation, criticism or interpretation.

Figure 8.1: Reprinted from Bert O. States: The Pleasure of the Play, p. 71. Copyright ©
1994 by Cornell University. Used by permission of the publisher, Cornell University Press

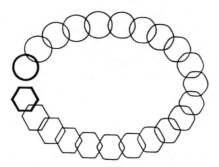

I find it difficult to think graphically. Charts, graphs, columns and models are
almost always lost on me. Their necessary simplicity seems to call too much
into question, and yet the more complex they are, the more they may distort
what they are supposed to clarify. However, occasionally I see a graphic
representation that assists in organizing my perceptions. A recent example is
the figure in States' (1994) book, *The Pleasure of the Play*, and reprinted in
Figure 8.1. These simple overlapping circles resonate for me with the separate
yet linked episodes of process drama, and it might be possible to adapt the
figure to that purpose.

For States, each circle represents a unit of dialogue and the area of overlap indicates the cause–effect linkage of any two units. The play appears to
move one step, or link, at a time in a probable direction. This direction gradually becomes elliptical, and there is a sense of convergence of all the parts as
the full potential of the drama is realized. All of the events are continuous,
since at no point is anything happening that is completely new. This kind
of development through a series of related and overlapping episodes is also
characteristic of process drama, which does not evolve through a merely linear
or chronological unfolding of plot (O'Neill, 1995, p. 48). Instead, each episode
or unit of action generates the next. The drama grows in an orbit through a
chain of events which yields its full dramatic potential.

Drama does not merely passively reveal, represent or reflect reality, but
provides a kind of geometry for organizing our perceptions. Whether in school,
studio or on stage, drama is a way of thinking about life, and organizing and
categorizing it. Many theatre artists explicitly recognize this by identifying their
efforts as a laboratory. The International Theatre Research Centre is Peter
Brook's title for his place of work, and he regards his dramatic experiments as
research focusing on the following questions: What is theatre? What is a play?
What is an actor? What is the relationship between them all and what conditions best serve this relationship? Brook's work is a quest, and the moment
something is successful it must be abandoned. It is research because it is trying
to discover something, and, as Brook tells his actors, discover it through theatre
so that the audience can be part of that discovery.

For Brook and other innovators, drama is a centre of psychophysical, sociological and personal experiment. Any experiment is a journey into the unknown, an entry to the labyrinth, and this quest can only be mapped after the event. Drama is always fundamentally experimental and provisional and any theory or research into drama or performance must recognize the elusive basis of the event itself. In other words, our work will always be directed 'Towards a Theory . . .' and, like drama itself, in the process of becoming.

The Discourse Community

Our efforts will become true research when they are soundly based on what Madeleine Grumet (1988) identifies as 'the clarity, communication and insight of aesthetic practice' (p. 89). In drama, as in other fields, inquiry arises from curiosity, from wonder, from speculation about the complex nature of the enterprise and the processes by which it comes to birth, but we will also want the results of our efforts to be generative. Higher thought, theorizing, is not an internalized dialogue. We claim to foster dialogue, collaboration and interpretation among our students and must not neglect these approaches in the wider research community. Genuine critical dialogue should not be replaced with contradiction, or fruitful ideas with mere irritable mental gestures. If we are to grow into scholars rather than remain students, we must always recognize and acknowledge the work of those who have gone before. It is better to admit to being a pygmy standing on a giant's shoulders than appear to be a pygmy struggling in the dirt of dissension with other pygmies.

We must not forget that we ourselves may become influential through our teaching, writing and research. The field of drama is peopled with charismatic figures, the effect of whose personalities and ideas can be mesmerizing and, at times, disabling. The tendency to reproduce ourselves spiritually among our students, co-workers and associates can be a formidable temptation. Unreflective and incompetent replication of philosophy and practice leads to a deadly inertia, while access to developing theory and effective research promotes and provokes dialogue and reflection in both students and professors.

This volume, and the institute from which it arose, mark the beginnings of a discourse community. There is discussion, mutual appropriation and negotiated meaning. Our mission is to transform the latent energy of our research and our deliberations into educational and aesthetic substance. Ideally, this will unite us in creating, sustaining and expanding a research community. We desperately need to work in dialogue, not just in our drama but as a genuine community of scholars, researchers and practitioners. As Dewey (1927/1984) puts it, 'Ideas which are not communicated, shared, and reborn in expression are but soliloquy, and soliloquy is but broken and imperfect thought' (p. 371). Collaborative learning and shared discourse, which are among the distinguishing features of drama, are not merely desirable objectives but essential for the survival of our work.

True research in drama will never be a question of creating theories and cataloguing facts. It will involve growth, or more precisely out-growth. Without abandoning its roots in practice and performance, we must find ways to show that drama can maintain itself as a discipline, integrating imagination and expression, and articulating through language and gesture the deepest concerns of our humanity. As we learn to present our theories and practice as avenues to coherence and integration in other disciplines, drama will grow outward without necessarily compromising its position as a discrete subject worthy of study. Drama has the power to enlarge our frames of reference and to emancipate us from rigid ways of thinking and perceiving. Its purpose is to bring about change — changes in practice, and changes in insight and understanding. As Heidegger (1971) reminds us, the arts guarantee us 'a passage to those beings that we ourselves are not, and access to the being that we ourselves are' (p. 53).

Conclusion

To return to my metaphor of the researcher in the labyrinth, it is wise not to forget that at the dead centre of the maze lurks our research topic, the monster, its jaws dripping with the gore of scholars it has already consumed. It may pounce upon us and destroy us too, immediately or slowly. The battle may be long drawn out with neither side yielding victory. Weariness of spirit and boredom may defeat us, and we may retreat from the monster to fight another day. Or — worst scenario of all — someone may have got there before us and the monster may be already lying dead. In plain terms, the book may be already published, or the dissertation defended, or the questions answered. But there are always other labyrinths and other monsters. We will continue to be driven by what Maxine Greene (1994) has identified as an affirmation of energy and 'the passion of reflection in a renewed hope of common action, striving for meaning, striving to understand' (p. 459).

Take your vorpal swords in hand, and go forth, armed with pencils and notepads, powerbooks and software. To paraphrase the words of Winston Churchill, we shall defend our theories and our dissertations, whatever the cost may be. We shall fight in the libraries and in the stacks, we shall fight in the footnotes and in the databases, and we shall never surrender!

References

ANDERSON, P. (1994) 'Four facts everyone ought to know about science', *Daily Telegraph*, 31 August.
BOLTON, G. (1979) *Towards a Theory of Drama in Education*, London, Longman.
DEWEY, J. (1927/1984) *John Dewey: The Later Works Vol. 11*, New York, Collier.
ECO, U. (1994) *The Limits of Interpretation*, Bloomington, University of Indiana Press.
GREENE, M. (1994) 'Epistemology and educational research: The influence of recent

approaches to knowledge', *Review of Research in Education*, **20**, Washington, DC, American Educational Research Association.

GRUMET, M.R. (1988) *Bitter Milk: Women and Teaching*, Amherst, University of Massachusetts Press.

HEIDEGGER, M. (1971) *Poetry, Language, Thought*, (trans. Albert Hofstadter), New York, Harper and Row.

HORNBY, R. (1986) *Drama, Metadrama and Perception*, Lewisburg, Bucknell University Press.

LANGER, S. (1953) *Feeling and Form*, New York, Scribner.

MEDAWAR, P. (1982) *Plato's Republic*, Oxford, Oxford University Press.

MERLEAU-PONTY, M. (1967) *The Phenomenology of Perception*, Evanston, Northwestern University Press.

O'NEILL, C. (1995) *Drama Worlds: A Framework for Process Drama*, Portsmouth, Heinemann.

PIPPARD, B. (1986) 'Complementary copies', in EGAN, K. (1991) (ed.) *Primary Understanding*, New York, Routledge.

POLANYI, M. (1962) *Personal Knowledge*, Chicago, University of Chicago Press.

ROETHKE, T. (1977) 'Dolor', in MOORE, G. (ed.) *The Penguin Book of American Verse*, London, Penguin.

STATES, B.O. (1994) *The Pleasure of the Play*, Ithaca, Cornell University Press.

STERNE, L. (1983) *The Life and Opinions of Tristram Shandy, Gentleman*, Oxford, Clarendon Press.

WITKIN, R.W. (1974) *The Intelligence of Feeling*, London, Heinemann.

YEATS, W.B. (1923) 'The Only Jealousy of Emer', in *Plays and Controversies*, London, Macmillan.

9 Art in Scholarship and Scholarship in Art: Towards a Poetics of Drama Research

John O'Toole

The Art in Scholarship: A Conversation with Cecily O'Neill

Cecily, in your chapter you quote W.B. Yeats (1905/1960, p. 281) to make an analogical leap. You remind us that Yeats, in exploring the nature of artistic impulse, describes the artistic enquirer as 'the sedentary soul in toils of measurement beyond eagle or mole'. Yeats invokes 'Archimedes' guess' as he discusses the artist's impulsion toward form. As you point out, Yeats might have been defining the research scholar as well as the artist: 'Time, observation, intuition, the guess and measurement are all part of the travail of the sedentary soul, as well as . . . soaring like the eagle and digging like the mole' (see page 138). Not a sedentary soul, though — your travails and mine have been on our feet, literally and figuratively, being invigorated by our discoveries and, as often, bruised in the errors of trial and error, where experience is what we get when we are looking for something else.

The notion of the sedentary soul seeking universal answers through research has now been challenged in current behavioural research methodology. Works with titles like *Beyond Method* reclaim research as an active pursuit:

> The pursuit of formal knowledge [is] but a particular form of human action, which because of its essentially social nature, must be understood as being as much an ethical, moral, ideological and political activity as it is an epistemological one. (Morgan, 1983, p. 373)

. . . or, for those with a head for heights and abysses, note the following from *Against Method*:

> Scientists do not solve problems because they possess . . . a method or theory of rationality, but because they have studied the problem for a long time . . . because they are not too dumb, and because the excesses of one scientific school are almost always balanced by the excesses of some other school. (Feyerabend, 1975, p. 302)

147

Like you though, Cecily, I liken my research to artistry. This is the second attempt I have made to write this paper — the first, before I read yours, could be considered a dramatic rehearsal. Its value was in scaffolding my understanding to be more receptive to your 'labyrinth'. Thinking about the form of your chapter I am reminded of the aesthetic in our work, and how we document that aesthetic.

Onward from its title 'Into the Labyrinth', there is an elegance about the chapter to which the reader warms. The poetry adds to our understanding. Our attention is captivated affectively and cognitively. True elegance of writing is not only cosmetic. A research paper has a form and, like any formal construction, the elements of that form are aesthetically responsive and manageable. Perhaps if more researchers were aware of this, their work would be pleasanter to read as well as being better scholarship.

For drama people, a double analogy with play directing may be helpful when comparing research to art: the writing style of a scholastic paper is like the design of a play. As any good play director knows, the design is not there just to decorate the animated playscript. The design is a living part of the performance text, which in one way or another interacts with writers' and actors' visions of what is happening, either to clarify these visions, resonate powerfully with them or, in bad design, to obscure them. One might further liken the researcher's use of references and quotations to a director's responsibility in making stage business, which is to illuminate the dramatic action, not usurp it. In *Twelfth Night*, if Sir Toby pulls a chair away just as Sir Andrew sits on it, and the purpose is to make the audience laugh, for all but the most naïve spectator it is tiresomely gratuitous. If in doing it we suddenly see something new in the text, Sir Toby's resentment and frustration, and the depth and invulnerability of Sir Andrew's egotistical complacency, it is adding artistic substance to the performance text. Some researchers, oppressed by conventional models of scholarship and believing that more knowledge is truer knowledge, read copiously and cram all the references into the text of their papers, believing or hoping that weight will generate wisdom. What really counts is not the quantity of what we read but the quality of how we read, so a paper full of endless references reiterating the obvious is as tedious as a comedy full of pratfalls.

There is a major implication here for the way in which we perceive scholastic papers, and the products of research in the behavioural fields. The thesis or paper is not just the hod in which we carry the lump, the preformed bricks of positive knowledge. As Halliday (1986) and Egan (1988) argue, there may be no meaning-making at all without language, and there is no useful learning without contexts incorporating language. Language not only gives form to the thought, it moulds the raw material of perception giving it shape. The discoveries of the social scientist or the drama teacher are not independent of their linguistic utterance. They are the products of conversation: the interaction with practice and the people spoken with over the years. Our dialogues are shaped by the linguistic forms in which they are expressed and the audience to whom they are directed.

Comparing three pre-eminent exponents of process drama, Dorothy Heathcote, Gavin Bolton and yourself, Cecily, I have observed that you each teach differently, and that you employ diverse thinking and writing strategies. Heathcote's writing, as her teaching, is bold, free-wheeling, snatching images and concepts from a wide range of disciplines, including history, mythology, and semiotics. Like her classroom dialogue, her writing swings between the domestic and classic, with liberal sprinklings of memorable phrases. Bolton's writing is spare, clear, light on metaphor, meticulously moving between anecdotal practice and theoretical conclusion, like his teaching. On the other hand, your writing beguiles with metaphor and poetic allusion, just as beguilement, metaphor and poetic allusion are your classroom currency too.

Here, the language qualities in the teaching and the writing are not those of cosmetic import only. They are part of the substance of how these teacher/writers both teach and write. Their truth by its nature is as subjective as it is objective, and can only interact with the reader in a negotiation of meaning, a dialogue. However, writers of research papers do not usually conceive of what they are making as anything other than monologues, because one of the dominant constraints of the form is that it is apparently monologic by nature and necessity. However, the readers all have their own contexts and assumptions, and, whatever the style, in the absence of access to the writer's own practice they will reconstruct the author's intent and find meaning in terms of their own. There is a dialogue.

The written word is a misleading medium, in that it makes monologue seem not only possible, but the natural way of operating. It also gives to the monologue the appearance of permanent substance. A spoken word's truth is vastly more vulnerable and fragile. For instance, my assertion that Heathcote, Bolton and yourself are pre-eminent exponents of process drama will stand tomorrow, even if I have changed my mind, and the reader has little choice but to accept or reject it. If it were spoken, you could bring your experience and knowledge into the debate, question my criteria and credentials and explore its validity for us both. Dialogue through the written word is not impossible, but it is laboured.

Just as conversation is a part of research, so research can be conversation, as Harste (1991) trenchantly asserts. Morgan (1983, p. 374) too, in his anthology of research methods likens research to 'reflective conversation', a term that can be used literally and metaphorically. After all, collaborative researchers working in the same place on the same project, whatever their research paradigm, frequently talk about little else. More than just conversing with our colleagues, however, in our research we must converse with our experience, our practice, as we reflect on that, and, in particular, on the lessons learned from practice. The more practice we have had, the more discoveries we have made, the richer will be the reflective conversation. It is worth noting the voices of good practice along with the newer voices of new disciplines, and remembering that new terminology just implies a new paradigm for observation that need not invalidate the old.

We must converse with the context in which that practice is set, not just the drama lesson, but the kind of school where it happens. We must ask ourselves, What are the motives and constraints that drive it? and, Why do the students think they are there? We also need to converse with our reading, and the theorizing of other workers in the same context. We may even be able to converse with analogous contexts. The drama researcher may learn from dance, or sport, or science. We must also converse with our assumptions and be helped or forced to recognize where we are coming from, and what the consequences and limitations of this entail.

It is a very small step now, linguistically and conceptually, from conversation to discourse; a step into critical theory and the analysis of those discourses which are and are not available to us in our research context. What I like most about the phrase 'reflective conversation' is that there is implied not an absolute truth, but transience, like theatre existing most validly in the moment of happening; in Barba's (1995) haunting phrase, '. . . a craft which, at the moment of its fulfilment, vanishes' (p. 8). As drama and theatre leave trails in the memory, so the knowledge which is realized in the reflective conversation is relative and fleeting, and will always need reprocessing in new conversations; in Gadamer's words (1975), our research is 'transformation into a communion in which . . . we make and remake ourselves as human beings' (p. 341).

Gavin Bolton (1979) cannily called his first book *Towards a Theory of Drama in Education* (my emphasis). In 1980, the first Australian drama in education conference held in Brisbane was entitled, 'In Pursuit of Meaning'. Both hint that, for the drama practitioner as for the poet, to travel hopefully is a better thing than to arrive. The titles indicate a sense of purposeful direction, and the direction is from practice, from the real context. It is no accident that the most influential theorists in process drama as in performance theory are virtually all outstanding practitioners. Their reflections may continue to refine their own practice and shape that of others, but they won their spurs in the field.

Our practice, and our ongoing inquiry into improving our practice, are our research, and, Cecily, you have aptly observed that drama not only happens through role-play but is essentially about role-play. What else is drama but the exploration of human behaviour in experimental situations, using activated models to replicate, confirm or challenge perceived social realities? Recent phenomenological paradigms in social science have even spawned a research method called 'dramatism' (Mangham and Overington, 1983, pp. 219–33). We may wince at the neologism, but we can take affirmation from the recognition of our craft within social science research, an area more traditionally known for its pursuit of scientific objectivity.

We can be confident in what we do. Research modalities like ethnography, critical theory, and reflective practice offer no more than a number of holding forms for our research. My context of practice is what drives me to pursue a research project, and I often do not know how to classify it until it is over. As we are researchers, we are artists, and for me there are three factors in the making of art which are directly relevant to the making of research: the *discipline of form*, the *operation of intuition*, and, the *social making of meaning*. These may be most easily examined in the artistic context.

The Scholarship in Art

I find it difficult to distinguish my work as playwright, drama researcher and drama teacher from each other. As a drama teacher, I inevitably work as a playwright. As a drama education researcher, I am conscious of the aesthetic dimension of what I do, of the art in the form. As an artist, a writer of plays and theatre in education programs, I usually have to research the subject matter.

Is the research the same? Is the investigation of an artist engaged in making art, research? It entails the same sorts of activities: reading books, interviewing and transcribing on tape, observational fieldwork, and, small-scale monitored experiments called improvisations. Like academic research, it emerges from a context of practice. It is bound or at least eventually bounded by the discipline of form, and the necessity to make social meaning. Playwrights and play assessors will verify that there are few more rigorous disciplines of inquiry and synthesis than writing a playscript, nor few more unforgiving referees than play producers or the paying public.

Playwriting and research demand intuition, and the operation of the back-brain. It may be helpful to scrutinize how this works. Since first drafting this chapter, I felt unease, and was intuitively aware that there ought to be more to say; the subject had been in my back-brain, unforming, coalescing and re-forming. With time and Cecily's chapter as catalysts, my first draft has transformed. My understanding of the research question has suffered a sea change.

The notion of a central question is common to all forms of research. Finding the central question for a project is the first crucial endeavour for all research students. In forming a drama, the playwright and the teacher-as-playwright are immediately confronted by those truistic but inescapable questions: What's happening? To whom is it happening? When? Where? and, What's at stake? (Heathcote, 1974). These questions are an effective way to focus research, too. Exploring them reveals a problematic issue that will be substantial enough for a play, a classroom drama or a thesis. While there are special differences among the ways the questions are approached, these spring from the differences of paradigm demanded by different purposes and products.

To work from example, I was commissioned to write a play on the childhood of Adolf Hitler. It has often been said that history is what is written by the victors: Byron (1812, iii, 48) called it 'History's purchased page'. Events are inevitably reconstructed in terms of the experiences of the present. A post-war American Army historian, a 1990s German historian, and a Jewish historian, however scrupulous in their integrity, when addressing the childhood of Hitler must come at the same material from quite different starting points. The stories of Hitler's childhood which they write are inevitably different histories, because their audiences and their starting points for research are different, and so are the questions that they choose to ask in order to begin garnering, interrogating and reconstructing material. What they have in common is that they are trying to make cognitive sense of the same welter of incomplete fragments of factual events that happened organically and with all the contingent coherences of chaos.

This is not what dramatists do. Just as historians' special truths are different from each other, their generic truth is different from dramatists'. These truths should not be incompatible, and historical truth must bear upon dramatic truth, yet they are different. When researching Hitler's childhood, my colleagues and I initially made a mistake. We went into libraries and immersed ourselves in thick books on German history, trying to uncover much information on the subject. We were quickly swamped. The way we got out of our swamp was to put all this information aside, along with our dependence on the front-brain.

If it were true that experience is what you get when you are looking for something else, then we had to look for something else. We found it in a modern Austrian picture book for young children called, *I am a Great Big Hairy Bear* (Janosch, 1976). It had nothing to do with Hitler, but we knew when we stumbled across it that it was what we were looking for, our moment of 'Archimedes' guess'. It had pointed the way to the play's form. We then returned to our history books, but with new eyes. We decided to cast through them, making a note of only those details which caught our fancy. These we explored through improvisation, deliberately taking them out of historical context while examining their applicability. This was our fieldwork. As content decisions were made, we returned to the library to check how the emerging drama matched up with written history, dramatic truth vis-à-vis historical truth. In belatedly trusting our back-brains — our fancy — to sort, select and reject, the details which caught our attention were not arbitrary or self-indulgent, and the amount of agreement and shared enthusiasm attested to the high level of social meaning-making, though our front-brains could not see their importance.

The seeker for *historical truth* is approaching the source looking for what can be verified externally to fit into an ideological paradigm concerned with illuminating the social political processes within that context. The seeker for *dramatic truth* approaches the source material looking for resonances that can be verified internally, implicitly, even subliminally by the percipients. Since drama works through irony, the strongest resonances may often be those which are quite contradictory to, and not consonant with, the attitudes that the audience and writer hold. What was most intriguing to us about Hitler's childhood was how little there was to suggest the man. His parents were not monsters; his mother was a gentle, sweet person whom Adolf loved deeply and nursed devotedly on her deathbed. We found no trace of anti-Semitism, but instead a nice Jewish doctor who treated his mother's final illness, and to whom Hitler sent Christmas cards while he sent other Jews to the final solution. This data is difficult for historians. Some have sought to construct Hitler's father — a customs official and expert beekeeper, a stern *paterfamilias* typical of his time, who actually favoured Adolf — into a monster and child-basher. In this form, it is more unambiguous to help explain the adult of later years.

For the dramatist, the contrast of these kind and humdrum people resonating with what we know of Hitler the adult is what is significant. A picture of a morose adolescent dreamer, who wrote poems to a girl he never had courage to introduce himself to, speaks with loud irony about the dreams which plunged Europe into war and holocaust. It implicates Hitler and the others who voted him into power, and it automatically implicates us all. The resonance is with ourselves and our own dreams. The dramatist's truth is problematic and moral, it gives no answers, but the very act of raising questions is an ethical deed.

Towards a Poetics of Research

Resonances are also the stuff of poetry, and this reminds us of the nexus between poetry and drama. Analyses of drama from Aristotle's *Poetics* to Dryden's *Defence of Dramatic Poesy* made no clearcut distinction between the two forms, and many non-European cultures of performance make none either (Qoopane, 1990). Perhaps the only difference from poetry in how dramatists research is that they must socialize the resonances, anchoring them in a living, concrete context, where the insights gained can be offered to an audience as outsights.

Poetry launched this chapter's conversation and has figured substantially in it. Poetic language is returning to the research conversation. Social science research, including drama and arts education, used to be replete with nouns, which confirmed the positivistic ambitions of the researchers, and affirmed the Newtonian universe which even science was abandoning. History, Pedagogy, Truth, Data, Information — they are all crushingly nominal. The researcher's favourite was Objectivity, which is a noun about noun-ness: observing and mapping reality in terms of static, observable, and, repeatable things. Its obverse was Subjectivity, into which category came poetry and conversation, which were excluded as unstable, unrepeatable, unverifiable and untrustworthy. Knowledge was a noun, finite and unbending. There was no difference in research methods between pharmacy and human behaviour. I prefer verbs like knowing and especially understanding, which were for a time, at least in my university, construed as less rigorous. Now research is more flexible, perhaps in belated reaction to the strident positivism of information age technology.

One word coming back into the research lexicon is wisdom, a word with strong poetic resonances that have been ironed out of its synonym, knowledge. Both words are used revealingly by an information age philosopher, in a debate about virtual reality: 'With a mind-set fixed in information . . . we become mentally poorer in overall meaning. We get into the habit of clinging to knowledge bits and lose our feel for the wisdom behind knowledge' (Heim, 1993, p. 10). Positivist Derek Pugh (1983) draws a distinction between 'wisdom:

a stock of insight' and 'knowledge: a set of substantiated findings', and asserts that knowledge, not wisdom, is the province of research (p. 48). He is clearly not into resonances, either. This definition turns upon assumptions which do not fit the way we work in drama: that the realms of the emotional and subjective are unknowable and unmanageable; that there exists a clear distinction between insight and outsight; and, that knowledge and wisdom consists of nouns, of answers. If we are contributing anything by our research in, through and about drama, surely it is not in drawing nominal distinctions between knowledge and wisdom, but in knowing what questions are wise to ask. Such will add to our stock of what we understand about human behaviour in context, understandings which are, in turn, the holding forms that will lead us to the next question.

Dramatic artists and teachers have stood just as aloof from research as the reverse, each with the arrogance of not really understanding the other. Acknowledging the rigour and artistry in art and research permits exciting possibilities for simultaneously or complementarily researching our art form and the art in our teaching as we practise them.

Cecily, to give Yeats another twist, our territory as artists, teachers and researchers is not *beyond* eagle or mole, but *between* them. We can use our dramatic art and research to find meaning and direction for ourselves and our students here on the ground, to help us navigate among the transient and shared truths where, in another haunting phrase by Yeats (1904/1960), 'Life drifts between a fool and a blind man . . . and nobody shall know his end' (p. 271).

References

Barba, E. (1995) *The Paper Canoe*, London, Routledge.

Bolton, G. (1979) *Towards a Theory of Drama in Education*, London, Longman.

Byron, G. (1812) *Childe Harold's Pilgrimage*, Canto iii, Stanza 48.

Egan, K. (1988) *Imagination and Education*, Milton Keynes, Open University Press.

Feyerabend, P. (1975) *Against Method*, London, Verso.

Gadamer, H. (1975) *Truth and Method*, New York, Seabury.

Halliday, M. (1986) *Spoken and Written English*, Geelong, Deakin University Press.

Harste, J. (1991) 'Research as conversation.' Keynote address to 'Talking Together' Conference, Toronto, Project Talk.

Heathcote, D. (1974) *Talks to Teachers*, Evanston, Northwestern University Film Library.

Heim, M. (1993) *The Metaphysics of Virtual Reality*, New York, Oxford University Press.

Janosch (1976) *I am a Great Big Hairy Bear*, Durham, Dobson.

Mangham, I. and Overington, M. (1983) 'Dramatism and the theatrical metaphor', in Morgan, G. (ed.) *Beyond Method*, London, Verso.

Morgan, G. (ed.) (1983) *Beyond Method*, London, Verso.

O'Toole, J. (1982) 'Establishing educational drama', *NADIE Journal* (National Association for Drama in Education), **7**(2).

O'Toole, J. (1986) *The Beekeeper's Boy*, Brisbane, Playlab Press.

Qoopane, F. (1990) 'Traditional performance in Africa.' Unpublished MA Thesis, University of Dar-es-Salaam.

Pugh, D. (1983) 'Studying organizational structure and process', in Morgan, G. (ed.) *Beyond Method*, London, Verso.

Yeats, W.B. (1905/1960) 'The Only Jealousy of Emer', in *Collected Plays of W.B. Yeats*, London, Macmillan.

Yeats, W.B. (1904/1960) 'On Baile's Strand', in *Collected Plays of W.B. Yeats*, London, Macmillan.

10 Reflections from an Ivory Tower: Towards an Interactive Research Paradigm

Jonothan Neelands

Rationale

In this chapter I want to explore my own position as a teacher-researcher. I am particularly interested in trying to locate myself in relation to classroom practitioners and their everyday realities. In other words, I want to establish the role of the university-based researcher in relation to school-based practice. I hope that this is more than an act of self-indulgent navel-gazing. There are a number of people, such as myself, who have recently moved into university after extensive classroom and consultancy experience. This move can involve an uncomfortable sense of dislocation. Many of my colleagues in the university have been immersed for many years in the rigour and discipline of academic life. At first, my own history of 'informal' action-centred research seems a poor preparation for entry into the research community of the university. But, I am also conscious that 'research' in one form or another has guided my own development as a practitioner and as a theorist. The fact that this research has always been grounded in classroom experience must be an asset, particularly if the seeds of academic research are expected to take root in the reality of classroom life.

Learning to Think

I should start by defining my own stance towards research practices more explicitly. I find that I am still broadly in sympathy with the values expressed in the first research project that I participated in as a newly qualified teacher in 1975. The *Talk Workshop Group* was a collection of teachers working at Vauxhall Manor School in London who spent five years analysing and classifying children's talk at home and in school. In terms of its methodology, the group was influenced by the work of the Rosens into the talk patterns in working-class communities and by the newly established *Classroom Action Research Network* (CARN) coordinated by John Elliot. Both of these initiatives sought to raise the value of teachers' own reflective accounts of what happens in their classrooms.

The findings of the Vauxhall Manor project were later published in a volume entitled *Becoming Our Own Experts*. This title was soon to become a 'war-cry' for a generation of young teachers, like myself, who found a mismatch between the preoccupations of university-based tutors and researchers and the realities of classroom life. For an older generation of 'radical' teachers the same phrase encapsulated a sense that they wanted to reclaim control over change in their classrooms — policies that were formulated outside the classroom did not reflect their 'expert' experience. This ethos is articulated on the first page of the book (Eyers and Richmond, 1982):

> . . . we, the teachers, must become our own theoreticians, our own experts. Our theory, our 'expertise' is in making sensitive inferences about an actual classroom experience, in noticing what is really going on. If the expert in the more usual sense, who stands back a little from the everyday reality of the classroom in order, ideally, to get a wider view of the scene, has a role in this process of discovery, it is simply to help the classroom teacher to discover more fully what is already there. Unrelated theory has no value in this context; it will quite rightly be dumped by the teacher as excess baggage . . . theory and practice must be married in the lives of the people who do the job. (p. 1)

I cannot underestimate the importance of this early influence on my professional life. At the time that the book was published I was working in a progressive English department in Nottinghamshire. The department was collegial and organized around regular staff–student dialogues about teaching and learning. From the outset I was encouraged to keep and share journals, to publish accounts of classroom practice and to be involved in alternative publishing of classroom materials and experiences. This activity, together with the value climate that enveloped it, gave me a sense of control over my professional life. It instilled in me the habits of 'reflective practice' (Schön, 1986) and it provided me with the confidence and experience to become a writer and workshop leader. But, whilst I was developing the skills and tools associated with classroom action research I was also hardening my attitudes towards other forms of research and researchers.

Because the department was considered to be at the 'cutting-edge' of practice we were frequently visited by university researchers who were keen to 'formalize' our findings. We were inclined to be suspicious and to be cynical about the motives of our visitors. After all, we were the ones who were actually doing the work rather than retreating to an ivory tower to contemplate it. I would never have imagined that twenty years later I would be working in a university and that my own contemplations on classroom practice would be published by mainstream, commercial, houses.

The Evolution of Action Research

The early enthusiasm of the Vauxhall group was further developed through the emergence of action research paradigms developed by John Elliot within CARN (Elliot and Adelman, 1973) and Lawrence Stenhouse in the *Humanities Curriculum Project* (Stenhouse, 1968, 1971). Elliot developed his notion of the 'action research cycle', which initially was a simple four stage model: identifying a problem, planning a course of remedial action, implementation of the action plan, and the review of behavioural outcomes.[1] This model was developed from the earlier work on behavioural objectives and curriculum development conducted by Kathryn Feyereisen and John Fiorno who first suggested an action sequence for school-based research (Feyereisen, Fiorno and Nowak, 1970). The cycle was intended to provide a continuous research process; as one problem was addressed, a new set of problems would emerge. In this sense, the action research cycle provided an ongoing dynamic of continuous inquiry. For classroom practitioners, the cycle was a form of professional development and a means of gaining control over pedagogic and curricular change.

The development of action research practices amongst teachers has subsequently been influenced by research activity in other professional settings, particularly by Schön and Argyris working with medical practitioners (Argyris and Schön, 1974). Their premise had an immediate attraction for teacher-researchers: 'All human beings — not only professional practitioners — need to become competent in taking action and simultaneously reflecting on this action to learn from it' (Argyris and Schön, 1974, p. 4). Argyris and Schön developed their methodology in response to a perceived flaw in many conventional approaches to research:

> Another important obstacle to the integration of thought and action is the current concept of rigorous research. The technology of rigorous research works best when it does not deal with real-time issues . . . this technology of rigorous research is based on diagnostic techniques that ignore or cannot cope with properties of effective action under real-time conditions. (1974, p. 4)

Schön and Argyris developed the concept of 'theories in use' to help explain the local and reflexive behaviours of professional practice. Actions are guided by operational theories. Actions can be understood in the context of the theory that informs them. Effectiveness is achieved through reflection on and modification of underlying 'theories of action'. Whilst Schön and Argyris once more foregrounded the professional working in a local context as the central element in action research, they also raised a new set of difficulties. Becoming one's own subject for research, exposing one's 'theories of action' to peer scrutiny, becoming involved in dilemma discussion and the simulation of professional problems as forms of research methodology is extremely challenging at a personal as well as at a professional level.

Action research and the 'Becoming our own experts' movement had its origins in small-scale research projects undertaken by professionals who were both committed to the need for research and voluntarily involved in the project. Very little consideration was given to identifying the human and ethical problems connected with professional disclosure. The problems and consequences in terms of increased levels of vulnerability and personal challenge, are greatly exacerbated when those teachers who become the focus for action research are neither committed to it nor voluntarily involved with it.

This, it seems to me, is a critical paradox. The practices of action research and reflective practice are designed to make the work of classroom teachers visible and central to the problem of understanding how teaching and learning can be made more effective. But, by turning the spotlight onto the teacher we are also exposing that teacher to public scrutiny — to the fear of being considered incompetent or inadequate.

The Professional is Personal

The issues surrounding the blurring of professional and personal identities was central to Fullan's analysis of professional change (Fullan, 1982). In this study, Fullan analysed the results of eighteen research-driven projects which were designed to improve professional practice. These were large-scale projects that focused on changing teachers' behaviours — the subjects and the objects of these projects, the teachers themselves, were often suspicious and cynical about the motives and assumptions underpinning these projects.

Fullan (1982) reaffirms the importance of involving classroom teachers in the processes of research needed to identify and manage change — indeed, Fullan demonstrates that change will only occur if those who are most effected are fully involved in these processes (1982, p. 91). But Fullan also identifies the 'practicality ethic' as the usual criterion of acceptance and rejection of change by teachers. The 'practicality ethic' refers to the degree of personal cost in terms of the time, effort and practicality that is implied by involvement in classroom research.

The obstacles to change that Fullan cites tend to be psychological and personal rather than bureaucratic or logistic — ambiguity and uncertainty over goals, isolation and loneliness, fear of censure, lack of interaction, lack of shared culture (1982, p. 122). Fullan's (1982) analysis also suggests that change only occurs through a combination of support and challenge and that this combination will inevitably produce a felt disturbance amongst those involved:

> . . . assume that conflict and disagreement are not only inevitable but fundamental to successful change. Since any group of people possess multiple realities, any collective change attempt will inevitably involve conflict.
>
> Assume that people need pressure to change (even in directions

which they desire) . . . Unless people are going to be replaced with others who have different desired characteristics, resocialisation is at the heart of change. (p. 91)

Institutionalizing Action Research

In 1987 I moved to Nottinghamshire to work for the Education Support Services as Head of the Dance and Drama Support Service. The service's operations were underpinned both by Fullan's work and by the currents and practices in action research which I have already identified. But this was a large-scale enterprise. Fullan's work on change and the action research cycle were applied at every level of operations. Those of us who were involved as 'managers of change' shared a background of involvement in small-scale action research neworks. We were now charged with the responsibility of involving every teacher and school in action research; whether they wanted to or not!

We responded to the identified needs of teachers, worked with them through action research processes, supported them in implementing the changes *they* wanted to see. This was a challenge. I had to place my own views about drama on the back burner and prepare to support a wide range of initiatives that were based on a multiplicity of views about drama and its functions — everything from puppetry to nativity plays! But the Support Services recognized the personal demands they were placing on teachers and increasingly began to incorporate clinical counselling skills and strategies into their support work in order to address the intra- and interpersonal consequences of becoming involved in professional change processes.

In order to institutionalize action research we also needed to institutionalize the quality of relationships required by such an approach. Teachers' interests needed to be formally protected and the personal risks delimited. The counsellor–client relationship seemed to offer an appropriate model. Contracts between support staff and classroom teachers were established that made goals, roles and responsibilities explicit and agreed. The model of professional support in Nottinghamshire was based on providing the five factors that Fullan identified as being essential to change programmes:

- Time
- Climate of support
- Desire to develop
- One-to-one support in the classroom
- Access to skills, knowledge and understanding of subject and the change process

The Support Services developed a set of principles which were designed to form the basis of the 'theory-in-use' operated by its support teachers. These principles draw together strands derived from action research, from Schön and Argyris's 'theory in practice', and from Fullan's work (NAIS, 1989, p. 14):

Four Fundamental Principles
- that every teacher is a curriculum developer;
- that curriculum development is integrally linked to professional development;
- that teachers learn most effectively when they are able to look at their classroom practice in a methodical and planned way; this process is considerably enhanced when it is shared in a supportive atmosphere with other colleagues and also when it is set within the context of real curriculum issues in the workplace;
- that the responsibility for decisions relating to curriculum and professional development issues remains clearly with teachers in schools.

The Support Services worked on the premise that all teachers were 'self-actualising' (Rogers, 1961). Support teachers operated a 'helping skills' model that mirrored and ran in parallel with the action research cycle. The 'helping skills' model was derived from the work of Gerard Egan (1986) which is often referred to as the 'diamonds' model of counselling because the process involves a series of exploratory and focusing episodes in four stages of problem solving: forming a contract; inviting change; action planning; doing and evaluating. By grafting this model onto the existing action research model, teachers were encouraged to address the personal challenges of researching their classrooms by taking ownership of the problems they identified and taking responsibility for planning and implementing change strategies.

In order to support teachers through this process, all management and Support Service staff were trained in 'helping skills' which included attentive listening; goal setting; conflict management; action planning; needs identification and stress management. These training programmes were derived from a variety of counselling sources including the work of Bauber in establishing 'I–thou' relationships (Bauber, 1958) and the work of Carkhuff and Hamblin who focused on the importance of matching the needs, feelings and emotions of clients to the resources for change which are available (Carkhuff, 1969; Hamblin, 1974).

The work of the Support Services were based on a specific and highly challenging hypothesis about teacher development outlined in Saville (1985). Saville's study placed the teacher's own behaviours and psycho-dynamic capacities at the centre of professional development. It explicitly addressed professional development as an essentially personal form of development in which the role of the observer/researcher has a critical function. The hypothesis suggested that change in a teacher's role is related to an ability to self-monitor relationships between actions, situation and personality. Self-monitoring threatens a teacher's professional self-esteem and confidence.

The development of self-monitoring competence requires a teacher to move from the less threatening to the most threatening in the following sequence of tasks — becoming aware of our actions; becoming aware of how these actions shape the learning; evaluating the extent to which we are to blame for what happens in the learning situation. This process depends upon the teacher getting honest and accurate feedback on performance. The hypothesis focuses on the relationship between third party observation and the acceptance of feedback. Initially teachers find it difficult to create sufficient openness and trust to ensure honest feedback from their students; they often require the assistance of a third party researcher in order to get access to honest feedback.

The researchers' ability to support the development of teachers' self-awareness is related to the success in initiating and sustaining a non-evaluative relationship. The more researchers perceive teachers as partners in research rather than as people to be evaluated, the more researchers are able to foster self-awareness by reducing the level of teachers' anxiety. The more teachers come to value themselves in a research role, the greater their capacity to accept a loss of self-esteem caused by self-monitoring.

The Nottinghamshire approach to professional development was swept aside by the curriculum reforms of the Tory Party during the 1980s and 1990s. The imposition of a National Curriculum effectively removed responsibility from teachers for curriculum development. The savage reduction in levels of funding to local authorities resulted in the collapse of the Support Services. Many teachers in Nottinghamshire became suspicious that 'helping skills' were being increasingly used as a management tool and it is the case that the growth of 'managerialism' in the commercial sector during this period did incorporate techniques derived from clinical counselling as a means of controlling the workforce. The Nottinghamshire experiment had sought to formalize and institutionalize the practices of action research, of teacher ownership over curriculum development, of 'helping skills' as a means of empowering its teaching force. But, perhaps all is not lost.

The ideals of the Support Services have found root back in Fullan's faculty at the University of Toronto, which is now merged with the Ontario Institute for Studies in Education, in the work of David Booth and Gordon Wells (Wells, 1994; Booth and Wells, 1994).

Communities of Inquiry

Booth and Wells (1994) propose 'communities of inquiry' as the site of teacher-initiated research in which teachers are 'given . . . a greater voice in educational decision making and encouraging them to develop their own expertise in planning and enacting the curriculum through critical inquiry into their own practice both individually and in collaboration with their colleagues' (p. 24). According to Booth and Wells, those who participate in a 'community of inquiry' demonstrate similar dispositions to those identified with the early development of action research:

> These inquiring reflective teachers see themselves as intentional learners. They actively observe what is happening in their classrooms and are willing to revise their plans and expectations in the light of what

they observe. This gives them the confidence to adopt a critical attitude to outside experts, testing proposals against their own beliefs and experience. . . . (1994, p. 27)

The 'communities' that Booth and Wells are initiating take full advantage of technologies, which were not available in the pioneering days of action research, in order to communicate and disseminate their findings. The groups make extensive use of video, fax and e-mail as a means of overcoming distance. Booth and Wells also raise a critical question about their own position within these communities:

> . . . If educational renewal and development are to come from within schools, as teachers and administrators seek to identify those areas in need of improvement and, together, plan and carry out the necessary changes, what is the role of university-based researchers and teacher-educators? How can we model and demonstrate the inquiry approach in our own courses and in our research? (1994, p. 27)

Despite the close collaboration of university-based academics, such as Elliot and Stenhouse, in the early development of action research teachers remained sceptical about their involvement in classroom affairs. As Phil Taylor (1993) has shown, this scepticism within the profession over the motives and methods of university researchers has continued into the 1990s. Taylor suggests that the hostility has been based on enmity towards the dominant research relationships and paradigms that are associated with university-based research. Those methodologies that have tended to objectify and quantify teachers' work have tended to alienate teachers or to fail to answer the problems they consider to be urgent.

Taylor goes on to argue for a shift of paradigm towards ethnographic methodologies, as a way of acknowledging and valuing the professional expertise of teachers. Ethnography approaches classroom experience as a set of 'social activities in a social world' (Geertz, 1993, p. 14) which is best understood through the participants' own explanations. Viewed from this ethnographic angle, the Vauxhall group were asserting the primacy of 'local knowledge' in the theorizing of classroom experiences. Like Geertz, this group was trying to:

> . . . turn away from trying to explain social phenomena by weaving them into grand textures of cause and effect to trying to explain them by placing them in local frames of awareness . . . to exchange a set of well-charted difficulties for a set of largely uncharted ones. (1993, p. 6)

Booth and Wells are attempting to relocate professional practice in 'local frames of awareness' by introducing their student teachers into 'communities of inquiry' and by developing in students the skills and attitudes of 'reflective practice'. In part this has also been my response. My final year students are

trained in action research methodologies and undertake twenty days of fieldwork in the school in which they completed their final teaching practice. The
students identify a problem with their colleagues in school, they observe and
hypothesize and action plan and test and at the end of the year they provide
an evaluation for the school which forms the basis of a viva/presentation for
assessment. But is that enough?

I am now undertaking consultancy visits to local schools, returning to the
support practices I learnt in Nottinghamshire, using these schools for my own
research and encouraging teachers to operate similar projects. The schools I
go into are also the schools my students go into for their practice. Perhaps a
community will evolve that will bring serving and student teachers together,
supported by the resources of the university.

Exploring My Potential

In this chapter I have tried to identify the influences and experiences which
have shaped my role as a researcher. These influences have come from action-
oriented and classroom-situated forms of research which are based on professional partnership between practitioners. In this section I want to explore my
potential to continue to operate from within this matrix of influence. How can
I positively use my position in a university to help teachers make sense of their
classrooms?

My history as a researcher has given me extensive experience of working
within 'communities of inquiry' from a teacher's perspective. I understand the
pressures of time, the fear of failure and censure, the suspicion of external
research/change agents. My role as a university teacher who has no managerial influence or authority in schools makes it easier for me to establish the non-
judgmental relationship that is essential to classroom research. I find that teachers
are less worried about what I think and are less concerned to put on a special
show now that I am removed from the local education authority.

The university has encouraged me to develop my skills as a consultant
and workshop leader. The university also expects me to research and to theorize but because I am also hired to offer schools advice and to deliver inservice
events for teachers, this theorizing is always grounded in the realities of classroom life. I have to filter theory through the 'practicality ethic'.

Like most other professionals, my work is multi-dimensional. My contact
with schools is varied. I go in, privately, to research my own practice. I work
with friends in their classrooms. I offer advice to principals. I run courses and
workshops. I supervise students. I negotiate education courses with school-
based staff. I make advisory/consultancy visits under contract from the local
authority. The variety of this contact must provide an excellent basis for developing useful and usable research relationships.

I work within an institute of education and I am therefore involved in both
teacher education and teacher training. My history as a classroom researcher

provides me with both the methodology and the insights to help students prepare for the actuality of classroom life. The students expect to be provided with the skills of classroom management and with a set of behaviours that will ensure effective practice. My focus has to be action-oriented and based on identifying and reproducing successful classroom practices.

The demise of local education authority support for schools has created new opportunities for university staff to become more involved in advisory and support work within schools and to provide a site for teacher networks.

Towards a Definition of Role

In the light of my own experience and the potential offered by my present position, I have framed a number of questions in order to help me to define my role as a researcher and to fix my orientation towards the improvement of classroom performance. The lead questions will take me into a consideration of related issues and also illustrate the 'package' of related professional skills which are necessary to a partnership approach to implementing research-driven change in classrooms:

- How can I reclaim my own research history and make it the basis for learning/developing new methods and paradigms?
- How can I begin to stop seeing research as a form of job security and begin to use it as a tool for development?
- How can I build supportive, teacher valuing, research relationships with classroom teachers?
- How can I ensure that my research activity is responsive to the identified needs of classroom teachers?
- How can I empower teachers to be the subject of their own research rather than being the objects of mine?
- How can I shift from offering teachers the products of research to engaging them in the processes of research?
- What are the most appropriate forums and networks for classroom teachers to share the processes and outcomes of their research activity?
- Is it the university or the school which is the most appropriate site for training in research methods?
- Is academic accreditation a sufficient validation of classroom research?
- Do research discourses have a superior or more legitimate claim to validity when compared to other modes of representation? Is this a view shared by teachers?

Note

1   This model has gone through a number of revisions. For an overview of current action research paradigms see Taylor 1993.

References

ARGYRIS, C. and SCHÖN, D. (1974) *Theory in Practice: Increasing Professional Effectiveness*, San Francisco, Jossey-Bass.

BAUBER, M. (1958) *I and Thou*, New York, Scribner's.

BOOTH, D. and WELLS, G. (1994) 'Developing communities of inquiry', *Orbit*, **25**(4), pp. 23–8.

CARKHUFF, R. (1969) *Helping and Human Relations*, New York, Houghton and Mifflin.

EGAN, G. (1986) *The Skilled Helper*, Pacific Grove, Brooks Cole.

ELLIOT, J. and ADELMAN, C. (1973) 'Reflecting where the action is; The design of the Ford Teaching', *Project Education for Teaching*, **92**, pp. 8–20.

EYERS, S. and RICHMOND, J. (1982) 'Talk Workshop Group; An introductory paper', in TALK WORKSHOP GROUP (eds) *Becoming our Own Experts*, London, Talk Workshop Group.

FEYEREISEN, K., FIORNO, J. and NOWAK, A. (1970) *Supervision and Curriculum Renewal: A Systems Approach*, New York, Appleton.

FULLAN, M. (1982) *The Meaning of Educational Change*, Toronto, OISE press.

GEERTZ, C. (1993) *Local Knowledge*, London, Fontana.

HAMBLIN, D. (1974) *The Teacher and Counselling*, Oxford, Blackwell.

NOTTINGHAMSHIRE ADVISORY and INSPECTION SERVICE (1989) *Classroom Support Service Review*, West Bridgford, Nottingham County Council.

ROGERS, C. (1961) *On Becoming a Person*, New York, Houghton Mifflin.

SAVILLE, C. (1985) 'The role of the local education authority adviser.' Unpublished PhD Thesis, Durham University.

SCHÖN, D. (1986) *Educating the Reflective Practitioner*, San Francisco, Jossey Bass.

STENHOUSE, L. (1968) 'The Humanities Curriculum Project', *Journal of Curriculum Studies*, **1**, pp. 26–33.

STENHOUSE, L. (1971) 'The Humanities Curriculum Project: The Rationale', *Theory into Practice*, **10**, pp. 154–62.

TAYLOR, P. (1993) 'Research design in educational drama', *Drama*, **1**(2), pp. 16–21.

WELLS, G. (1994) *Changing Schools from Within: Creating Communities of Inquiry*, Toronto, OISE press.

11 Light the Lights! Research Writing to Communicate

Margot Ely

Did I hook you with my shameless theft of a phrase from Stephen Sondheim's lyrics? I surely hope so. In fact, in my wild and far-ranging dreams about this chapter, I once thought I'd title it 'Everything's Coming Up Roses'. But those bittersweet overtones didn't quite hit the mark.

So, let me tell you what these pages are about and what powered them. This chapter considers research writing as an important, nay essential, aspect of both doing the research and casting a wider net so that the research will be read. My assumption here is quite straightforward; there comes a time when we must reach out and communicate with others. Familiar to drama and arts educators?

This chapter is an expansion of a speech and article I created for the Collaborative Action Research Network in Great Britain. These spurred my work on a forthcoming book with my colleagues Margaret Anzul, Maryann Downing and Ruth Vinz (Falmer Press, forthcoming) about qualitative research writing.

I talk here to qualitative researchers at whatever stage of experience because the qualitative research umbrella best fits all of the research traditions, except one, discussed in this book. But even as I write these words, I feel I could make a good case that all research — including empirical in its various guises — would be immeasurably improved were we to do more 'lighting the lights' on writing.

I have no question that qualitative research is often exciting and powerful to the researcher in personal, near-to-home ways. It has, for example, charged and changed me as no other professional activity — and I've had my share. In fact, I'll go one step further: Unless doing qualitative research has essential, personal impact, there is no use going further. I am here talking to people who aim to go further. This is sorely needed. I'd love to learn how you, my reader, feel about that when you've read these pages.

My purpose in this chapter is to consider with you what it might mean to write a research report that is believable and interesting — a report that is worth reading. After all, no matter one's reason for doing research, writing is involved and almost always a final written document is part of that. The purposes for such a final report might vary — but they do exist, i.e., to help oneself make sense, gain direction, receive beginning support, receive continued support, and publish articles and books. (Note the order, please!) It seems essential to me that we consider more deeply how to be increasingly believable to ourselves and to others in that document.

When I planned this paper, I felt that it goes without too much saying that the shaping of a believable final product is part of a seamless whole research process — ethically conceived and carried out. But in my enthusiasm to speak of the final report, I might give the impression that it is or can be a separated event. Of course, it cannot be. Lynn Becker says it well:

> I think that the believability of my writing has been dependent on the trustworthiness of my method . . . If I had been careless or dishonest in my method, then this also would have been reflected in the report. To me, the writing of final reports is a process of 'going meta' that seems to be a built-in way for researchers to check and reassess their own data. For me, the best way to remain trustworthy as a writer and researcher is to write so I can distance myself from what I have already written and concluded.

I do what Lynn describes in my final writing. Parenthetically, I flinch some even at a separated picture of 'final writing' because I know that final writing begins the moment I put my first words to paper in my log.

I feel that the state for qualitative research has never been better. We are less in the thrall of mystique and more able and willing to make our process public. Qualitative research is coming out of the closet. However, in my experience, the spotlight on writing our stories, our reports, has lagged behind. I'll address some possible reasons for this as I go along.

There is now an expanding literature about how qualitative research may be written and assessed. I find the work of Atkinson (1990, 1992), Guba and Lincoln (1989), Van Maanen (1988), Wolcott (1990), and Zeller (1987) provocative and useful. But, overall, to me the literature on this topic seems a bit ponderous and overcomplex. Perhaps this is because writing believable research reports is also a complex matter?

What is more, in my opinion, certainly the literature on qualitative research is far less helpful than it must be about the writing of reports. It is almost as if the authors are saying, 'Well, you've done it! You've collected data — thought about them — acted on them — and so forth. Now you're on your own with the final report. Good luck.' This is for many researchers a time of tremendous stress. I believe that in order to escape the trauma of that point, many qualitative researchers do one of two things — freeze, or revert to what I call a headlong flight into more data collection. There seems to be a myth about that the more data one collects, the more chance one will have a meaningful and believable study. And I believe that this myth is promulgated by much qualitative literature.

At this point, I am ready — albeit with fearful heart — to say to people,

'Try not to burden yourself with more data than you need — with data over-load. Think. Write more about your data all the way through the research process. And study and consider all through the process how your report might be crafted. Do not wait until some arbitrary point called *final analysis and writing*.' It is through the continuous, recursive process of thinking/col-lecting/writing/reading — the same process by which we create our ongoing research strategies — that our search to discover the essence of what we are studying must mesh with our search to communicate these essences in worth-while ways.

In this chapter I'd like to highlight criteria about writing, about rhetoric of qualitative research reports, because I'm of a mind that these are the heart of the matter in creating a believable and effective piece. My plan is to provide some context for what is meant by rhetorical criteria — and in this I've been much inspired by Lincoln and Guba (1990). Then I'll share the writing of some people as they plan the forms of their research reports and how this links to believability and interest. Next, I'll provide a few examples of people's pre-sentations and their reflections on them. Last, I want to consider with you some personal ripples about the whole process.

In what follows I use quotations from my students and graduates with their permission, and I rather freely interchange the terms action, qualitative, and ethnographic research. I have quoted purposefully from the writings of people in a wide variety of professions because I am convinced that all of them speak directly to you as drama and arts educators and researchers. From this point on, there is mention of some rhetorical devices — first-person story, layering, vignettes. I hope these will become more clear as I proceed.

Rhetorical criteria talk to how the presentation is crafted by the writer so as to enlist the reader into entering the story, living it the way the researcher has experienced it, and understanding the grounds upon which the conclu-sions and inferences are based. The aim here is to communicate as richly, creatively, and bravely as possible the essence of the experience — to bring people to life (and this includes the researcher) — to build a story line and rhythm so compelling that there is no question but that readers choose to stay. No small tasks. But, happily, tasks many qualitative researchers find worth striving for. Usually, these rhetorical tasks are quite different from the dis-tanced, rote ways of writing that have been our lot in the past.

Perhaps because of this history, our heads may still be back in the very transmission-oriented experiences of reading and writing that were part of our early schooling. Laurie Diefenbach expressed the experiences of many fledg-ling and not so fledgling researchers when she wrote:

> Most of us 'learned to write' in an academic setting, but there were only certain acceptable forms one's writing could take in that set-ting . . . The only 'official' writing done during my school years was usually of the dead, lifeless, five-paragraph essay . . . I think many of the qualitative researchers in our support group were frightened at

first because they had become so used to the 'academic' style of writing
. . . the cramped, uncomfortable style that is usually expected.

In the words of Vivian Gussin Paley (1992), 'The natural connections between
storytelling and learning are often obscured in school.'

Rhetorical criteria assume that the researcher produces something in writing, however raw at first. This, in itself, is not always as easy as it sounds. For
Jill Schehr, school psychologist, it produced an insight about how the very act
of beginning her final writing engendered her to move toward creating a
believable report:

> Writing always seems so definitive to me. This may be one reason
> why I've had such a difficult time 'writing up' my experiences. How-
> ever, in response to reading Wolcott (1990) and *Circles Within Circles*
> (1991), I decided that perhaps I was dawdling and creating excuses.
> I never do, after all, think I've gotten enough information about
> people . . . life is so complex and reactions and feelings so diverse and
> fluid. I certainly did have some nascent understanding of the prison
> nursery community that I was part of, so why not begin to commit
> myself to paper? I forced myself to begin by giving myself permission
> this way: 'This is only an exercise. Write "freely"; this is just a rough
> draft.' I told myself that I was only committing myself temporarily and
> began to compare this writing exercise to the experience that I was
> having as a participant observer. In studying my prison nurseries, I
> observed, interviewed, analyzed, reflected . . . and learned, only to find
> out what I didn't know. In similar ways, 'writing up' this experience
> enabled me to further understand and question. This, in turn, gave me
> more faith that I would eventually produce a credible account.

The crafting and recrafting that are demanded by qualitative report writing highlight for all of us our concern with how language is used. Is what I
am writing clear? Does it avoid the overblown? Am I inviting my readers in
close, or am I setting a barrier? How do I use natural language? Does it avoid
generalization? How does it give voice to the people I studied? to me? Generally, is my report reader-friendly? For some, and I am among them, these
concerns with language use relate to the very core of how we wish to represent ourselves. And so we search to find a voice that is compatible with our
personal vision. Rebecca Mlynarczyk, professor of writing and English, writes:

> It has recently occurred to me that much of my dissertation is written
> in the same rather pedantic style of my male mentors — I'm thinking
> of people like Jerome Bruner, Howard Gardner, and John Van Maanen.
> Don't get me wrong. I've learned a lot from these folks. I like them.
> But do I want to write like them? In picking up Bruner's *Actual Minds,
> Possible Worlds*, I quickly spotted the type of language I have in mind.

Rebecca continues:

> This kind of writing does seem characteristic of a certain type of male
> academic writing that assumes a rather 'clear' and 'simple' cause-and-
> effect stance toward the universe. I have read so much of it that I can
> easily mimic it in my own voice that emerges in my own reflective
> writing . . . I find more compatible the personal and probably more
> 'feminine' use of such devices as 'I statements' and layered stories and
> plan to experiment with them. I am very impressed with the power of
> metaphor and am hoping to get away from my usual concreteness
> and literal-mindedness to get some of this power. There are no easy
> answers to complicated questions like the connection between gender
> and language. But I'm glad that these issues have surfaced in my
> consciousness. *I didn't wait 47 years to write a dissertation in some-
> body else's voice.*

Sharon Shelton seems assured that she and others can write with cohesion
and impact. Perhaps this is because she is a writer:

> So much academic writing seems unclear and disorganized to me, and
> I view with suspicion those writings that aren't coherent and power-
> ful. How can you trust a researcher whose narrative is muddled? If
> someone cannot recreate a situation, how can we trust their experi-
> ence of it?

But Sharon knows that actual re-creation is not possible. After all, putting
words on paper is not what happened in the classroom, on stage, on the
street, in a hospital. What then is the aim for writing? For what are we striving?
Rebecca grapples with this issue:

> It is important to be aware of the difference between 'facts' and 'truth.'
> The great masterpieces of literature, works like *Hamlet, Middlemarch,*
> or *Anna Karenina* are fictional, but they are also true to the psycho-
> logical processes of their characters and the societies in which these
> characters live. Their authors have captured the essence. In contrast,
> works of nonfiction are sometimes factually correct but not true in the
> sense of getting at the essence.

Rebecca continues:

> I certainly don't wish to suggest that ethnographers are budding fiction
> writers, that they can blithely ignore the facts in trying to get at the
> truth. Far from it! The ethnographer's job is to get at the essence of
> what is being studied through the most accurate observation and
> analysis possible. Facts should never be ignored, but they are just the
> beginning. Making meaning of the facts is the hard part.

I, Margot, like the distinction Rebecca makes between facts and truth, and I have found the search for 'essence' to be a goal many qualitative researchers seem to understand tacitly. Tyler (1987) uses a different term, that of 'evocation', to highlight this aim. Atkinson (1992, p. 51) talks of writing for 'readability' and 'representation'. He says, 'The ethnographer is undoubtedly an artisan who crafts narratives and representations.' But it is an illicit sleight of hand to refer to these products as 'fictions' just because they are 'made'. And the historical writer David McCullough (1992, p. 62) provides what I think is a splendid thought. In describing his aim for writing, he quotes the French artist Delacroix, who said, 'What I demand is accuracy for the sake of the imagination' (*The New York Times*, 12 August 1992).

The idea here seems to be similar. We are striving to present the heart of the matter as we have distilled it from our experiences, knowing all the while that creating exact copies is impossible, even if we wished to do so. *Oh how often my colleagues and I struggle with this idea and what it means in action.*

And now, in a linear fashion that is never true of the recursive process of crafting a research report, comes the question of form. What ways, devices, will I use to communicate the essence of the experience? What forms will best do justice to the people who were my participants? What data will I include so that my readers have sufficient bases to understand how I came to my insights and/or to help them come to their own? How do I create a partnership with my readers? How do I keep the thinking open rather than neatly closing it off? From whose point of view will I present the narrative — or better, how many points of view will communicate sufficiently the complexity of what I studied and learned? How can I come across as a person and as a person who is a researcher?

Jill Schehr, who previously shared her thoughts on getting started, writes now about a point in time somewhat further along:

> Tentatively, I have, somewhat grandiosely, decided to produce on an epic scale. The cinematic techniques I have employed in the field reflect my wish to describe the social culture of the prison nursery I am studying. Broad descriptive writing, from an observer's view, is how I intend to present this wide-angle camera 'pan.' I have tried it, and it seems just the brush I need to paint the backdrop. But I have also learned the value of 'layering' from another vantage point. For example, while describing the social context of the prison nursery, I can 'zoom' in on the individuals who comprise this community: inmate mothers and their babies. Closer still, I can write about a mother's experience, at times from her viewpoint, using knowledge gained from hours of observation and interview. Thus, what started out to be a distanced descriptive account now comes more to life with the use of these new writing techniques.
>
> As I became more familiar with my data, I also became more comfortable painting more 'close-up' vignettes. Thus, I painted backdrops

and zoomed in on vignettes . . . to my surprise, what evolved seemed 'alive' and true to my experience. I became proud of my ability to lift the 'doctoralese' censorship that had often encumbered my writing. This writing was much more personal than even I had been used to . . . and why not? This participant-observer experience had touched me way down deep. However, I still have a nagging feeling that my hard work will not be taken seriously . . . I am afraid that perhaps it is too passionately painted.

In the following excerpt, Ken Aigen, professor of music therapy, shares his thinking about form. It is clear that Ken wants both to do justice to his participants and to move beyond the usual forms of discourse of his profession:

Besides having a concern for the welfare of the study participants, my respect for them has led me to want to find a way for their voices to speak in whatever form my final report takes. How a Music Therapy group is experienced by the participants is not something that has been written about extensively, but it is something which is of ethical concern and professional interest. Yet this task is quite difficult in the group under discussion because these children have significant communication disorders. One way I have discovered to get around this difficulty is to employ narrative devices such as constructs, critical incidents, and themes.

First, in order to differentiate my research efforts from clinical documentation, I thought that it would be interesting to present the therapy group as a social system, including, of course, the therapists. In this way, I would move to a level of description and analysis not typically aspired to by clinicians themselves. I also became interested in communicating the evolution of the repertoire of the group because I saw the unfolding of group process in the themes underlying the various song activities. Currently, my orientation point has been looking at the ways in which spontaneity and improvisation characteristic of therapy are manifest in the group setting. However, I am still not absolutely certain that this will be the central theme around which I organize my report of findings. In fact, it may turn out that the final focus will emerge as I put the findings into some form to be shared with others.

Carol di Tosti, teacher and school administrator, did a study of a small number of 'Whistleblowers' on corruption in education. Here she is talking about one superintendent of schools. She calls him 'my superintendent'. He went so far as to wear a wire at meetings to record for authorities what was happening:

During the interviews, reading through transcripts, viewing the commission reports, I found the experiences of my superintendent to be fascinating, mythic, compelling. My superintendent feels very strongly about the failure of American public school education to overturn what he deems to be the murdering of children every day in our schools. He is an impassioned man. He has, as I discovered both in interviews and through other accounts, devoted his life to serving children. His experiences of thwarting corruption in his district testify to the magnitude of his desire to thwart a system that he now believes refuses to reform itself toward producing quality life and learning. Hampered, encouraged, stirred, and burdened with my insights, I considered: Here is drama; here is a life of impact. Do I use forms which capture this life to make it vivid, vibrant, real? Or do I do what my various teachers have 'taught me so well?' 'Just do it and get it over with?' I made my decision; I had to be just to my superintendent. I had to be just and ethical to myself. I was compelled by conscience, thank God, compelled by myself and my support group to select the forms, the genres of revelation. Thus, I wrote stories, poems, acts of a longer play. As I began, I became more involved in the understanding that not only must I strive for accuracy of content, the spirit and flavor of my superintendent's drama, I must be ever vigilant about how I unfolded those dramas. To him, his life and actions held great meaning. The genres I selected should also signify and relate this meaning; the fusion of form and content should be complete.

It is probably clear by now that in my, Margot's, qualitative research work, I lean toward writing a report in a variety of forms. There are differing opinions about that. Sticking to one form has worked well for many researchers. For example, Oscar Lewis's books in firsthand accounts have the compelling nature of fine novels to me. I am of the mind, however, that combinations of rhetorical devices function in the service of the report in specific ways. The combinations may consist of, for example, vignettes, constructs, themes, first-person accounts, layered stories, plays, poetry, 'autobiography', biographical data, allegories, diaries, parodies, songs, picture strips and their narratives, direct quotes, multivoice accounts, collage (Atkinson, 1992, talks of bricolage and pastiche), and, of course the researchers' own stories, musings, and, very important, the connecting narrative. The devices depend heavily on figures of speech — metaphor, synecdoche — that serve as tools for understanding, thinking, and feeling about the study. For me, such narrative combinations present a fairer feel of the complexities we study, better help communicate multiple realities, and more easily draw the readers in near, as well as provide distance when distance is desirable. What is more, different rhetorical forms can signal that different jobs are asked of the reader.

I am not alone in this, of course. Many qualitative researchers have come to conclude that the sole use of prescribed narrative devices or those that have worked well up to now is to reduce what we can relate and close off the possibility that our readers can create their own alternative insights. What I am suggesting is that qualitative researchers open up to the possibility of integrating a variety of narrative devices, genres, and voices in the service of the report. This view of presentation counters the myth that there is 'one correct way' to write qualitative research reports.

And yet I have often wondered why such an obviously sensible (to me) view about writing in useful and interesting forms would find so much disapproval with so many academics and other professionals — including arts and drama educators. Perhaps it is because many of us like to hold onto the known, the tried: 'If it was good enough for me, it must be good enough for my students.' Perhaps it is because some people have formed a deep distrust of interesting writing: 'If it is interesting, how can it be scholarly?' Perhaps it is because many of us choose not to butt heads against an established orthodoxy that oftentimes has its way anyhow.

Be that as it may, the shapes and content of research presentation must not be chosen primarily to amuse, shock, or entertain, although they often do that. Certainly, they must not be chosen to manipulate. The overriding aim must be to communicate with people in order to involve them in living our research experiences and in thinking about them.

Generalizations about forms don't hold. So, while I do not hesitate to communicate my opinion about multiple forms, I also watch carefully not to force it. In the final analysis, decisions about form must be based on what seems to the researcher-writer to be most honorable in telling the story. Thus, it is a decision about quality, not quantity of form.

In order to bring this presentation more to life, it seems fitting to share several rhetorical devices created by researchers. I offer them with the proviso that you understand they are lifted out of context; they are not the entire research report.

Lynn Becker studied life in one kindergarten. Here, as some small context for her 'Playlet in Two Voices', a section of which follows, are two of her field log entries. On 11 October, she wrote:

> I decide to spend the next few minutes at the table where Walter has been playing with the dominoes. When I return to that table, Walter is sitting next to another boy, and they are both working on puzzles. Walter is telling the other boy (William) that he will be his friend and that William won't have to worry about not having any friends in the classroom. As Walter is saying this, William silently works on his puzzle. Sue, the teacher, comes over and separates the boys to different tables.

On 8 November, she wrote:

> At one point, she (Sue) tells Walter, who is sitting on a chair, that he didn't put his jacket away properly and that he should go back and fix it. Walter says, 'Oh yeah. That's right,' and rushes back to his cubby to pick up his jacket. As he starts to walk back to his chair, he says,

'May I?' and Sue cuts him off and says, 'No, you may not get a mat. Now sit down quietly.' Walter has a pained expression on his face, and he looks as if he is about to cry. He sits down at the table and says, 'I want to lie down for my nap.'

And now, a piece of Lynn's 'Playlet in Two Voices — Kindergarten'. Please read it aloud. See what it brings.

A Playlet in Two Voices:
Kindergarten

[*Walter's voice is inferred by the researcher, Lynn Becker*]

Walter: It's nap time, and I'm so glad Miss Harris let me have a mat today. Last week I was so tired, and all I wanted to do was lie down and rest before snack time.

Teacher: I'm going to put on a record that I know all of you will really like. It's from Peter Pan.

Walter: My favorite Peter Pan song. I can fly! I love this song. I have to sit up to hear this. I want so much to sing along with this.

Teacher: Close your eyes and listen carefully. Relax every part of your bodies.

Walter: I want so much to sing along with this. I have to sit up.

Teacher: Keep your bodies still. Relax your toes, and your feet, and your legs.

Walter: I can fly! I can fly!

Teacher: Keep still now.

Walter: I'm superman!

Teacher: Your mouths shouldn't be moving.

Walter: I have to take my sweater off. I'm so warm now.

Teacher: Relax your stomachs and your arms.

Walter: I'll just hold it in my lap and she won't care.

Teacher: You should be wearing that.

Walter: I wish I could really fly like superman.

Teacher: Keep your bodies still and lie down while you listen to the music.

Walter: I can't sit still anymore. I want to fly out of this room.

Teacher: Put it on now. You just got over being sick.

Walter: Maybe I could turn my sweater into a great cape.

Teacher: *NOW* Walter!

Lynn wrote the following reflections on the playlet:

I saw this particular piece of writing as more than an attempt to express classroom life from Walter's point of view. It was my attempt to understand how Walter thinks and to experience something of his struggle for a sense of power and voice in this environment. For me this kind of writing is not 'frills' in qualitative research. It seems to be an important and necessary part. 'Becoming the other' or using the first-person 'I' helps me get beyond the limits of being in the 'researcher' mode. This kind of writing seems to be more honest in some ways than writing that aims to be 'objective.'

Sharon Shelton crafted several stories and poems from her log data as part of her report about experiences in a third-grade classroom. Here is a piece of Sharon's first-person story about Amanda, a third-grader. This story might be considered a contextual ground for the poem that follows it. The classroom is labelled 'whole language'. It is the showpiece of the school district.

No A for Amanda

Mmm. Popcorn! I am so hungry. It's almost lunchtime, and I only had a bao, a Chinese bun, for breakfast. I can smell that popcorn. I want to eat it right now. But first we have to make our names and glue popcorn on them. Or make popcorn people. I know! I'll do both. Ms. Thompson will be so happy when she sees I'm doing both.

I wish my hair were blonde instead of straight and black. I'm glad my pencils are sharp. I'll draw my letters as carefully as I can. I am going very slowly on the sides of my A to make them touch each other at the top. A for Amanda. I don't want my lines to wobble. Ms. Thompson doesn't like wobbly lines.

Mimi is saying she's writing her name. I'll bet she doesn't draw a picture, too, though. I like Mimi's shoes. They look like grown-ups' shoes. I wish I had clothes like Mimi, but my mother always says we wear the same clothes as long as we can. She always says, 'Three years new, three years old, three years patched.'

Ms. Thompson is stopping at our desk! She is dressed in a purple top and pink pants. Pink is my favorite color in the whole wide world. Ms. Thompson looks so pretty today. She's picking up my picture! What's happening, though? She's turning it over. Why is she turning it over? She's walking away. What is she saying? What does she mean, 'Start over. Too small?' Doesn't she see my neat lines? Doesn't she know I am going to draw a girl, too?

Don't cry. I mustn't cry. Good girls don't cry in class. Start over. Just start over. Remember to make my A bigger. Remember to make my lines straight. Remember to be quiet. Always remember to be quiet.

Here is Sharon's poem that follows 'No A for Amanda'.

Amanda 1992

It feels like 1949
To me
Watching you there,

Bright sparrow eyes
Your wings folded,
Cold,
No singing.

You pick at crumbs
Of learning
Flung unthinking,
Unseeing.
Your mind flitting
Through
Other people's stories,
Other people's songs.

I was once a fledgling,
Caged in silence,
Frozen by obligation,
Hungering for spring,
Longing to take wing,
Crying, dying to sing.

Sharon wrote:

> I was happy with the poem I wrote about Amanda, comparing her to
> a bird who could not yet sing or fly. I identified with Amanda, and
> expressed great hope for her through my poem. I feel that it was
> coherent and had unity and clarity. I think that the poem captures the
> essence of the story, but I am pretty sure that the order and com-
> bination — story followed by poem — are crucial at getting at the
> meaning of Amanda's experience. Neither my story nor the poem
> alone would do that for me.

It seems it is also important to mention here that not all classroom research pieces have been as sad as the two I shared. Indeed, in her large report,
Sharon did an interesting and necessary job: she presented a sympathetic story
from the point of view of this teacher, a story that highlighted the constraints
under which she felt she worked. Also, of course, many people document
victories . . . in process and grand. The bottom line is that qualitative research
holds an enlarging mirror up to our imperfections, our humanity. To accept
this and to go on to do something about it — only to reach another stage of
imperfection — seems the key for me. What is sure is that studying oneself
usually (dare I say always?), carries with it some discomfort as well as heightened
self-awareness. For example, Rebecca writes:

> And yet I continue to struggle with my desire for control. Now, in the
> spring, as I transcribe the last audiotape, I hear my own voice far more

than anyone else's. When I begin to worry about whether the students will pass the Writing Assignment Test, I 'control' my own panic by trying to do everything I can to help them although I know deep down that they need to learn to help themselves.

As the vignettes from my life as a teacher reveal, some themes have remained relatively constant: an interest in and respect for the students as individuals and as writers, a fascination with the processes involved in teaching and learning, a tendency to reflect on my practice and to attempt to change. But also running through these vignettes, almost like a litany, is my struggle with the issue of control. There seems to be an ongoing conflict between my desire to maintain control as a teacher and my understanding that, in the final analysis, only the students can control their learning.

Judy Walenta, a nurse, did her research about Sonny, a young adult labelled autistic. In her four-person layered story of one event, Judy approached what might be called a Rashomon-like rhetorical presentation. She reflects on the experience:

The pieces which I wrote in 'One Day in the Park' are impressionist in nature. My pieces are 'impressions' of a scene or, in the case of Sonny's story, a life seen through someone else's eyes, with the purpose of inviting the reader into another reality. The hope is that the reader will make her/his own observations about the scene and individual being presented and draw his/her own conclusions. I choose to present my layered story through the eyes of four people in order to help me get a better look at what might have happened on that day.

The story concerned an event that took place when Sonny was in the park with some counselors and some other residents from his group home. I had concluded earlier that he had had a seizure from the way the counselors told the story, [but] Sonny's mother disagreed and felt that the counselors were just covering up for negligent acts on their part. Sonny's story — the construct — seemed important to present. He is the silent one who speaks for himself rarely and then in one- or two-word messages. I needed to see it from Sonny's point of view, from his mom's, and from the perspective of two counselors — one who saw the event and one who was with him afterwards. I did not write the story to entertain, but as an exercise in experiencing someone else's point of view.

Michelle Haddad studied a principal on the job. Following are some pieces from what I call a construct — her introductory picture of Marty, the principal. Much of what she includes are Marty's own words, edited and written around to present a whole 'photograph':

'I'm Not a Rebel, Just a Maverick'

It's been said that I don't care about the outside educational bureaucracy. That's not so. I don't consider people outside the school the enemy; they're just secondary. They are not bad people trying to destroy us. It's not a fight; it's just that, you know, they think they need something, and it's important to them.

Listen, I do what is my priority, which is the internal. I recognize responsibility for external authority as well because you can't just say, 'I'm not going to do anything they want or need.' They have their needs, too, and they have their purposes, but it's basically unimportant. And, of course, the other part of the responsibility that I have is I can't punish my children or my teachers by not doing what the outside authorities say they need to do in order to go on to high school. We do what the children need, and everyone else be damned. There are rules and regulations for everything, and those rules and regulations are sort of parameters. You try to the extent possible, and where it makes sense, to stay within them. But I break rules and regulations continuously.

I don't mean to say I'm always right, or that the system is always wrong, but sometimes the system makes mistakes. Take, for example, the Iraq war. We were mandated to have shelter drills. Now, we haven't had shelter drills since World War II. They said you should have the children duck under the desks. And I said no, because the kids are scared as it is that some of these Scuds might be here. They don't understand a distance of 8,000 miles away. This is wrong. They said, 'Oh, no, no, you've got to have it.' The answer was, I never had the drills. I got back a note saying, 'You have to have shelter drills.' I just didn't respond to it. I just ignored it, that's all.

Most principals did it, though. You know, it's easier not to disobey. It's easier just to do it. The answer is, you pick your battles. Let me put it this way: I'm really going around the side. I'm flanking them. Because, if you butt them, then they're going to fight you back. And then they have the authority to say, 'You're not meeting your mandated needs,' or whatever it is. So I say, 'Okay, I understand. Okay, I'll see you next year.'

Yeah, I love beating the system, because the system stinks. It really does. And one other thing. It's lovely to have tenure.

Shelly reflects about this sort of form:

Writing about Marty in first person was and still is very difficult. I had a lot of trouble with even daring to attempt to write in first person, believing that to make a statement in Marty's voice would be presumptuous. What right did I have to assume that I could speak for Marty? My study group convinced me to take the plunge. I felt like I was holding my breath and saying to myself: One, two, three, jump! On an intellectual level, I thoroughly agree that everything is subjective, relative to interpretation, and that writing in first person is no more presumptuous than writing in third person. But it still is hard. There must be something in our conditioning as academic writers that triggers a 'dare not tread' feeling about writing that is not impersonal.

Next is an example of what I label 'a snapshot'. This one is a brief, first-person, historical picture written by Elizabeth Merrick about Marisol, a Black unwed teenager in a culture of poverty who is pregnant and who chooses to have her baby.

Marisol

You want to hear about my life? Well, I wasn't raised by my mom — my real mom. When I was little, I lived with my grandmother's friend. They took me in when I was young . . . real young . . . when I was born. My mother didn't want me. My grandmother couldn't take care of me because she was taking care of my other cousins, so my grandmother's friend took care of me. Understand?

I lived with them from then until I was about four and my mother came back to town. Who knows where she'd been. I always remember that day she came and got me. You gotta understand I was just four years old. The people I was living with never told me that they weren't my mother and father so I always thought they were and their sons were my brothers. They never told me for fear it would hurt me.

And when she came and got me, I was crying. I always remember that day because it was hard. This lady coming in and she was like 'I'm your mother' and all this foolishness. And I was screaming, 'No! No, you're not!'

So she took me from then on until I was seven. And she used to lock me in the house by myself. I had to wash my own clothes and cook my own food and stuff. When I got to be like 10 or 11, I knew how to ride the trains by myself and so I ran away from my mother and went back to the people who raised me.

At times, the use of different voices and the interchange of forms is so subtle that the artistry slides past unless we stop for a while and look. Here is a seemingly deceptively simple paragraph from Philip Taylor's work about drama and action research in a seventh-grade social studies classroom:

'While we're doing the glitter,' Susan dictated to Madelene, 'Joyce steps into the time machine'. Susan was describing how she felt her group's film should begin. This film was going to recreate the journey back to Boston through the eyes of Joyce, a time-traveler. 'No, that would take too long,' Madelene insisted, 'the camera will pick up Joyce preparing.' The problem was, it seemed, would there be sufficient glitter, a prop used to suggest a flashback, to enable Joyce to set up for the next scene? Susan clearly thought there would be.

In this paragraph Philip braids his participants' voices with his own. Look at the information this small paragraph holds. We are privy to Susan and Madelene's process. We hear their verbal interactions. We learn what they are doing. We are witness to their negotiation/disagreement. Philip's narrative sets the job at hand into a broader context. Toward the end of the paragraph he moves from having been a tour guide to being an analyzer, all the while talking to his readers.

Some narrative devices are very brief and very powerful. See the change of type on page 172, lines 14–15, to denote that I am talking to what I had just written. I am having a conversation with myself. This device can just as well be used to talk to what others write. Another brief device was highlighted by a colleague who spoke of a study she came across — *Worlds of Pain* — in which Lillian Rubin, sociologist, psychologist, and activist, explores the experience of blue collar families. My colleague found that she could not put it down, even though, as she read, she almost did not want to know that much. Rubin culled statements from her many hours of interviews with each family. After each statement, she identified the speakers:

- Woman, aged 28, eleven years married, 4 children
- Man, aged 32, twelve years married, 3 children

By this simple form, she kept the quoted words bound to the worlds from which they came, and she hammered home to me how young these couples were and how soon burdened. And I am reminded once again that I learn the most about writing qualitative research reports by reading the great ethnographers — Wolcott, Mead, Steedman, Paley, Spradley, Benedict.

It is through story — through narrative of all sorts — that we understand ourselves and our worlds. Barbara Hardy has said that narrative is:

> . . . a primary act of the mind. [There is an] inner and outer storytelling that plays a major role in our sleeping and waking lives . . . for we dream in narrative, daydream in narrative, remember, anticipate, hope, despair, believe, doubt, plan, revise, criticize, construct, gossip, learn, hate, and love by narrative. In order really to live, we make up stories about ourselves and others, about the personal as well as the social past and future. (in Meek, 1978, p. 12)

My narrative represents who I am as Margot — what and who I value — what and who I disdain. It helps me to set events into time and context and links me to others. My writing allows me to consider and reconsider my actions. It is never neutral, even when I try to make it look that way. It is selective.

I cannot 'get' or write everything. My writing always sends personal, political, and/or ethical messages even if I am not consciously aware of them. Because of this, what and how I write become crucial to me as a qualitative researcher and must be attended to. Awesome!

But we are in a wonderful position because of the match between certain basic assumptions that power both qualitative research and the transactional theory of language — in this case, that theory about reading, writing, and literature. It is not strange to either field to believe that what we know we construct contextually, that it is partial, multifaceted, and shifting. We celebrate our subjectivity because that is all there is; yet we care deeply to link with others, to reach for binding, in-process understandings. As writers of qualitative research reports, this makes it imperative to share our stances and processes in responsible ways. After all, for our readers what we write is the 'field' that we have studied. The 'better' we write, the 'better' we may help people to understand and assess those pieces we saw as important. There is no escape. Our readers will not read our minds, even if we are our own readers. They will read our texts, our writing. This alone demands that we face head on some of our own ways of seeing the world.

Jill does what I believe to be a splendid job in writing about just some of the issues she found she needed to face in order to produce a credible report:

> Apart from my professional experience, there are personal experiences which may often serve to distort my perceptions. I am a mother who is raising two children. In some ways, this humbling experience has made me more sensitive to the complexities of the job of mothering, and counteracts my tendency as a clinician to be unsympathetic to parents (especially when encountering abuse and neglect). But, as a mother, I have slowly developed a personal philosophy of parenting and constantly have to guard against its intrusion into my observing and writing about other mothers.
>
> The majority of the mothers in the nursery, and general prison population, are women of color. Poverty and deprivation are often the common melody running through their stories. I have been raised in a different cultural environment. I am now immersed in a social culture with rules and customs that are diverse and, at times, very new to me. It is a challenge for me to try to 'understand' in so foreign a culture, and yet there are many commonalities that we share as women and mothers. As a psychologist, I have to consider how these different cultural aspects influence what I observe . . . guarding against relying on theory for understanding. As a mother, I have to guard against judging the quality of other mothering which I may not understand as it stems from different cultural practice.
>
> Finally, I am working with women who are behind bars. Some of the women speak openly about their crimes, while others profess their innocence. Although they have been judged and stripped of their

freedom, they have been allowed to raise their babies for one year. As a mother, I have strong emotional reactions to each inmate mother who is forced to send her baby away. As a citizen, I have a response to antisocial behavior. As a woman, I am aware of the victimization some women, especially from minority groups, experience in their relationships and in their treatment by authority. It is my job to listen to their stories, remaining aware of how my biases may interfere with a new way of understanding and writing about what I observe and experience. I have confidence that my personal and professional philosophy of looking within and without at the same time will keep me 'on my feet.' It is in this area of transition between self and other that my stance as a researcher continues to evolve.

Witherell and Noddings (1991, p. 1) point to the power of story — of rhetoric — to engage us in more than getting the facts when they say that 'story fabric offers us images, myths, and metaphors that are *morally resonant* and contribute both to our knowing and *our* being known' (p. 1). Witherell and Noddings bring me full circle. The process of writing — of striving to meet rhetorical criteria in a qualitative research report — often has personal consequences equal to or more important than producing the report itself. I have shared with you Sharon's coming to an expanded and less negatively stereotyped picture of the teachers she studied, Rebecca's conscious struggle to understand and harness her own control as a teacher, and Carole's fight to conquer her fear to take writing risks (she calls it cowardice; I do not). There are so many other vignettes about the personal consequences, the ripples from writing, but I would like to bring only one more to your attention. Here, Judy grapples with what she calls the 'White Knight Syndrome'. See also how she uses metaphors:

> With my helper/healer background, I think the greatest danger to my detachment was the temptation to cast myself in the role of savior for Sonny, or even for all of the residents in the group home. I received the most assistance in my attempts to avoid this approach by some of the participants themselves! I was surrounded by images of saviors: parents, direct care workers, group home administrators, even teachers. Several of these individuals saw themselves as the only one or ones who truly understood Sonny and other people labelled autistic. Staff defended the residents against parents, parents against staff. Administrators blamed the parents and even the school for everything that went wrong. The only group that appeared to attempt some neutrality was the teachers, although I did not have sufficient contact with them to verify this perception.
>
> Through all of this, I constantly worked on seeing and writing about a variety of points of view. Frequently, when I felt myself getting up on my high white charger and grabbing a lance, I consciously slowed

down to a trot and initiated a mental dialogue with all parties concerned. This did not come naturally and easily at first and still requires constant effort. But it has been very rewarding. I am now much quicker to realize the white knight syndrome and to remedy it. All that armor is just too heavy, too confining.

When all is said and done, to me the greatest value of working toward a believable and effective report lies in its affirmation of the self — the researcher — as a central, ethical, powerful, flexible, fallible, learning human being.

Finally, as what I consider a particularly apt capstone to this chapter, I offer you a quotation by Salman Rushdie (1991, p. 88) — a statement about the importance of self, the importance of self in writing:

'Our lives teach us who we are.' I have learned the hard way that when you permit anyone else's description of reality to supplant your own — and such descriptions have been raining down on me, from security advisors, governments, journalists, Archbishops, friends, enemies, mullahs — then you might as well be dead. Obviously, a rigid, blinkered absolutist world view is the easiest to keep hold of, whereas the fluid, uncertain, metamorphic picture I've always carried about is rather more vulnerable. Yet I must cling with all my might to my own soul; must hold on to its mischievous, iconoclastic, out-of-step clown instincts, no matter how great the storm. And if that plunges me into contradiction and paradox, so be it; I've lived in that messy ocean all my life. I've fished in it for my art. . . . It is the sea by which I was born, and which I carry within me wherever I go.

Acknowledgment

My deep appreciation to these colleagues: Ken Aigen, Margaret Anzul, Lynn Becker, Laurie Diefenbach, Carol di Tosti, Maryann Downing, Michelle Haddad, Rita Kopf, Elizabeth Merrick, Rebecca Mlynarczyk, Jill Schehr, Sharon Shelton, Philip Taylor, Judy Walenta.

References

ATKINSON, P. (1990) *The Ethnographic Imagination: Textual Construction of Reality*, London, Routledge.

ATKINSON, P. (1992) *Understanding Ethnographic Texts*, Newbury Park, Sage.

ELY, M., ANZUL, M., DOWNING, M. and VINZ, R. (forthcoming) *Qualitative Research Writing: Crystal Reflections*, London, Falmer Press.

ELY, M., ANZUL, M., FRIEDMAN, T., GARNER, D. and McCORMACK, A. (1991) *Doing Qualitative Research: Circles within Circles*, London, Falmer Press.

GUBA, E. and LINCOLN, Y. (1989) *Fourth Generation Evaluation*, Newbury Park, Sage.

HARDY, B. (1978) 'Narrative as a primary act of the mind,' in MEEK, M., WARLOW, A. and BARTON, G. (eds) *The Cool Web: Patterns of Children's Reading*, New York, Atheneum.

LINCOLN, Y. and GUBA, E. (1990) 'Judging the quality of case study reports', *International Journal of Qualitative Studies in Education*, **3**, pp. 53–9.

McCULLOUGH, D. (1992) 'Thoughts on writing history', *The New York Times*, 12 August, p. 62.

PALEY, V.G. (1992) 'You can't say you can't play: Free choice, friendship, and fairness among young children.' Address delivered at the Eleventh International Human Science Research Conference, Rochester, Oakland University.

RUSHDIE, S. (1991) 'Interview with Salman Rushdie', *The New York Times*, 12 December, p. 88.

TYLER, S.A. (1987) *The Unspeakable: Discourse, Dialogue, and Rhetoric in the Postmodern World*, Madison, University of Wisconsin Press.

VAN MAANEN, J. (1988) *Tales of the Field: On Writing Ethnography*, Chicago, University of Chicago Press.

WITHERELL, C. and NODDINGS, N. (eds) (1991) *Stories Lives Tell: Narrative and Dialogue in Education*, New York, Teachers College Press.

WOLCOTT, H. (1990) *Writing Up Qualitative Research*, Newbury Park, Sage.

ZELLER, N. (1987) 'A rhetoric for naturalistic inquiry.' Unpublished doctoral dissertation, Bloomington, Indiana University.

Afterword: Drama as Research

Gavin Bolton

At the 1995 Institute of Drama Education Research held at Griffith University, interest was expressed by not a few delegates in the possibility of seeing drama itself as an investigatory tool, and one or two leaders introduced some exploratory exercises that required us to role-play. It is not the place here to give full account of these experiments, but they raised issues of general interest to research in drama. In this chapter I would like to discuss some of those issues.

There seems to have been three broad assumptions. The first, the firmest link to traditional research, was that dramatic representation, usually some form of role-play, could be used as part of orthodox research. The second was that the reflective processes espoused by certain kinds of action research are critical to process drama. The third was that classroom drama practice can empower students to investigate a problem or issue as researchers. I will discuss each of these under separate headings. In order to do so I may occasionally rely on brief references to draft research papers and exercises pertaining to the 1995 Institute. These may cause some passing frustration to people who were not there, but they raise matters that go well beyond the narrow perspective of that institute.

The Use of Role-play in Research

Since Maier, Solem and Maier (1956, p. 2) laid out the benefits of role-play and guidelines for its usage in their handbook on role-play technique, its efficacy in 'reproducing the conditions of a life situation' has persuaded a minority of researchers to employ role-play as part of their research design. Although it seemed sufficiently established as a research methodology for Cohen and Manion (1980) to give it a separate chapter in their account of research methods, in a publication of the same period by Hamilton, Jenkins, King, MacDonald and Parlett (1977) role-play does not get a mention anywhere within its pages.

The history of its usage is not without notoriety, derived from its more spectacular cases. For example, for a year in a sustained act of infiltration and deception, Frank Coffield (Patrick, 1973) role-played a Glasgow gang member in order to record and analyse how such a city-gang functions. Contrasted with this blatantly unethical form of inquiry is an experiment conducted without any attempt to deceive anyone, but which turned out to have disastrous consequences for the human guinea-pigs who were required to role-play being a prisoner or a warder in a mock prison set-up.[1] It was intended that these roles should be sustained (harassment by the guards was to be permitted, but no physical abuse) for up to fourteen days, but such was the degree of stress felt by the prisoners that the experiment was hurriedly terminated by the sixth day, two severely disturbed participants having been released from the game on the fourth day. The disregard of ethical standards in this second experiment derived not from deception but from the tacit permission that role-playing a power position gives. The researchers foresaw the dangers of physical abuse — and amended the rules accordingly — but failed to anticipate the relish with which the guards would employ psychological abuse, even when they could perceive (or perhaps *especially* when they could perceive) the genuine discomfort of their victims.

Not only can the use of role-play in these kinds of circumstances appear to give permission to the participants to behave outside their normal moral constraints, there is also a tacit assumption that the person in charge of organizing the game is taking on ultimate responsibility for what might happen. Thus the participants need not see themselves as responsible beings; they are to be *relieved* of that tiresome burden and can enjoy their temporary release from it — it's only a game and, what's more, someone else has asked us to play it.

But this apparent release from responsibility rarely (the exceptions may include young children or card-sharpers!) extends to breaking the rules of the game. There is something culturally sacrosanct about protecting the rules. Not to play the game may be to invite loss of face. Researchers interested in using role-play may need to give attention to this by delineating participant goals and delimiting strategies. It may be necessary, for instance, to reconstruct the responsibility displaced by the setting up of the game. It no doubt would have led to a very different prison experiment if the warders had been told that, 'You have been nominated for promotion within the prison service on the grounds of your ability to combine authority and respect in your dealings with prisoners.'

The need for some qualifying measure of this kind does not just apply to large-scale research experiments. Even the most informal game can slide into less than responsible behaviour — as some of us at the Griffith University Institute found out! It was an amusing, light-hearted example of the use of role-play to draw attention to some of the problems of research. In groups of two to four people we were invited to invent a piece of research that required us (in our fictional roles as researchers) to use a methodology with which we were unfamiliar. Having given some thought to planning it, we had to submit it orally to some funding authority — and we were given a bad time! We could very well have been prisoners to our funding committee's brutal warders. For they, quite legitimately within the rules of the game, played their roles as arrogant bastards, out to demolish our proposal and us with it. Fortunately, it only lasted a few minutes. Now, no doubt, if the leader who had set up the exercise had intended a more serious investigation into presenting a research project to a funding body she would have written in a 'Give them a chance to present their case' clause into the rules. Indeed, when it became our turn to play the 'Come in; do sit down' roles, you can imagine, after our bitter experience, how we leaned over backwards to be the perfect listeners!

Role-play is indeed a slippery device. Because of its improvisational quality, what starts along one pre-chosen route can slide imperceptibly onto a different track. This is especially true when the leader wants his group to replicate some specifiable context — an attempt to examine, through simulated roles, for example, reception procedures in a hospital outpatients' department can become overtaken by creative interactions (confrontations, where status is involved) from the role-players. This is not entirely a matter of indiscipline from the participants. It is in the nature of dramatic invention that it readily becomes multi-layered and the social dimension is likely to take over. In our research institute an attempt to set up a discussion by employees (in role) on the problem of banning smoking in the work premises wandered off target in some groups because the relationship between employees became of overriding interest.

That the social dimension can take over can actually strengthen some research. Margaret Donaldson (1978) ably demonstrated the deficiency of Piaget's (1956) experiment in which he measures a child's ability to decentre by changing the relative positions of a house on a mountain side and asking the child to describe whether the house could be seen by someone placed the other side of the mountain. In her experiment, Donaldson adopted an *as if* hypothesis, something like, 'If I were a policeman looking for a naughty boy, could I see him if he was there and I stood here? Can you hide the naughty boy so that the policeman (and then two policemen) can't see him?' Donaldson discovered that given this make-believe invention, children of a younger age group than that designated by Piaget, were capable of decentring.

Perhaps the most controllable dramatic behaviour in research occurs when a prepared video performance by the research team or by uninvolved others is shown to the research target group, with a view to recording their reactions. For instance, Louis Cohen of Loughborough University, England, recently showed a series of very brief acted episodes (the scripts had been devised and acted by secondary theatre arts students) of teacher/pupil interaction, some of which demonstrated racial prejudice. The purpose of Cohen's research (to be completed) is to assess the extent to which student-teachers watching these tapes were (a) aware of, and (b) disturbed by the examples of prejudice.

The Kinship of Drama with Reflective Thinking in Research

Phil Taylor (1992, in press) and Peter Millward (1988) both based their doctoral investigations on the researcher's own practice. Whereas Millward's massive study draws on the audio tape and transcript and analyses every word of the drama-making with a view to discovering how 'people accomplish the dramatic presentation of experience', Taylor's purpose is an indepth study of the teacher's (i.e., his own) pedagogic processes, particularly of those moments 'where uncertainties, dilemmas or conflicts were felt' (1995a, p. 34). Both examples of qualitative research, both involving teacher-in-role, Millward's might be described as a case study from which conclusions about drama-making as dramatic art can be drawn with only passing interest in his own contribution; Taylor's falls under the category of reflection-in-action research, closer in purpose to professional development than Millward's, with central interest in his own contribution.

It is the notion of reflection in action, taken from Schön (1983/87) and expounded with such clarity by Orton (1994) that has excited drama researchers. Schön maintains that those moments in the classroom when artistry rather than logic determine the way through uncertainty are most ripe for analysis for they reveal professional competence. How a teacher reflects *during* such moments is something other teachers might learn from. Implicit in Taylor's writing is that process drama, *par excellence,* fulfils Schön's conception of indeterminate zones of practice. (It would be instructive to invite Schön's response to this view.)

While not wanting the term teacher-artist to be displaced by teacher-researcher, I can see the value in attempting an analysis of those occasions in collaborative creative work when a teacher is faced with a problem of rescuing, containing, reviving, challenging, re-shaping, refocusing or clarifying a piece of work. Drama education has a history of anecdotal, self-analytical accounts of drama lessons and Cecily O'Neill, David Booth, Philip Taylor and Brian Edmiston have recently pursued this kind of reporting with increasing rigour, although any indepth analysis of a particular moment of teacher decision-making in a way that allows the reader to understand the relative status of available choices still eludes most pens, and yet this is what reflection-in-action appears to demand. We are sometimes impressed by the strategy selected by a teacher at those moments in a lesson when nothing seems to be working (see, for example, the fascinating account by Philip Taylor in Chapter 1 in this volume, and forthcoming, of his 'rat' lessons) but we cannot always learn from that kind of account as the range of options in terms of both the students' needs and possible drama strategies are rarely made available to the reader.

Even to speak of such a range of options serves to mask the, often unacknowledged, teacher–school value systems controlling what that range might be. Indeed, any real change in teaching can be only brought about by checking on personal, organizational, political and ethical values inherent in every teacher decision. As Chris Day (1993, p. 86) suggests, it may be a deficiency in Schön's notion of reflective practice that he appears not to embrace these deeper levels which may be only penetrable by others in dialogue with the practising teacher.

Perhaps more than any other school activity, process drama is representative of the 'swampy lowlands' (Schön, 1983) of action research. It is difficult to think of a parallel curriculum activity in which the teacher may be so vulnerable. For this reason, probing the personal, cultural and ethical values implicit in a teacher's choice of action may be far from straightforward. Irving and Williams (1995) suggest that it is not easy for practitioners (these authors were particularly interested in counselling) to recognize their true theory-in-use, a term taken from Argyris (1976), referring to a person's assumptions and beliefs about the world. They argue that practitioners' espoused theories, the ideals they may believe they are following, often successfully masquerade as a true account of practice, not from deliberate intention to mislead, but because theory-in-use is so deeply embedded and skilfully disguised that the practitioners are also deceived.

Thus, it may be that a drama teacher's declared intention to be open to the children's ideas, non-judgmental, risk-taking, sensitive to class and individual feelings, without a personal agenda, tolerant of temporary confusion, may be underpinned in practice by an urge to operate unilaterally, with a strong sense from years of experience of what will and what will not work, and an underlying determination to come out of it smelling of roses. As Irving and Williams (1995) put it, 'it is all right if everyone wins as long as I don't lose! (p. 111)' And the participants may be quite blind to these incongruities.

Now if we are to participate in that form of action research that depends solely on the teacher's own reflection-in-action, then in asking ourselves questions about choice of strategy that go beyond merely reconstructing practice to deconstructing practice, we will surely, in our attempt to answer the deeper set of questions, fall back once more on the declared values of our protective espoused theory, without realizing that we are on the slippery slopes of self-deception. And we will not develop professionally because no-one is making us acknowledge our theory in action. It may be that Laura McCammon's (1995) suggestion of a *third eye* provides a solution, but not if such an outsider were merely operating as a fellow researcher, for that has positivistic overtones. That third eye should be a counsellor, framing the questions that prompt the teacher-researcher to probe her value-system with honesty. Philip Taylor (1995b) is optimistic that 'teachers can develop that third eye within themselves' (p. 50). This may be too much to ask. A more realistic solution, however, lies in triangulation and cystallization, which Taylor explores in Chapter 1 of this volume.

Pupils as Researchers

The idea was voiced in Brisbane by a number of participants in the institute that process drama, almost by definition, was a form of research. Certainly the general trend of process drama lessons seems to require pupils to explore something . . . a theme or a topic. For instance, in Taylor's research referred to above, drama served the social studies curriculum on the topic of the Boston Massacre. Although he does not refer to his seventh-graders as researchers, one can perhaps understand why a teacher, given this kind of remit, might be tempted to frame a class in this way with a view to stimulating a serious investigation.

More explicitly labelled as research is the drama conducted by Brian Edmiston and recorded in Chapter 4 of this volume. Edmiston's teaching situation is similar to Taylor's inquiry: a class of students, this time in connection with a unit on civil rights, are invited in their separate groups to use drama to explore their chosen topic . . . Hank Aaron, the Mafia, the Great Depression, the Holocaust. They are to choose a research question and be prepared to modify it in light of the drama experience. They had done already a considerable amount of academic work on their topics before involving themselves in the new perspective that dramatic exploration was to bring. This was obviously, from the comments of the students, a highly successful educational experience. This is one such comment: 'Our job wasn't just to find out stuff that was already out there, but to *make* stuff — to find out how it felt and to show other people'.[2] This student is effectively summarizing the purpose of process drama — making/discovering/communicating. Edmiston's argument is that the quality of learning is enhanced by having the students see the drama work as a research project. In the kind of context Edmiston describes, such an argument is persuasive, but much process drama is fiction and not tied to, say, social studies. Is the methodology still akin to research?

It might be argued that even when a fiction is being created by the class, once the given or pretext is accepted as a starting point, a series of investigatory tasks is often set up, perhaps inventing a past and pursued as though researching the facts of the past. A classical example of this latter case is Cecily O'Neill's (1995) Frank Miller drama which begins with the teacher announcing that: 'I received this note today. It says Frank Miller is coming back to town' (p. vii). From then on the class set about either inventing his past or anticipating what might happen now. Even as they act events in the present, the sense of 'finding out how it was or demonstrating how it is' is sustained throughout. But I would be reluctant either to have the class see themselves as researchers or to see what they are doing as research.

Is it the case, then, that process drama confined to investigating the 'real world' might qualify as research? I am not convinced that even this is viable as a general policy. The framework of research that stimulated rigour in Edmiston's classroom might well become a straightjacket, for both student and teacher, in other circumstances. The idea of persistently seeking the intellectual link between the drama and a research question may be too confining for everyone — and *may militate against the creation of theatre form*. The students may also feel cheated, unless they have chosen to take a research approach and not just accepted the invitation of a nice teacher.

The context of Brian Edmiston's example is significant, and we can learn from it. The students he worked with *already saw themselves as* 'students required to work on their final projects', before starting any drama. In other words, they were already framed in the functional role required by 'drama as research'. This, it seems to me, is the key to the method. A teacher cannot simply label his students as 'researchers' and thereby depend upon their good-will in going along with the idea. The role must seem absolutely logical to the students *outside* the drama. That is, their *real* context (in this case, their school context) must frame them as people who need to investigate something. That is who they *are*. And then, as researchers, (not, 'researchers') they can take on any role the drama might demand of them, whether that be Helen of Troy or Albert Schweitzer.

This is the secret of Dorothy Heathcote's 'Mantle of the Expert' approach to education (Heathcote and Bolton, 1995). She works with her students at establishing an enterprise of experts (professional, managerial, scientific) before they reach the key issue related to the curriculum which they are due to study. Whatever role they play, they are experts, not actors, trying out their parts. Attention to detail is meticulous; source material is authentic and adult; recording what they have learnt is paramount. The work is ideally conceived of as long term, so that over a number of weeks, or even months, their function as 'experts' becomes part of their total identification in the classroom: that is *who they are*.

I suggest, therefore, that Brian Edmiston has articulated a valid thesis, vividly exemplified by his account of his own teaching. That validity becomes strained, however, in my view, if the frame of researcher or expert is seen as something that can be hung around the students' necks as a temporary measure to suit the methodology. If, on the other hand, they already see themselves as researchers, they may very well, as part of that research, use drama to investigate something.

Notes

1 This was conducted at Stanford University in 1971 and recorded by Banuazazi and Movehedi (1973).
2 This student quote and others are taken from a draft paper, 'Drama as research: Students and teachers as qualitative researchers,' which Edmiston distributed at the Institute of Drama Education Research at Griffith University, July, 1995.

References

ARGYRIS, C. (1976) 'Theories of action that inhibit individual learning', *American Psychologist*, **31**, pp. 638–54.

BANUAZAZI, A. and MOVEHEDI, A. (1973) 'Interpersonal dynamics in a simulated prison', *International Journal of Criminology and Penology*, **I**, pp. 69–97.

COHEN, L. and MANION, L. (1980) *Research Methods in Education London*, Croom Helm.

DAY, C. (1993) 'Reflection: A necessary but not sufficient condition for professional development', *British Education Research Journal*, **19**(1).

DONALDSON, M. (1978) *Children's Minds*, London, Croom Hill.

Hamilton, D., Jenkins, D., King, C., MacDonald, B. and Parlett, M. (1977) *Beyond the Numbers Game*, Basingstoke, Macmillan.

Heathcote, D. and Bolton, G. (1995) *Drama for Learning: Dorothy Heathcote's Mantle of the Expert Approach to Education*, New Hampshire, Heinemann.

Irving, J.A. and Williams, D.I. (1995) 'Critical thinking and reflective practice in counselling', *British Journal of Guidance and Counselling*, **23**(1).

Maier, N.R.F., Solem, A.R. and Maier, A.A. (1956) *The Role-Play Technique*, San Diego, University Associates.

McCammon, L.A. (1995) 'Commentary on "reflective practice and drama research" and "Our adventure of experiencing"', *Youth Theatre Journal*, **9**, pp. 45–8.

Millward, P. (1988) 'The language of drama.' Unpublished Doctoral Thesis, University of Durham, England.

O'Neill, C. (1995) *Drama Worlds: A Framework for Process Drama*, New Hampshire, Heinemann.

Orton, J. (1994) 'Action research and reflective practice: An approach to research for drama educators,' *NADIE Journal: International Research Issue*, **18**(2), pp. 85–96.

Patrick, J. (1973) *A Glasgow Gang Observed*, London, Eyre Methuen.

Piaget, J. and Inhelder, B. (1956) *The Child's Conception of Space*, London, Routledge and Kegan Paul.

Schön, D. (1983) *The Reflective Practitioner*, New York, Basic Books.

Schön, D. (1987) *Educating the Reflective Practitioner*, New York, Basic Books.

Taylor, P. (1992) 'Our adventure of experiencing: Drama structure and action research in a grade seven social studies classroom.' Unpublished Doctoral Dissertation, New York University.

Taylor, P. (1995a) 'Our adventure of experiencing: Reflective practice and drama research', *Youth Theatre Journal*, **9**, pp. 31–44.

Taylor, P. (1995b) 'Wanting more or demanding less? A response to McCammon', *Youth Theatre Journal*, **9**.

Taylor, P. (Forthcoming) 'Reflective practitioner research', in Wagner, B.J. (ed.) *What Classroom Drama Can Do*, New Hampshire, Heinemann.

Taylor, P. (in press) *Our Adventure of Experiencing: Teachers Researching Process Drama*, New Hampshire, Heinemann.

Notes on Contributors

Gavin Bolton retired as reader emeritus in drama education at the University of Durham in 1989. His publications include *Towards a Theory of Drama in Education, Drama as Education, New Perspectives on Classroom Drama*, and *Drama for Learning*.

John Carroll is a senior lecturer in drama at Charles Sturt University, Australia. He works extensively in the area of drama and sociolinguistics focusing on the relationship between language, role and learning. Both his MEd and PhD are in this area of research. He is an active member of the National Association for Drama In Education (NADIE, Australia) and is a past director of publications. His current research interests include the areas of dramatic role and television acting as well as computer-based qualitative research methods.

Brian Edmiston is an assistant professor at the University of Wisconsin-Madison, USA where he directs the Theatre and Education Program. He has received several research and teaching awards. In addition to his interest in writing about teacher research and the structuring of classroom drama he is currently writing about his monster-hero dramatic play with his 5-year-old son, Michael.

Margot Ely is an instructor, collaborator and mentor in qualitative research. Her professional base is New York University, USA. She sees learning–teaching–research as interconnected and writ large, with important implications for human relations, liberations, and creations. She believes these endeavors must be passionately felt. She loves networking, travelling, working, the arts, crossword puzzles, mysteries and having a good laugh.

Sharon Grady is an assistant professor at University of Texas at Austin, USA where she teaches process drama, theatre in education, and research methods. Her publications have appeared in *Theatre, Youth Theatre Journal*, and *The Drama Review*. She is currently completing an ethnographic case study of how participants make meaning in TIE programs, *Between Production and Reception*.

Maxine Greene is professor of philosophy and education and the William F. Russell Professor in the Foundations of Education at Teachers College, Columbia University, New York, USA. The author of six books and the recipient of several honorary degrees, Greene is former president of the Philosophy of Education Society and the American Educational Research Association. She also served for many years as a member of the John Dewey Society executive council. Recently, she was honored with a New York University alumni award for her outstanding achievements in education and philosophy.

Jonothan Neelands is a lecturer in drama and cultural studies in the Institute of Education, University of Warwick, UK. He has worked as a classroom teacher in elementary and secondary schools and as an advisory teacher and adviser.

Angela O'Brien is an associate professor and Dean of the school of studies in creative arts at the Victorian College of the Arts, The University of Melbourne, Australia. She has taught English, drama and theatre studies in secondary schools, TAFE colleges and tertiary institutions in Australia and the UK since 1971. She is foundation chairperson of the Victorian chapter of the Shakespeare Globe Centre. Her doctoral study was in the left-wing theatre in Australia (1920–1960).

Cecily O'Neill works with students, teachers, directors, and actors throughout the world, lecturing and conducting drama workshops. O'Neill divides her time between London and the United States, where she is associate professor of speech/theatre at The Ohio State University. Her publications include *Drama Structures, Drama Guidelines, Dorothy Heathcote: Collected Writings on Education and Drama*, and *Drama Worlds: A Framework for Process Drama.*

John O'Toole is associate professor of drama at Griffith University, Australia. His many publications include *The Process of Drama, Dramawise* and, the first book on TIE, *Theatre in Education*. He is also a playwright and director, but first and foremost a practising drama teacher from primary to PhD levels.

Johnny Saldaña is a professor of theatre at Arizona State University, USA and director of the theatre education/teacher certification program. He is the author of *Drama of Color: Improvisation with Multiethnic Folklore* (Heinemann), and has conducted and published numerous research studies on child audience response and multiethnic issues.

Lowell Swortzell, professor of educational theatre at New York University, USA has published fourteen plays for young audiences and six books, including *All the World's a Stage* (*New York Times Book Review* 'Outstanding Book of the Year' award); *The International Guide to Children's Theatre and Educational Theatre* ('AATE Distinguished Book of the Year' and *Choice* awards). He was inducted into the College of Fellows of the American Theatre in 1992 and received a Fulbright grant to lecture and study in Australia in 1995.

Philip Taylor is a NYU graduate and teaches drama at Griffith University, Australia. He has been a journal editor for the American Alliance for Theatre and

Education and the National Association for Drama in Education (Australia). His award-winning study on teacher research and process drama is soon to be published by Heinemann, New Hampshire.

Jeffrey Wilhelm has been a teacher of reading and the language arts at the middle school and secondary level for the past thirteen years. He currently is an assistant professor at the University of Maine, USA where he teaches courses in middle and secondary level literacy. He is also the recent recipient of the NCTE Promising Researcher Award (1995) for his dissertation entitled *Developing Readers: Teaching Engaged and Reflective Reading in the Middle School*.

Lin Wright is the retired chair of the department of theatre at Arizona State University, USA. She has been principal investigator for several theatre curriculum research projects and most recently chaired the writing committee for the theatre portion of the US *National Standards for Arts Education*.

Delegates at the Institute of Drama Education Research

Griffith University
Brisbane, Australia
7–12 July 1995

Barta-Martinez, Fernando

Brunning, Barbara-Jo

Burton, Bruce

Chamberlain, Noel

Darvell, Liz

Donelan, Kate

Epstein, Shira

Fairhead, Wayne

Grant, Ian

Hempenstall, Peter

Lee, Tracey

Kempe, Andy

Manley, Anita

McLean, Judith

Millett, Tony

Morgan, Norah

Nicholson, Helen

O'Mara, Joanne

O'Neill, Maureen

O'Rourke, Chris

Pascoe, Robin

Rasmussen, Bjørn

Saxton, Juliana

Kao, Shin-Mei

Somers, John

Swortzell, Lowell

Taylor, Philip

Venter, Estelle

Weiss, Suzanna

Wissler, Rod

Wright, Peter

Bolton, Gavin

Bundy, Penny

Carroll, John

Chung, Myoung-Cheul

Davis, David

Edmiston, Brian

Eriksson, Stig

Grady, Sharon

Hafnor, Carl Jacob

Hoepper, Christine

Ilsaas, Tove

Lepp, Margaret

Martin-Smith, Alistair

Miller, Carole

Morelos, Ronaldo

Neelands, Jonothan

O'Brien, Angela

O'Neill, Cecily

O'Toole, John

Oakley, John

Prior, Ross

Roberts, Vera

Scheurer, Pam

Simons, Jennifer

Voss Price, Lucy

Swortzell, Nancy

Warner, Christine

Warren, Kathleen

Whatman, Jennifer

Wright, Lin